ANTON QUINTANO

RICASOLI, MALTA
History of a Fort

Publishers Enterprises Group (PEG) Ltd

Published by
Publishers Enterprises Group (PEG) Ltd
P.E.G. Building, UB7 Industrial Estate
San Gwann SGN 09, Malta
http://www.peg.com.mt
e.mail: contact@peg.com.mt

in association with
The Kalkara Local Council

First Published 1999

Cataloguing in Publication Data

Quintano, Anton, 1956–

Ricasoli, Malta: History of a Fort / Anton Quintano -

p.   : ill.

1.   Malta - History of Fort Ricasoli - 1670–1999
2.   Malta - Military and Local History - 1670–1999
I.   Title

DDC: LC:
Melitensia Classification:

ISBN: 99909-0-243-7

Printed in Malta by P.E.G. Ltd

to Stephanie,
Augusto and Desirée

Acknowledgements

I am grateful to Mr Roger Vella Bonavita who supervised my original Bachelor of Arts (Honours) thesis on Fort Ricasoli at the University of Malta between 1975 and 1977. I am also indebted to Dr Anthony Luttrell for his generous advice and for translations from Spanish; as well as Mr Dominic Micallef, Miss Josephine Zammit and the late Chev. Joseph Galea for translating difficult passages from French. Chevalier Galea gave me much valuable advice about the Hospitaller Order of St John and their archives at the National Library of Malta. He also spurred me on when the apparent dearth of documentary sources was disheartening me. Mr Emanuel V. Borg helped me describe the architecture of the chapel of St Nicholas in the fort. Mr Raymond Camilleri of the Lands Department and Mr Joseph Magro Conti of the Planning Authority facilitated my visits to the fort. Carmel Camilleri was responsible for the drawings of the fort and the parts of baroque fortification. Finally I am grateful to my parents, for encouraging me during the earlier part of the work; and to my wife Stephanie, son Augusto, and daughter Desirée, for creating a home environment conducive to study and academic work.

Contents

List of Illustrations, Maps and Plans

List of Tables

Abbreviations

Archives

AAF	Archiepiscopal Archives, Floriana
AOM	Archives of the Order of Malta (at NLM)
ACCV	Archivum Collegium Canonicorum Victoriosae
NAM	National Archives of Malta (at Rabat)
NAM (Mdina)	National Archives of Malta (Mdina Section)
NLM	National Library of Malta (Valletta)

Other

BL	breach loading
gr.	*grano/grani*
HAA	heavy anti aircraft
HMS	His/Her Majesty's ship
KOMR	King's Own Malta Regiment
MAS	*motoscafo anti-sommergibile* (anti-submarine motor torpedo-boat)
MLI	Malta Light Infantry
MTL	*motoscafo turismo lento* (baby submarine carrier)
MTM	*motoscafo turismo modificato* (motor torpedo boat)
MTS	*motoscafo turismo silurante* (baby submarine flotilla leader)
NCO	non commissioned officer
QF	quick firing
RA	Royal Artillery
RE	Royal Engineers
RMA	Royal Malta Artillery
RMF	Royal Malta Fencibles (Regiment)
RML	rifled muzzle loading
RTD	Recruits Training Depot
SLC	*siluro a lenta corsa - maiali* (torpedo baby submarine)
sc.	*scudo/scudi*
t.	*taro/tari*

Abstract

The Grand Harbour of Malta is a depository of history. The fortifications which surround it are witness to that. Much has been written about the history of Valletta or the three cities, and the fortifications have comprehensively attracted the interest of historians too. However, each and every fort has a history of its own - not only in the military aspect, but also in the demographic, social or even the ecclesiastical; and not only for the Knights' period (1530-1798), when most of them were built. The forts around harbour continued to perform their original function right through the British period. Indeed some forts, including Fort Ricasoli, experienced events which made them the focus of attention of the whole Maltese population. Each and every fort around Grand harbour warrants a particular and detailed study of its own, although one should never lose cognizance of the oneness of the Grand Harbour defence system. To date brief histories of Fort St Angelo and Fort St Elmo have been published; and two very detailed historical surveys of Fort St Elmo and Fort Manoel have been submitted to the University of Malta for theses, and remain as yet unpublished. This present book is the first one published about the history of Fort Ricasoli. It narrates and analyses different aspects and events in the history of Fort Ricasoli. Whenever possible, a comparative analysis with other similar forts such as St Angelo and St Elmo has been made in all aspects discussed.

Preface

Although Fort Ricasoli lies at the periphery of the Grand Harbour region of Malta, it controlled the access to Malta's major port since its construction in 1670. Since early modern times Malta's population has been dependent on the importation of food supplies from Sicily or other lands, and the Grand Harbour had to be fortified in order to secure such supplies. Another reason why the harbour was fortified is that after 1530 the governing Sovereign Order of St John, who were a Hospitaller and Military Brotherhood of Knights, carried on their corsairing war against the Turks with Malta for their feudal principality and base. Ottoman retribution was always feared.

The present book is not merely the history of a fort in Malta - it is an extensive overview of the military history of the whole island, with particular reference to the harbour area. It also delves into the demographic, social and economic history of the fort and it attempts to profile the lay dependants of the garrison. The origin of this history of Fort Ricasoli is a Bachelor of Arts (Honours) thesis in History[1] submitted by the present author to the University of Malta in 1977. Since then the author has worked on its update and re-editing.

Fort Ricasoli was one of the last harbour forts to be built, and its history in the time of the Knights is devoid of any great wars or events. Nevertheless the present book is the first one to illustrate the daily social life inside and around an eighteenth century fort in Malta: Ricasoli lies on a promontory and weathering is constant, therefore, continued rebuilding was necessary ever since its construction; in case of invasion, a contingency plan for the defence of the south-east part of Malta was devised, including Ricasoli as a final keep of the retreating forces; St Nicholas Chapel in Fort Ricasoli was a conventual parish of the Order, and its history is also surveyed.

Events suddenly took a dramatic turn after 1797. Shortly after that Mikiel Anton Vassalli,

---

[1] A. Quintano, 'Fort Ricasoli: An Historical Survey, 1670-1798'.

the francophile father of Maltese literature was imprisoned there, Napoleon Bonaparte first set foot on the Maltese soil precisely at Ricasoli steps when he toured the fort before proceeding to Valletta. The ensuing siege and blockade of the French by the Maltese insurgents is analysed.

In contrast to the Hospitaller period, the British occupation of the fort is highly eventful. The British period started off with the infamous mutiny by the Froberg Regiment in 1807, during which the mutineers threatened to engage the defence of Valletta in battle before surrendering to the loyal troops. In 1837, six hundred old people from the *Ospizio* (hospital) in Floriana were moved to Ricasoli because of cholera. Almost four-hundred of them died in horrendous conditions there within three weeks. King Edward VII visited Ricasoli Point in 1903 on the occasion of the laying of the foundation stone of the breakwater. During the First World War, Ricasoli again served as a hospital for the wounded soldiers of the Gallipoli, and later the Salonika campaigns. Before dawn on 26 July 1941, a flotilla of Italian navy E-boats attacked Grand Harbour and Ricasoli's gunners contributed in the routing of the valiant but ill-fated seamen. Meanwhile there was slow but steady infrastructural development inside the fort. This is also investigated in the present book.

For the past thirty-five years Fort Ricasoli lay in a state of neglect. Although the Planning Authority has issued a development brief for the fort, a developer is urgently needed so that its fortifications be restored to their former grandeur. One hopes that any development at Ricasoli will not impair the historic parts of the fort as happened there in 1977, or as happened elsewhere in the fortresses of Malta and Gozo. This history of Fort Ricasoli is the first one ever attempted. It should serve as a reminder to all responsible Maltese authorities that something urgent needs be done to save it from total and irreversible ruin. Fort Ricasoli should not be allowed to fall.

Anton Quintano
Attard, Malta

Part I

The Hospitaller and French Periods

1

Before Ricasoli

The knights Hospitallers

The knights of the Hospitaller and Military Order of St John of Jerusalem were homeless in 1523, having been ousted from Rhodes by Sultan Suleiman the Magnificent after a siege which lasted many months. So they found their way to Rome where Pope Adrian VI, and then Clement VII welcomed them. They were trying to find support in Europe so that they may establish themselves in a state of their own. The knights of St John had for centuries proved to be the bulwark of Christendom against the Muslim powers, more especially the Ottoman Turks.

The Order of the knights of St John had been founded as a religious brotherhood and their primary aims in the Holy Land had been to care for the sick pilgrims as hospitallers.[1] But from a comparatively early period they acted as armed contingents to defend pilgrims whenever necessary.[2] It was in the early thirteenth century that the brotherhood became para-military, and they started to build medieval castles all around Palestine.[3] The Christian defence there, however, collapsed and with the fall of Acre in 1291 the knights withdrew firstly to Cyprus,[4] then to Rhodes where they developed also as a naval power. The Ottoman threat, however, created pressure upon the Order of St John until Rhodes became untenable. The Order was expelled on 1 January 1523. With the experience gained in the East, the knights became consummate fortress builders, as well as a naval force.[5]

---

[1] J. Riley Smith, *The Knights of St John in Jerusalem and Cyprus, 1050-1310*, (London 1967), 34.
[2] Ibid., 45.
[3] J. Quentin Hughes, *Fortress: Architecture and Military History in Malta*, (London 1969), 25. For the best rendering of the Hospitaller castles in the Holy Land, see P. Deschamps, *Les Chateaux des Croises en Terre Sainte* (3 vols), (Paris 1934, 1939, 1973); S.C. Spiteri, *Fortresses of the Cross: Hospitaller Military Architecture (1136-1798)*, (Malta 1994), is an erudite study of all fortresses built by the Knights Hospitallers of St John.
[4] Riley Smith, 197.
[5] Hughes, (1969), 26.

The Order had to find a permanent home and that was what their head, Grand Master Philippe Villiers de l'Isle Adam asked for at the various European courts he visited in the 1520s. Above all, the Order wanted a home which was independent of any Christian power, although they also wished to stay on the frontiers of Islam. When the knights accepted Malta for their convent in 1529, these two requisites were satisfied to a great extent, although Emperor Charles V as King of Spain and Sicily, gave Malta to them as a perpetual fief.

Malta and its harbours in 1530

In 1524, the knights had sent a commission to Malta to report on the state of the island before they accepted the Emperor's offer. When one analyses the report,[6] one realises why the knights were not fully pleased with these islands. Malta was a barren island, small and economically dependent on Sicily. The old city of Mdina had weak defences. What these commissioners saw positive were the harbours of the island. Certainly the latter were one of the main reasons why the knights came to Malta.

Malta's harbours are of extreme importance because of their strategic position in the central Mediterranean. Nature has formed the harbours into a symmetrical pattern around their centre which is Sciberras Peninsula on which Valletta and Floriana were later built. They offered shelter for shipping inside the two main channels which are very deep, but more especially inside the various creeks between the promontories which, with regard to Grand Harbour jut out towards Sciberras Peninsula on a south-east, north-west axis. With the Order of St John established in Malta, the harbours became of great importance: both to Christian Europe because they were used to confront the Ottoman threat; and to the Order of St John since the knights depended on income from their lands in Europe, and in case of siege on arrival of relief forces, in order to survive.

Dividing the harbours is Sciberras Peninsula, about two kilometres long and 800 metres wide. The harbours on both sides are made up of a channel 400 metres wide . The one on the south-east of Valletta is Grand Harbour; the one to the north-west is Marsamxett Harbour. Grand Harbour is divided into creeks and promontories. Ricasoli Point is the first promontory to the north-east of Grand Harbour, lying between the open Mediterranean Sea to the north-east and Bighi Bay or Rinella Creek of Grand Harbour to the south-west. The area was originally called Rinella. Ricasoli Point also lies about 450 metres distant from St Elmo Point across the mouth of Grand Harbour. It is about 800 metres long and 300 metres at its widest. Rinella Creek is about 150 metres wide. Next comes Bighi which is a short but broad peninsula. Strategically Fort St Angelo and Vittoriosa (or Birgu), to the south-west of Bighi across Kalkara Creek were much more important. Fort Ricasoli is 800 metres away from Fort St Angelo.[7] Beyond Fort St Angelo are Dockyard Creek, Senglea, French Creek, and Corradino Heights.

---

[6] G. Bosio, *Istoria della Sacra Religione et Illustrissima Militia di S. Giovanni Gerosolimitano*, (Venice 1695), vol. iii, 30.
[7] National Library of Malta (NLM) (manuscript) 647, no pag(ination).

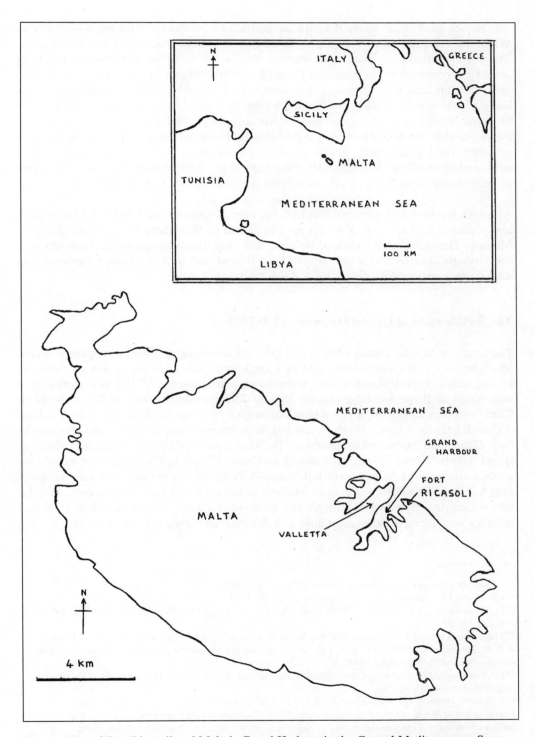

The position of Fort Ricasoli and Malta's Grand Harbour in the Central Mediterranean Sea.

21

The names used in the above description are the present day ones for rapid orientation. When the commission of the knights came in 1524, these places had different names. The only fortified place within the harbour area was Fort St Angelo which was lightly armed but could cover the mouth of Grand Harbour with gun fire in case of attack. The only built-up area was Vittoriosa, the suburb of St Angelo. Almost all the peninsulas had different names: Valletta was called Mount Sciberras; Senglea was called l'Isola or St Julian's Hill or even Pietralonga; Vittoriosa was called Borgo; Bighi was called Salvatore Hill; while Ricasoli was called Rinella Point[8] or Ponta l-Irqieqa, the Maltese synonym for Punta Sottile. It was called so on account of its triangular shape which narrowed gradually to Rinella (later Ricasoli) Point.[9] This promontory had a backbone or ridge from Punta Sottile to Zonqor Point, five kilometres to the south-east.[10]

Although the harbours were not fortified, the commissioners described them favourably and reported that they should become the centre of the island if the Order came to Malta.[11] Besides its poor state of defence, the only disadvantage of the harbours was the *Gregale* (north-east) wind. It could be violent and to it the Grand Harbour was dangerously exposed.[12]

The fortification of Grand Harbour, 1530-1565

The Order of St John came to Malta in 1530, and assuming that the Sultan would attack Malta because of their corsairing activities, the knights started to strengthen the defences of the island. Fort St Angelo was modified and strengthened.[13] Defence works were undertaken at Birgu and after that the famous Turkish corsair Turghut Reis (known in Christian states as Dragut) entered into Marsamxett Harbour in 1551, Grand Master Juan d'Omedes realised that a fort was needed at Sciberras Point to secure the entrance to both Grand and Marsamxett Harbours. The Order had not enough time and money to spend to fortify both sides of the mouth of Grand Harbour. The knights obtained two goals with one work. Rinella was left barren.[14] Pedro Prado, the engineer who designed Fort St Elmo, also designed Fort St Michael at the neck of l'Isola promontory, and the city of Senglea started to be built shortly afterwards. Faurè[15] suggests that in 1556 two military engineers, Baldassare Lanci and Bartolomeo Genga, made a project for the

---

[8] F. Balbi da Correggio, *The Siege of Malta*, (Copenhagen 1961), 85.

[9] G.F. Abela, G. Ciantar, *Malta Illustrata*, (Malta 1772), I, 14.

[10] H. Bowen-Jones, J.C. Dewdney, W.B. Fisher, *Malta: Background for Development*, (Durham 1961), 24.

[11] Bosio, iii, 30.

[12] These winds often blow for three consecutive days and account for 15 per cent of all winds in Malta. A.St.B. Harrison and R.P.S. Hubbard, *A Report to Accompany the outline plan for the region of Valletta and the Three Cities*, (Valletta 1945), 9.

[13] J.F. Darmanin, *The Phoenico-Graeco-Roman Temple and the Origin and Development of Fort St Angelo*, (Malta 1948), 32.

[14] J. Quentin Hughes, *The Building of Malta: 1530-1795*, (London 1967), 16. A. Hoppen, *The Fortification of Malta, 1530-1798*, (Edinburgh 1979), illustrates all aspects of the building of the fortifications and the circumstances of the building of each particular Hospitaller fort in Malta.

[15] G. Faurè, *Storia ta' Malta u Ghaudex*, (Malta 1913), iii, 1215-1215.

Bighi Hospital (now school) as seen from Fort Ricasoli.

Fort Saint Angelo across Bighi Bay as seen from Ricasoli Point.

Fort Saint Elmo across the mouth of Grand Harbour from Ricasoli Point. The Ricasoli arm of the breakwater is in the forground at the centre.

erection of a tower on Rinella Point, and that in 1560 Girolamo Cassar and Evangelista Menga prepared other projects for the same purpose. However Faurè does not give any documentation. Neither does Guillaumier[16] who is the only other author who mentions these projects. In 1565 these fortifications were tested during the Great Siege of Malta. But an important development at Rinella Point occurred in the meantime.

Gallows' Point

It was soon after the arrival of the knights at Malta when two slaves, Kara Saim Rais, and Kara Mustapha, tried to take over Fort St Angelo while some of their friends tried to escape by boats to bring back reinforcements from Barbary (North African) coast. The revolt failed.[17] The two rais, together with ten other leading escapees were sentenced to death and hanged from two gallows made up of two posts and crossbar each at Punta Sottile. Hence Punta Sottile or Rinella Point took the name of Gallows' Point[18] until Orsi Tower was built there a hundred years later. Every time there was an execution,

---

[16] A. Guillaumier, *Bliet u Rhula Maltin*, (Malta 1972), 169.
[17] Bosio, iii, 100.
[18] Ibid., 101.

the corpse of the victim was hung from these gallows as a warning to other wrong-doers, slaves, and also for newly arrived persons. From 1531 onwards, the first sight that met the eye on entering Grand Harbour was usually some sun-dried bodies swaying in their chains on this spit of land.[19]

Gallows Point and the Great Siege of 1565

On 18 May 1565, more than 30,000 Turks invaded Malta from all over the Empire and lay siege to the fortified area of Grand Harbour, starting from Fort St Elmo, in the hope of berthing their fleet in Marsamxett Harbour instead of the more open Marsaxlokk Bay in the south of the island. The Turks had come for three reasons: firstly in retaliation to the piratical activities of the knights in the Aegean Sea and the Levant; secondly to deal the Order with a final mortal blow; and thirdly to secure a naval base lying midway between the Ottoman possessions in the East and the newly established regencies in North Africa. The Turks thought that Fort St Elmo, being a very small fort would capitulate in a very short time, possibly within ten days. But the knights and their soldiers there, including many Maltese put up a brave resistance and the Fort was only occupied on 24 June. The delay later cost the Turks the war, since they did not conquer Vittoriosa and Senglea by 7 September, when they finally decided to withdraw. By that time stormy weather used to be expected at Malta[20] more than nowadays, and the Turks could not possibly winter here because of lack of provisions.

When the siege started the Turks could not hope to force the entrance to Grand Harbour under cover of a battery at Gallows Point because of Fort St Elmo. Gallows Point could serve the Turks in two ways, both of which were discovered quite late in the battle of Fort St Elmo by the corsair Dragut. As a master of siege warfare and artillery work Dragut knew that it was heavy fire from many points of the compass which finally wore down the defence. He pointed out that the batteries which the Turks had erected at Sciberras Hill were well enough sited, but Fort St Elmo was only being engaged from one direction - the narrow landward, or south-westerly flank. Therefore Dragut gave orders to erect a battery at Gallows Point, which together with a new battery at Dragut Point (now ignè Point, Sliema), were to engage St Elmo from a further two quarters. Cross fire from many directions was the easiest solution for the destruction of a bastioned fort. The other reason why Dragut wanted a battery to be placed at Gallows Point was for it to cut the communications by boat between Forts St Angelo and St Elmo. St Elmo's strength lay in the fact that the Grand Master, Fra Jean de la Valette could reinforce its

---

[19] E. Bradford, *The Great Siege*, (London 1961), 94. The gallows on Gallows' Point are clearly portrayed in Matteo Perez d'Aleccio's frescoes of views of the Great Siege in the Magistral (now President's) Palace, Valletta. In 1820, the British Authorities did the same with the corpses of four English seamen turned corsairs. See Chapter 11.

[20] That was sixteen years before the Gregorian correction of the Julian calendar, when 5 October 1582 was declared 15 October. Therefore the sun's position and weather obtaining on 7 September 1565, was slightly more inclement than that of 17 September nowadays, also because the 'little ice age' (c. 1550-1700) had just started.

Zincotype engraving showing a general view of the battle of Fort St Elmo during the Great Siege of 1565. Note Gallows Point marked F; Salvatore (later Bighi) promontory marked G; Fort St Elmo marked A; Fort St Angelo marked H; and Żabbar marked L

garrison by means of boats by night.[21] Dragut gave the order on 30 May. Fortunately for the knights, on 4 June the Turkish admiral Piali Pasha showed reluctance to land the number of guns required from his ships until Marsamxett Harbour had been secured. Although Dragut managed to get a small battery of four small guns established on Gallows Point the day after, it was not strong enough to ensure that no boats could cross from Fort St Angelo to Fort St Elmo.[22]

---

[21] Bradford, 94.
[22] C. Sanminiatelli Zabarella, *Lo Assedio di Malta 1565*, (Torino 1902), 244-245.

Zincotype engraving showing the Rinella area during the attack on Birgu (Vittoriosa) by the Turks in the Great Siege of 1565. Note Gallows Point marked K; Fort St Elmo marked G; a Turkish battery on Salvatore Promontory at H; artillery pieces and gunners being transported by boat (I) to Gallows Point from larger ships at Wied Ghammieq (M).

Sometimes at night, the phosphorescent water gave away the movements of the boats. The Turks detected these boats from Gallows Point. On 1 June the Turks slipped out in small boats from Rinella Creek and intercepted them. One of the Maltese boats was overwhelmed. In a second attack on 2 June, the Turks suffered the loss of their boats. After that, they contented themselves with bombarding the relief boats with cannon and musket fire.[23]

---

[23] Bosio, iii, 539.

Neither was this battery safe. The guns from Fort St Angelo occasionally fired at it[24] and it only lasted a few days. It was destroyed by a cavalry sortie led out of Vittoriosa by the knight Grand Marshal Guillaume de Coupier.[25] On the 11 June Dragut decided to build an even stronger battery. This time it was no half hearted affair. Dragut's men landed in full force on the rocky spit and established strong guards on the landward side, so that there would be no more question of de Coupier's cavalry surprising their gunners. They established a really powerful battery on the point. Several of the heaviest guns were brought ashore from the ships. Four were deployed on Gallows Point and labour corps troops began to erect ramps and defensive palisades.[26] This battery was henceforth able to command the sea approaches between Forts St Angelo and St Elmo. They could now attack St Elmo's south-east walls facing Grand Harbour, and in due course they would be able to turn on the weight of their fire power upon Fort St Angelo too.[27] After the general assault on Fort St Elmo of 16 June, it was clear that reinforcements would soon be totally intercepted from Gallows Point and from Grotte dell'Alliata (tal-Ghalja, below the Lower Barracca). Bradford suggests "the moment that happened, all was lost".[28] Gallows Point had proved decisive and of great consequence in the conquest of Fort St Elmo. Words attributed to Dragut make the point that "by withdrawing the nourishment which St Elmo like an infant drew daily from Borgo, his mother`s breast - the fort must necessarily fall and perish".[29]

A fort on Gallows Point could have been very useful to the defence of Malta. When St Elmo fell, the Turkish fleet was stationed just outside Gallows Point. St Angelo's fire could not reach them from such a distance.[30] Gallows Point was of great strategic importance. It was only Dragut who noticed that at the end of May 1565. Next time there was a siege, if St Elmo was to remain isolated, the occupation of Gallows Point would be vital for both sides. As events turned out, however, with the building of Valletta in 1566, the importance of Gallows Point was somewhat reduced, because the batteries of Valletta were also meant to safeguard the entrance to the harbours and Valletta could dominate Gallows Point by means of her fire and its higher ground.

The fortification of the Grand Harbour area, 1565-1670

Hughes suggests that Fort Ricasoli was built "to complete the defences of the Grand Harbour",[31] and that in 1670 there remained only one outstanding requirement in the

[24] Bradford, 112.
[25] R.J.D. Cousin, *A Diary of the Siege of St Elmo*, (Malta 1955), 83.
[26] Ibid., 100-101. This battery is featured in Domenico Zanoi's engraving (Venice 1565) as reproduced in W.H. Tregellas, 'Historical Sketch of the Defence of Malta', in *Journal of the Royal Engineers Institute*, paper viii, vol.iii, no. 10, (1897), 185-211, (Backpage plate).
[27] Sanminiatelli Zabarella, 280-281.
[28] Bradford, 127.
[29] Cousin, 122.
[30] Balbi da Correggio, 87.
[31] Hughes, *The Building of Malta*,(London 1967), 33.

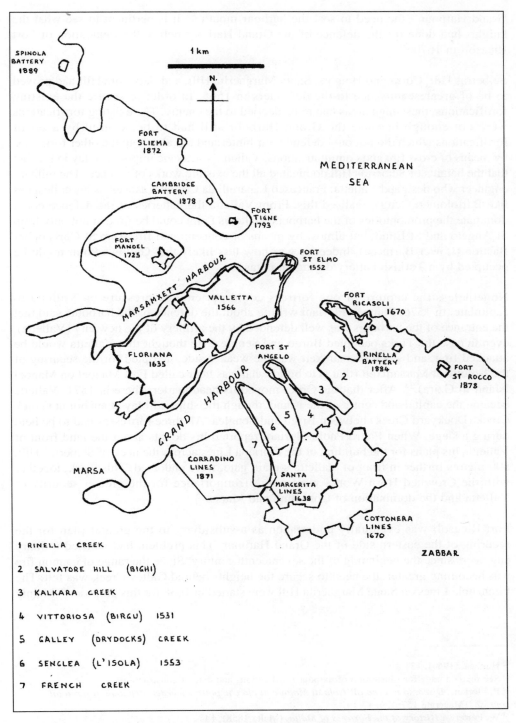

1 km

N.

SPINOLA
BATTERY
1889

FORT
SLIEMA
1872

MEDITERRANEAN
SEA

CAMBRIDGE
BATTERY
1878

FORT
TIGNE
1793

FORT
MANOEL
1725

MARSAMXETT HARBOUR

FORT
ST ELMO
1552

VALLETTA
1566

FORT
RICASOLI
1670

FLORIANA
1635

FORT ST
ANGELO

1

RINELLA
BATTERY
1884

FORT
ST ROCCO
1878

2

GRAND HARBOUR

3

5 4

6

7

CORRADINO
LINES
1871

SANTA
MARGERITA
LINES
1638

COTTONERA
LINES
1670

MARSA

ZABBAR

1 RINELLA CREEK

2 SALVATORE HILL (BIGHI)

3 KALKARA CREEK

4 VITTORIOSA (BIRGU) 1531

5 GALLEY (DRYDOCKS) CREEK

6 SENGLEA (L'ISOLA) 1553

7 FRENCH CREEK

The position of Fort Ricasoli and the development of the defence of the Malta Harbours.

Grand Harbour - the need to seal the harbour mouth.[32] It is pertinent to see what the knights had done for the defence of the Grand Harbour before the foundation of Fort Ricasoli in 1670.[33]

Sciberras Hill, Corradino Heights, Santa Margherita Hill, and Salvatore Hill had proved to be of greatest nuisance to the defenders in 1565. In order to secure the existing fortifications, these high areas had to be decried to the enemy. The existing fortifications were not enough because the Grand Harbour still had to be secured by a set of fortifications which did not only defend their hinterland but also help the other fortresses by means of cross fire and communications. Valletta's strategic importance lay in the fact that the heights of Sciberras Hill dominated all the existing works of defence. The military engineer who designed Valletta, Francesco Laparelli da Cortona, as well as his colleagues like Bartolomeo Genga, realised this. From Valletta the batteries of the defence could dominate the promontories of the harbours. Gallows Point could be fired at not only from St Angelo and St Elmo, but almost by means of concentrated fire from St Christopher Bastion (Lower Barracca). Indeed it was now less likely that Gallows Point might be occupied by a Turkish battery during an invasion.

Nonetheless the capture of one fortress could put enough pressure on Valletta to capitulate. In 1576, Pompeo Floriani writing about the defence of the harbours said that the entrance of the harbours was well defended by the artillery of the new city (Valletta), even in case the Turks occupied Borgo and Senglea. He thought that Valletta would be attacked first, and since Marsamxett was the weaker side, he opted for the securing of the Isolotto at Marsamxett (that is to build what was later called Fort Manoel on Manoel Island in Gzira).[34] After that the Order moved its headquarters there in 1571, Valletta became the capital and centre of the island, though the ships still lay at anchor at Galley Creek (Dockyard Creek) between Birgu and Senglea. All three fortresses had to be held during a siege. When Pietro Paolo Floriani reported his doubts about the land front of Valletta, his plans for the building of the Floriana Lines across the neck of Sciberras Hill, 800 metres further in front of Valletta's main gate, were endorsed. This work, together with the Crowned Horn Works were only of importance for the greater security of Valletta and the domination of Corradino and Marsa.[35]

Fort Ricasoli was eventually undertaken as a subsidiary to the greater plan for the securing of the eastern side of the Grand Harbour. This problem had worried military engineers since the beginning of the seventeenth century. Since the range of cannon fire was becoming greater, the need to secure the heights behind Galley Creek was felt. The Firenzuola Lines on Santa Margherita Hill were started in 1638 for this purpose.[36] Mainly

---

[32] Hughes, (1969), 131.

[33] See map on page for illustration of harbour fortifications and date of construction.

[34] P. Floriani, *Discorso intorno all'Isola di Malta e di ciò che potrà succedere tentando il turco tal impresa*, (Macerata 1576), 6, 17-19.

[35] W. Porter, *A History of the Fortress of Malta*, (Malta 1858), 143.

[36] J. Crocker, *History of the Fortifications of Malta*, (Malta 1920), 5.

due to lack of funds, and also because before they were finished the Cottonera Lines were started 800 metres further afield in 1670, the Firenzuola (or Santa Margherita) Lines which envelop Cospicua (or Bormla) were only completed in the eighteenth century, wasting much of the time and money of the Order. So by 1670, when construction on Fort Ricasoli started, the main and most important works of defence for the Grand Harbour had been already tackled. However, one can take exception because although these works were completed or under construction, more could be done for the better defence of the place. Valletta was not yet totally secure from Marsamxett, while Salvatore promontory and Corradino heights could be better secured by actually building forts there and not just by bringing the fire of the other forts to bear on them. There were always new defensive works which could be undertaken, and had the Order had greater funds, and had there been a greater population to man the walls, Fort Ricasoli would not have remained the fort which "completed"[37] the defence of the Grand Harbour.

The building of Orsi Tower, 1629

On 8 August 1602, the Grand Master and the Council of the Order ordered that a ravelin be built at Gallows Point to deter slaves from escaping by boat. The ravelin would be armed with some bombardiers with muskets. All crafts would have to show licence to leave port in order to proceed. For one reason or another, it seems that this construction never materialised.[38] Indeed slaves were very numerous in the early seventeenth century and it seems that there were many attempts at escape on boats. On 29 January 1629, Fra Alessandro Orsi[39] built a tower at his own expense on Gallows Point near the entrance of the harbour, after that his project was sanctioned by the members of the Council of the Order who deemed it necessary.[40] He was prompted in his action by the occasional escape of slaves and not by any consideration of military strategy. The tower was not meant to counter any invasion or any enforcement by sea of the Grand Harbour - it was built to stop the slaves from escaping. This is why it stood on the inner side and not on the outer side of Gallows Point, facing the Grand Harbour rather than the open sea.[41] The following two years things happened which might have occurred in direct consequence of Orsi's act of liberality. In 1630, on the intervention of Pope Urban, Alessandro Orsi was created a knight Grand Cross of honour of the Order.[42] A year later Fra Orsi was appointed Governor of Vittoriosa and Senglea.[43]

---

[37] Hughes, (1967), 33.

[38] Hoppen, 91.

[39] An Italian knight from Bologna. He entered the Order on 7 June 1585. Archives of the Order of Malta (AOM) (Manuscript) 442 no pag. He was Captain of the galley *San Filippo* in 1603. B. dal Pozzo, *Historia della Sacra Religione di Malta*, (Verona 1703), I, 482.

[40] AOM 109, f. 164v. See Appendix I.

[41] P.P. Castagna, *Malta bil-Gzejjer Taghha*, (Malta 1865), I, 163, suggests that the tower also served to guard against invasion.

[42] Dal Pozzo, I, 788.

[43] Ibid., I, 799.

Detail from painting *Prospetto della Città di Malta dalla parte di Gregale l'Anno 1968*, showing Orsi Tower at the point of the newly garrisoned Fort Ricasoli.

An interesting feature about Orsi Tower is that it was a round tower, unlike the many martello watch-towers built under the Grand Mastership of Fra Martin de Redin in 1658, and it had a casemate, together with its own ditch and drawbridge and a small room for the soldiers.[44] It was about ten metres in diameter.[45] Another peculiarity was that the design was made by Orsi himself.[46] The tower was originally called Torre San Petronio,[47] after the patron saint of Orsi's home city Bologna, but the Maltese called it either *Torri Teftef*, after a nickname of an artillery commander who served in it, or more commonly *Torri ta' l-Ors* (Orsi Tower). Another Maltese name which Orsi Tower had was *Torri l-Hamra tar-Rikazli*, which is the Maltese translation of Orsi corrupted into

[44] NLM 142 d, f.458.
[45] NLM Plan 17. The tower was destroyed by a storm on 8 February 1821. NLM Plan 10.
[46] AOM 109, f.164v.
[47] A. Mifsud, *La Milizia e le Torri Antiche in Malta*, (Malta 1920), 27.

rossa (red).[48] Over the main gate of Orsi Tower was a marble slab with the following inscription recording its foundation:[49]

SUB SERMO PRINCIPE

MAGNO MAGISTRO DE PAULA

FRATER ALEXANDER URSUS

NOB BONONIEN

COERCENDAE SERVORUM FUGAE

SPECULAM FUNDAM

AERE SUO CONSTRUCTAM EXCITAVIT

ANNO DOM MDCXXIX

The flag of the Order of St John flew above the tower. After the building of Fort Ricasoli it was only armed during summer with a commander of artillery and with two gunners and four soldiers from Ricasoli. The tower was left outside the walls of Fort Ricasoli in the re-entrant point bastion. After some attempted escapes by the slaves during the Christmas period of 1746 it was again rearmed permanently.[50] Orsi Tower became part of the fort after 1670 in temporal and spiritual jurisdiction.[51] Between 1629 and 1670, Gallows Point was called Orsi Point.

Reasons for the building of Fort Ricasoli

The launching of new defence projects

The reasons behind the building of Fort Ricasoli are varied. One can look at the proposals for the building of a fort on Gallows (or Orsi) Point by previous military engineers in order to appreciate the strategic value and the necessity of a fort there. Whenever there was a war scare, the knights would give an added impetus to the defence works. They would normally invite one of the best military engineer of the time, who were mostly Italian in the seventeenth century and French in the eighteenth century, in order to report on the state of defence and suggest additions and alterations. The visiting engineer might plan a totally new work, for which he would prepare plans, wax or plaster models and see to the laying of the foundations before returning to his country. Of course the plan would have been vetted and criticised by other engineers abroad; by the knight members of the Commission of War and Fortifications (the equivalent of the War Ministry); and by the resident chief engineer of the Order, before being approved by the Council of the Order. All this activity usually led to conflicting strategic projects, and one might have been started when it was superseded by a totally different project which rendered the first one obsolete, as happened in 1638 and 1670, when after starting the Firenzuola

---

[48] NLM 142 d, f.458.
[49] Mifsud, 27 footnote.
[50] NLM 142 d. f.457v. See also Chapter 4.
[51] Ibid., f.465v.

Lines, the knights then approved a grander project, the Cottonera Lines just 800 metres afield, to defend the same area.

Early proposals for a fort

It was the architect of the Firenzuola Lines himself, the Dominican Cardinal and engineer Vincenzo Maculano da Fiorenzuola,[52] who first commented on the security of the entrance to the Grand Harbour after that Orsi Tower was built. According to Fiorenzuola, the enemy would never occupy Salvatore Hill or Orsi Point if the Santa Margherita (Firenzuola) Lines were built, since the guns at the new Lines would surely cut them.[53] A year later, Captain Domenico Guazzo, although agreeing with Fiorenzuola over the need of the Santa Margherita Lines, thought that it was necessary to fortify Orsi Point because without it being secured, the enemy would occupy it, rendering impossible the entry into harbour of any relieving force.[54] The debate over Orsi Point resumed in 1640 when the Italian military engineer, Giovanni Medici, the Marquis of St Angelo visited the island. In principle he agreed with Guazzo and advocated the building of a fort for which he produced plans. He said that a fort at Orsi Point together with two ravelins outside Vittoriosa were the last two pressing needs for the completion of the defences of Malta.[55] Four years later the Grand Master said in the Council, that everything Medici had proposed about the major fortifications had been carried out, although this is not true with regard to Orsi Point. Medici's proposal had been very peculiar. He proposed that Fort St Angelo should be transferred both in name and garrison to Orsi Point, also to honour his title which was Marquis of St Angelo. This shows that Medici considered the strategic importance of Orsi Point highly. Although the Commissioners of Fortifications were ordered by the Council to discuss and report about Medici's proposal,[56] no such document is extant in the archives of the Order. However, before 1670, nothing was done on Orsi Point, and on 18 June 1658 the Council approved the expenditure of 10,000 *scudi* to put Fort St Angelo in a better state of defence, so that Medici's plan was definitely shelved.[57]

In 1644, the ships of the Order's navy captured a great Turkish galleon laden with valuable cargo, and women thought to have belonged to the harem of the Sultan himself. A great Turkish expedition against Malta was feared, and the knights doubled their efforts in defensive works. An anonymous letter received in the Chancery of the Order exhorted the Council to build the proposed fort that was so necessary at Orsi Point.[58] On 8 July 1645, the engineer Bartolomeo Bandinello Pallavicini commented to the Commissioners of War that Orsi Point was important for the conservation of Grand Harbour, same as

---

[52] He came to Malta in 1638., Hughes, (1967), 210.
[53] AOM 6554, f.47-48v.
[54] Ibid., f. 53.
[55] Ibid., ff. 33v-34.
[56] AOM 257, f. 162.
[57] AOM 260, f. 37.
[58] AOM 6554, ff. 69, 71, 71v., 72v.

Vittoriosa, Senglea, Santa Margherita Lines and Mdina were for the defence of Malta. He agreed with those who said that in case of siege, the Turks would still be able to mount a battery at Orsi Point, making havoc of any relief force, and he also thought that a fort there would secure Salvatore hill. He came out with a new idea. He suggested that even if the central Fort St Angelo fell, a new fort at Orsi point would still be able to hold out until a relief force would come to Malta. Pallavicini produced plans with his report, but unfortunately they do not survive.[59] That same year the Count de Pagan criticised the plan which Medici had produced for a fort at Orsi Point. Medici had planned an escarped front facing Salvatore Hill (or Grand Harbour). Pagan preferred a simple parapet running all around the peninsula instead, so that its cannon would be able to fire *a fleur d'eau* that is, raking the water's edge, against approaching vessels. He proposed a central keep in the form of a tower so that the small garrison required would be able to retreat there until reinforcements arrive, and also in order to dominate the whole region. He was of the opinion that it was difficult for the enemy to occupy San Salvatore Hill, because Orsi Point Fort, Valletta, Vittoriosa and Santa Margherita's cross fire would reach them from many quarters.[60] Five years later in 1650, Fra Giovanni Bichi built his villa on Salvatore Hill, hence that peninsula was also called by the name of Bighi. Obviously he thought the place was safe enough.

It is clear from the above reports that a fort at Orsi Point was necessary for the better defence of the Grand Harbour, especially its entrance. The expected Ottoman onslaught materialised at Crete in 1645, rather than at Malta. The real need for speeding up with military projects was only felt in the late 1660s. Meanwhile only an entrenchment capable of twelve cannon was built in 1656 in the Rinella area, more exactly at Wied Ghammieq, in order to defend the south-east coast and approaches to Grand Harbour.[61] Certain observations can be made out of these reports. What is for sure is that Orsi Tower was not strong enough to counter an attack. A fort at Orsi Point was needed because although the existing forts could not be forcibly engaged by ships outside harbour, a ship lying about two kilometres due east of the harbour could fire at Rinella, Kalkara Creek, and Salvatore (Bighi) promontory without being molested. The batteries at Fort St Elmo and Santa Margherita would be out of range in this case.[62] Also there was nothing that could stop the Turks from repeating their feats of 1565 when they landed with boats at Wied Ghammieq and Kalanka tal-Patrijiet and engage Wied Ghammieq Battery and Orsi Tower. The proposed fort was not built before 1670 because the Grand Master and the Council of the Order did not feel the great urgency to make the necessary expenditure. The urgency came in 1669 following alarming developments in the East.

[59] Ibid., ff. 75, 75v, 80-81.
[60] Ibid., ff. 85, 85v.
[61] Guillaumier, 165.
[62] The average range of heaviest guns was of two kilometres approximately. AOM 6543, no pag.

2

Ricasoli's Foundation

The War of Candia (Crete) 1645 - 1669

When the Order's navy routed a Turkish flotilla and captured a Turkish galleon in 1644, the Turks unexpectedly invaded Crete instead of Malta. The Sultan accused Venice, which ruled Crete, of benevolent neutrality towards the Order of St John, so he asked for a base at Crete in order to check the Maltese corsairing caravans. He even made the Venetians believe that the vast Turkish preparations for war were directed for Malta and it was in the light of this war scare that engineers Medici, Pagan and Pallavicini had been entrusted to report on the defence of the island.[1] In the actual war at Candia the Order played a prominent part.[2] In 1648 the Maltese galleys sailed to help the Venetians and greatly distinguished themselves.[3] In 1656 a Venetian squadron defeated the Turkish fleet at the Dardanelles. These were helped by seven of the Order's galleys under the command of Fra Gregorio Caraffa, who later became Grand Master.[4] With the exception for a few lulls, for example when France and Spain were at war against each other in the 1650s, the Order's galleys always found time to go to Greek waters to harass Turkish shipping directed to the war theatre in Crete. Under the Grand Mastership of Fra Raphael Cotoner (1660 - 1663) the squadron of the order was constantly cruising in the Mediterranean, more especially around Crete,[5] and there was an increase of corsairing activities in the 1660s.[6]

In 1660, the Order sent to Crete a squadron with four hundred Maltese soldiers and seventy knights.[7] Again in 1667 under the rule of Fra Nicola Cotoner, the Council sent

---

[1] G. Ferrari, *Le Battaglie dei Dardanelli, 1656-1657*, (Citta di Castello 1913), 2.
[2] T. Zammit, *Malta - The Maltese Islands and their History*, (Malta 1926), 196.
[3] Dal Pozzo, ii, 169.
[4] Ferrari, 29.
[5] Zammit, 186-188.
[6] P. Earle, *Corsairs of Malta and Barbary*, (London 1970), 110-111.
[7] Dal Pozzo, ii, 185.

another squadron to help the Venetians against a further Turkish onslaught.[8] Two years later, another squadron was sent to Crete but the Turks, in spite of desperate opposition, did at last take the island which had resisted them for a quarter of a century.[9] The Venetians found it impossible to withstand the large number of Turkish forces brought to Crete and surrendered the fortress of Candia in 1669. The conquest of Crete transformed the Eastern Mediterranean into a Turkish lake as never before and considerably strengthened the Ottoman Empire.[10] In 1669 there was real fear and danger that the Sublime Porte was heading for glories reached only under Sultan Suleiman I more than a hundred years earlier. The capture of Crete rendered the position of the Maltese Islands very perilous. With the fall of Candia Malta found herself at the front line of the defence of Europe. The knights feared a Turkish attack on Malta in retaliation for the persistent help which they had given to the Venetians in the War of Candia. The Grand Master had to turn all his attention to problems of defence.[11]

The Cottonera Lines project

Back in Malta, on 23 October 1663 Fra Nicola Cotoner became Grand Master. He was a Spanish knight of the Langue[12] of Aragon and his mind was filled with grandiose schemes and an intense desire to perpetuate his name through the creation of a monumental line of fortification which would once and for all solve the problem of the land front of the three cities and the cover needed by the galley port, which were exposed to higher ground.[13] It is difficult to gauge the extent to which Cotoner was moved by pride or by need. Certainly Cotoner only saw to the island's needs of defence at a critical moment in the Order's military history at the fall of Crete when he had already been Grand Master for seven years. On the other hand one is kept asking why he chose to start a new set of fortifications rather than completing the Santa Margherita Lines which were left unfinished. Cotoner's modesty can thus be questioned.

The military engineer entrusted with the perfection of Malta's fortifications was Antonio Maurizio, the Count of Valperga. He was born in a noble Piedmontese family in Turin. He was the chief military architect to the House of Savoy and wrote various books about military defence.[14] On 27 March 1669, the Council of the Order decided to ask the Duke of Savoy to send Valperga for some months in order to advise the Grand Master on the design of new fortifications and to take charge of the completion of unfinished works.[15] A day later the Common Treasury announced that it would sustain all expenses of

---

[8] Ibid., 338.
[9] Ibid., 345.
[10] A.N. Kurat, 'The Ottoman Empire under Mehmed IV', in *New Cambridge Modern History* (Cambridge 1961), v, 510.
[11] dal Pozzo, ii, 383..
[12] The knights were housed into eight different medieval nations called *Langues*.
[13] Hughes, (1969), 126.
[14] Ibid., (1967), 222.
[15] AOM 261, f. 131v.

Grand Master Nicola Cotoner under whose magistracy Fort Ricasoli was built. Cotoner also founded the garrison of the fort.

Valperga's voyage.[16] Valperga travelled to Augusta in Sicily and Captain Fra Simone Rondinelli was sent there to fetch him. They arrived at Malta on 9 February 1670.[17] As can be noticed, military engineers were highly esteemed persons. He was shown around the fortifications and by 2 April 1670 he had already produced his report and drew the plans for Santa Margherita Fort (that is the Cottonera Lines), and the fort at Orsi Point (Fort Ricasoli). Valperga submitted them to the Council which approved the two new projects after a vote.[18] The main project designed by Valperga was a two kilometre continuous line of fortifications to include eight bastions, two demi- (half) bastions and nine curtains surrounding Birgu, Cospicua and Senglea. These were named Cottonera Lines after the Grand Master.

Valperga's plans for Fort Ricasoli

Valperga also designed the plan for the fort at Orsi Point, later to be called Fort Ricasoli. What Valperga wrote on 2 April 1670 is not extant, but in a subsequent report of his dated 16 October 1670 he repeated his own convictions in favour of the fort which he had traced on Orsi Point.[19] Valperga thought that the gravest danger to Malta was that it could remain without a harbour as the latter was surrounded by hills and could be reached not only by cannon shots but also in several places by lighter guns and muskets. He cited Medici and Fiorenzuola to emphasise his argument. These engineers he said had been consulted and the remedy found had been to start Santa Margherita Lines which up to 1670 had been neglected. Valperga made use of experience gained at Crete and was of the opinion that the Turks could winter here. A fort at Orsi Point was of the greatest value to a successful defence of Malta because only by building such a fort were relief forces guaranteed security on entering the harbour. The Order depended on reinforcements in case of siege and the European powers would be reluctant to send a relieving fleet unless the entrance of the harbour and Galley Port were safe. Valperga stated that this fort was an integral part of the whole system of defence of the Grand Harbour from the south-east shores because without it he considered the Cottonera Lines as most incomplete. Valperga also emphasised the similarity of his views to those of previous military engineers with regard to the actual plan of the fort.

Valperga's general plan included two lines of fortification: one running from Cottonera to Marsa Creek to envelop Corradino Heights; and another from Cottonera to Fort Ricasoli to envelop Bighi promontory. The military engineer, however, did not insist with the Grand Master that these should be built at once, because like Medici he thought it impossible for the Turks to establish themselves on Bighi because of cross fire from the

---

[16] AOM 645A, f.232.

[17] AOM 6560, no pag., and NLM 1301, f. 30.

[18] AOM 261, f. 161v.

[19] Before leaving the island, the military engineer would supervise the laying of one course of stone wall all around the outer shape of the new fort so that whoever would take over the work would know exactly where to dig for the foundations.

other forts. Together with his plan which is not extant with the report, Valperga prepared a wax model of the proposed fortifications.[20]

Approval of the project and financial contributions

On 8 April 1670 Grand Master Nicola Cotoner, as an example for further contributions, offered 100 *scudi* a month from his income to be directed towards the building of these fortifications. During the same sitting, the Council of the Order decided that the Commissioners of War and Fortifications should meet to discuss and find ways and means of raising capital for these new projects including the fort at Orsi Point.[21] Much of the capital which the Order of St John needed for the running of the Convent[22] originated from rents which the knights drew from various lands they possessed in their native lands, especially France, Spain and Italy. Even for carrying out public works or fortifications, the Maltese were rarely taxed, except for being obliged to give a days' work on Sundays. Since Malta belonged to the Order under title of a feudal deed, they could only tax the Maltese by permission of the Pope. However, these two projects were gargantuan by the standards of the day especially when compared to the small population and economy of the island. Since the Maltese people, especially those of the harbour region, stood to gain by these works, they were this time asked to contribute their share of the burden. On 13 May the Commission of War and Fortification suggested that a new tax on all immovable property in Valletta, Senglea and Vittoriosa be levied by permission of the Pope. Other revenue could be forthcoming from the King of France who had bought the St Christopher Islands from the Order of St John; from the selling of forests belonging to the priories of the Order in France; the return of debts owed to the Order; and the employment of a new, and hopefully more efficient director of the postal service which was costing 8,000 *scudi* per annum.[23]

Up to that time and even for a month after, the project for the fortification of Orsi Point was considered part of the Cottonera project. Hence this money was originally also destined for the fort at Orsi point until Fra Giovanni Francesco Ricasoli made his donation. As a result of the financial measure regarding the new tax, Pope Clement X did grant permission to the Grand Master to impose the tax, but only on 5 December 1670, when other funds had been found for Fort Ricasoli.[24] During the 1670s, all the energies of the island were directed towards this great effort to make the defences of the Grand Harbour impregnable - an effort comparable only to that which took place a century earlier when the walls of Valletta were completed in five years. This time it was the turn of the south-eastern defences to be perfected.

---

[20] AOM 6402, ff. 305 - 307v. The defence line which Valperga designed to envelop Corradino Heights was only built with great modifications by the British in the 1870s, while the other line from Cottonera to Ricasoli was never built.

[21] Ibid., f. 162.

[22] The country where the Order was ruling, therefore Malta, was considered the knights' Convent.

[23] Ibid., ff. 164v-165v.

[24] NLM 705, no pag. Some of the money accruing from the new tax was still spent on Fort Ricasoli when the money given by Fra Ricasoli was expended.

The Grand Master and Council of the Order adopted the report of the Commissioners of War and Fortifications on 10 June 1670. The fort at Orsi Point and Cottonera were to start and be continued in earnest. The Common Treasury destined 8,000 *scudi* a month for the projects.[25] It can safely be asserted that the commencement of works on Fort Ricasoli took place shortly after 10 June 1670.

The foundation of the fort by Fra Giovanni Francesco Ricasoli

The foundation of Fort Ricasoli took place on 15 June 1670. Answering to the Grand Master's example of liberality in forwarding money for the fortifications, Fra Giovanni Francesco Ricasoli donated 20,000 *scudi* to the Order for the fortifications.[26] The Grand Master called Ricasoli to the Council where the members thanked the generous Italian knight and by unanimous vote applied the money to the fort being built at Orsi Point which henceforth would be named Fort Ricasoli. The founder's coat of arms was to be placed at the most conspicuous place at the fort with an inscription in his honour.[27]

Fra Giovanni Francesco Ricasoli

Giovanni Francesco was born in Florence in 1602, in a noble family which traced its origins in Jeremy son of Hildebrand in the turn of the tenth century. He was the fifth son of Baron Paolo Ricasoli (1561-1620), and his wife the Contessina Serristori.[28] On 20 September 1617 he became a knight novice of the Langue of Italy, and on 21 December 1618 he started his career in Convent as page-boy to Grand Master Fra Alof de Wignacourt.[29] He settled permanently in Malta in 1630 and served in the Order's navy for a long time This was the shortest way for promotion in the Order's government. He performed many obligatory and voluntary six-month periods of duty on the Order's warships called caravans, distinguishing himself in many combats at sea not only because of his courage, but also for his insight towards navigation and command. He was therefore appointed Captain of a galley. In February 1641, Ricasoli was Captain of the flagship which was returning to Malta from Syracuse in convoy with another three galleys. Suddenly a storm arose and the flagship was shipwrecked at Calarossa near Cape Passero. Meanwhile Ricasoli upon seeing the ship being violently rocked by the high

---

[25] AOM 261, f. 166.

[26] Ibid. The sum given by Ricasoli varies according to different authors. Dal Pozzo put the figure at 30,000 *scudi*. (dal Pozzo, ii, 390.). With him agree the majority of subsequent writers who obviously did not consult the archives. Only Mifsud (page 33.) agrees with AOM 261. NLM 647 (no pag.) gives the figure at 20,300 *scudi*.

[27] Ibid. For the full text of the entry in the Council's register of the foundation of the fort see Appendix IV.

[28] L. Passerini, *Genealogia e Storia della Famiglia Ricasoli*, (Florence 1861), Tables VI and IV, opposite pages 95 and 57. See Appendix II for full genealogy. An indirect descendant of Fra Ricasoli, Baron Bettino Ricasoli, served as Prime Minister of Italy in the 1890s. The same noble family is still a well known producer of Chianti and other wines in Tuscany.

[29] Passerini, 100.

Bailiff Fra Giovanni Francesco Ricasoli, founder of the fort.

sea tried to save her by tying a cable around his waist and swimming to a nearby promontory to which he tied the galley. Although the ship was lost, most survivors owed their life to him that day.[30] Two months later he was appointed Captain of the galley *Pretoria*.[31] On 9 June 1642 Ricasoli again showed his courage when together with other Captains of the squadron of galleys, he sailed in boats into the harbour of Tripoli by night in order to sabotage vessels. Only one ship was destroyed, but that was by Ricasoli and his men.[32] On 30 May 1644, Fra Giovanni Francesco Ricasoli was appointed a senior knight or Bailiff (Balì), having been in possession of a Commandery for five years.[33] In 1661, while he was Captain of the galley *Patrona di Malta*, he narrowly escaped capture by the Turkish flotilla which met the Maltese squadron near Milos.[34] In fact he hurled himself on to a Turkish ship while boarding was taking place and after fighting courageously, took possession of the prey with its exceptionally rich cargo.[35] Together with a brother of his, Giovanni Francesco Ricasoli contributed a large sum of money for the marble decoration of the organ loft in the church of Santa Maria Nuova in Florence.[36] In 1664, he prepared and paid for his tombstone in St John's conventual church, now the co-cathedral, in Valletta.[37] After 13 January 1668, he resided in the large house called *Banca dei Giurati* or *Palazzo della Città* in Merchants Street, Valletta, (now used as the Public Registry office).[38] He died on 26 July 1673.[39]

Fra Ricasoli had obtained the sum he later donated for the Fortifications in a curious manner. While Captain of a galley of the Duke of Tuscany in the Eastern Mediterranean[40] on a mission of reconnaissance in search of a Neapolitan galley, presumed lost, he fought against some Turkish ships and was wounded. So he was given 25,000 *scudi* as recompense for his enterprise.[41] Ricasoli could also raise money from his various rents because he held many commanderies in Italy such as the commanderies of San Giovanni delle Padule in the Priory of Capua;[42] that of Santa Lucia di Viterbo; and that of San Filippo di Osimo (both in the Priory of Rome); that of Caltagirone in the Priory of Messina; the Bailiwick of Cremona in the Priory of Turin;[43] as well as the commandery of San Giacomo in Campo Corbolino of the Priory of Pisa.[44]

---

[30] Dal Pozzo, ii, 63-64, And Passerini, 100.

[31] AOM 470, f. 122.

[32] Dal Pozzo, ii, 65-66. Little did Fra Ricasoli realise that the men in the fort he founded in 1670 would foil a similar attack by the Italian navy three hundred years later!

[33] AOM 470, f. 133v. A number of caravans entitled a knight to a Commandery or the rents accruing from a large estate in the country of his Langue. A number of years as Commander qualified the knight for the title of Bailiff, or senior knight.

[34] Dal Pozzo, ii, 293.

[35] Passerini, 100.

[36] Ibid., 101.

[37] For the inscription on his tombstone see Appendix III.

[38] V. Denaro, "Houses in Merchants Street, Valletta," in *Melita Historica*, ii, no. 3, 164.

[39] Ibid., and Passerini, 101,

[40] The sailor-knights were still allowed by the Order to serve the navies of their native countries.

[41] AOM 482, ff. 153v, 154.

[42] AOM 470, ff. 164, 164v.

[43] Ibid., ff. 133v.; 139v.; 159, 159v.; 721v.

[44] AOM 482, ff. 144, 144v.

Tombstone of Fra Giovanni Francesco Ricasoli in St John's Co-Cathedral, Valletta.

It must be noted that it was the Council of the Order that had decided about the precise destination of the money donated by Ricasoli. The Bailiff had only indicated that the money should be spent on the fortifications. On the recommendation of the Duke of Tuscany[45] who had also obtained the necessary brief (letter of instructions) from the Pope,[46] and also as an act of gratitude, the Council of the Order bestowed upon Fra Ricasoli the privilege to wear the golden Grand Cross of honour of the Order on 15 September 1670. Throughout its long history, members of the Order had distinguished themselves by giving donations for the furtherance of the Brotherhood. The donation of Fra Giovanni Francesco Ricasoli was an example of the liberality of individual

---

[45] AOM 1444 no pag.
[46] AOM 482, ff. 153, 153v, 154.

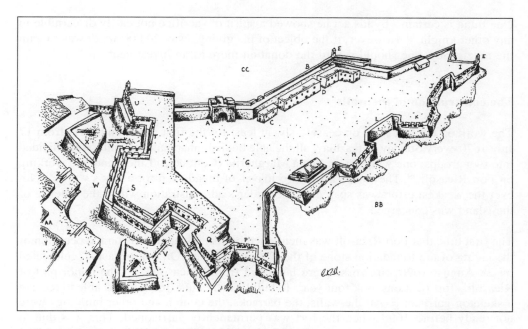

Artist's impression of (Hospitaller) Fort Ricasoli including:

A.	Porte Cochere behind Main Gate with Governor's House
B.	Tenaille (Grand Harbour) Front
C.	St Nicholas Church
D.	Officers' and Married Quarters
E.	Vedettes
F.	Gunpowder Magazine
G.	Place of Arms (Parade Ground)
H.	Soldiers' Barracks
I.	Bastion No 1
J.	Curtain No 1
K.	Bastion No 2
L.	Curtain No 2
M.	Bastion No 3
N.	Curtain No 3
O.	Bastion No 4
P.	Curtain No 4
Q.	Bastion No 5 (St Dominic demi-bastion)
R.	Curtain No 5
S.	Bastion No 6 (St Francis bastion)
T.	Curtain No 6
U.	Bastion No 7 (St John demi-bastion
V.	Caponnier of communication
W.	Ditch
X.	Ravelin
Y.	Glacis
Z.	Traverses
AA.	Covertway
BB.	Open Sea
CC.	Rinella Bay in Grand Harbour

knights, to be followed by other knights and Grand Masters who had the well-being of the Religion (as the Order was sometimes called) at heart.[47] Fra Ricasoli was a very noble, rich and powerful knight who had spent most of his life in the service of the Order. There is every reason to believe that Ricasoli was aiming for the magistracy. His act could have gained him support in any eventual election. However, Ricasoli died before Grand Master Cotoner did and we can never know what his real intentions were.

---

[47] A. Mifsud, *The English Knights Hospitallers of the Venerable Tongue of England*, (Malta 1914), 17.

One thing is certain - by his act he showed a spirit of sacrifice not easily discernible in any other knight.[48] However, if the object of his giving away 20,000 *scudi* was to gain the magistracy, one should regard the donation more as an investment.

The construction of the walls

The work on the fort went on ceaselessly, at least for the first few months. As from 17 July 1670 every Sunday or feastday, all the able bodied inhabitants of Malta were divided into two groups: one working on Santa Margherita (Cottonera) Lines; and one working on Fort Ricasoli.[49] They were given two loaves of bread each for a day's work.[50] Not ever the weakest effort was spared by the Order's administration where the defence of the island was concerned.

The first time that Fort Ricasoli was mentioned by its new name was on the occasion of the laying of the foundation stone of the Cottonera Lines. On that occasion, celebrated on 28 August 1670, fireworks were launched from "Ricasola".[51] The major part of Ricasoli's fortifications took four years to build. On 12 June 1674, it was able to receive a skeleton garrison.[52] All the walls, the barracks, the church and other buildings were not ready before 1698 when the fort was permanently garrisoned. This was due to financial and other constraints. Until 1693, about 100,000 *scudi* had been spent on Fort Ricasoli by the Common Treasury. The 20,000 *scudi* Ricasoli gave did not serve for its completion[53] and in 1676 Malta was visited by the most deadly bubonic plague ever, which killed about 11,000 people out of an estimated 55,000.[54] The physical, economic and social devastation wrought by the plague was horrifying. All large projects stalled for many years.

Description of the fort[55]

The fort as built by Valperga has undergone only a few alterations. The major changes are the building of a retrenchment by the British at the neck of Bastions 4 and 5; and the building of the outworks, especially the counterguard in the 1790s. It is a bastioned fort, almost triangular in shape, with three distinct fronts, two facing the sea and one facing land approaches. The front facing south-east or the area known as Rinella is the land front, composed of one centre bastion and two lateral demi-(half) bastions, thus

---

[48] In 1749, Fra Jacques-Francois de Chambray donated a sum of money for the completion of the Fort at Ras it-Tafal, overlooking the harbour at Mgarr, Gozo. It was similarly named after him, Fort Chambray. Spiteri, (1994), 453.

[49] Although this is what the documents say, we must believe that this is an exaggeration.

[50] AOM 261, f. 167.

[51] Ibid., f. 169v.

[52] AOM 262, f. 30v.

[53] Hoppen, 92.

[54] J. Micallef, *The Plague of 1676; 11,300 deaths*, (Malta 1984), passim.

[55] See plan on page .

Aerial photograph of Fort Ricasoli from outside Grand Harbour. Note the Number 1 curtain with casemated battery for six 80 pounder RML guns next to Ricasoli Point (Number 1) Bastion. An oil tanker is being cleansed at the tank-cleaning facility.   (Courtesy: DOI)

forming a crown-work. The front which faces north-east or the open Mediterranean Sea (or open sea front), is also made up of bastions, four in all. The trace chosen for the front which faces south-west or the Grand Harbour front is *tenaille*, that is composed only of long straight walls called curtains built in the shape of a gentle zig-zag.

The three land front bastions were named from left to right: St Dominic demi-bastion flanking the open sea;[56] St Francis bastion, being the central one; and St John's demi-bastion, flanking Rinella Creek in Grand Harbour. These three bastions were later renamed Bastions Number 5, 6, and 7 respectively by the British. These bastions are linked by two curtains. This land front is two tiered, so that there is actually a double line of fortification; the upper walls proper and a lower fausse-braye. A fausse-braye is a line of defensive walls built in the ditch between the counterscarp and the bastions and curtains proper. The object of Valperga had been to increase the number of guns on the main front by doubling the walls, as was done later at Fort Manoel, and the right flank of St John's Bastion of Cottonera. The inner upper line is really a number of linked cavaliers, or towers. The flanks of the bastions are right angled according to the composite Dutch and Italian systems of fortification.[57] The whole land front is 350 metres long.

---

[56] AOM 1016, f. 263.
[57] NLM 34, f. 15.

47

Pre 1976 aerial photograph of the Land Front of Fort Ricasoli from above the open sea coast looking towards the south-west to Rinella Bay in the right background. Most of the fortifications visible in foreground were destroyed in 1976 to make way for the new road. Note the fausse-braye; the caponnier of communication at the centre; St Francis (Number 6) Bastion; the oil tanks; the left ravelin with shed below its scarp; the counterscarp; and the main barracks' roof and arches in the right. Beyond Rinella Bay is Salvatore Hill. (Courtesy: DOI)

Starting with the upper terrace, both the faces of the bastions and curtains are 63 metres long, while the flanks are 25 metres. St Dominic upper bastion was demolished after 1714.[58] The dimensions of the lower walls, that is the fausse-braye are 88 metres for St Francis and St Dominic (originally 75 metres),[59] while St John's are 75 metres. The

---

[58] NLM 290 map.
[59] Ibid.

48

Aerial photograph of the bastioned Open Sea Front of Fort Ricasoli with Valletta and Mdina in the background. Note the Married and Officers' Quarters on the left and the Ricasoli arm of the breakwater with the bull-nose light at its point. (Courtesy: DOI)

curtains are 38 metres and the flanks about 8 metres.[60] All around the land front is a 25 metres wide ditch with counter-scarp. Across the ditch are two ravelins. Each one of their faces is 60 metres long.

The front of the fort which faces south-west flanks Bighi Bay in Grand Harbour. It is known by different names, including Marsa, or Salvatore front since it faces those places.

---

[60] AOM 6402, f. 48v.

49

Aerial photograph of Fort Ricasoli showing the Grand Harbour *tenaille* front from Ricasoli Point to the Main Gate. Note the circular moat of Orsi Tower below the re-entrant bastion at the Point. The main casemated barracks at the back of the land front bastions are visible in the background. Three searchlight towers are conspicuous on bastions 2, 3 and 4.   (Courtesy: DOI)

It is made up of four curtains in the form of a gentle zig-zag called *tenaille*. Each curtain is about 125 metres long on average.[61]

The front of the fort which faces north-east flanks the open Mediterranean Sea. It is a four bastioned trace with small curtains in between. The first one is Ricasoli Point bastion whose salient angle faces Fort St Elmo. During the British period these four bastions were named Numbers 1 to 4, starting from Ricasoli Point being Number 1 Bastion, and moving towards the south-east to St Dominic demi-bastion (Number 5). The total length of the fort from the salient angle of Ricasoli Point Bastion (No. 1) to the salient angle of St. Francis (No. 6) bastion is 575 metres. This makes Fort Ricasoli the largest fortress

---

[61] AOM 6402, f. 48v.

The right flank of Saint Dominic demi bastion with the fausse-braye on the lower ground.

in Malta excepting the five fortified towns of Valletta, Floriana, Vittoriosa, Cospicua and Senglea. The average height of the parapets is between 15 and 20 metres. Outside the ditch is the glacis which is 50 metres at its widest. On Valperga's specific instructions, the parapets of the sea fronts were made three metres wide, while those of the land front were four metres wide. The average thickness of the walls was about 2.35 metres (excluding the casemated parts).

The number of embrasures on the land front was originally two on each flank on the fausse-braye and one in each flank of the upper bastions. On all the other bastions' flanks and faces there were at least two embrasures in each.[62] During the eighteenth and nineteenth centuries, these embrasures were increased considerably. The upper flanks of each bastion now have five embrasures each, while the flanks of the fausse-braye still have two each. St Francis bastion of the fausse-braye has thirty embrasures, while the upper terrace has nineteen. St Dominic bastion has 57 embrasures. St John Bastion needed least artillery since it faced Cottonera. It has two embrasures.[63] The two ravelins have a total of twelve embrasures; three on each of their four faces.[64] During the British period, all these embrasures were complemented with guns and small expense magazines.

---

[62] AOM 6551, ff. 48-48v. This number is according to Valperga's instructions
[63] Guillaumier, 170.
[64] Castagna, I, 161.

General view of Fort Ricasoli from Saint Francis Bastion looking towards north-west. Saint Nicholas Church is on the left; married quarters at centre; and recreation establishment is on the right.

The parade ground is the largest in any fort in Malta being 100 metres long.[65] All around the two sea fronts of the fort, casemates were dug for effective fire across the waters. The internal buildings of the fort were constructed starting from 1680s through the nineteenth century by the knights and by the British. The first constructions erected with the fort were the casemated barracks, both of the south-east land front and those by the south-west Grand Harbour front.

There were three main gates: one for daily use with drawbridge facing south-west; and the other two in the middle of each land front curtain, one facing south-east between bastions number 6 and 7, and one facing east between bastions number 5 and 6. These two gates were always sealed and without drawbridge. Fort Ricasoli had also three other false gates: two of them sealed, one facing east and the other facing north-east. These were provided in case of any need for sorties during a siege. Another gate faced north-east and was opened according to the needs of Orsi tower.[66] The Main Gate is baroque in style and is unique in Malta; unmistakable with its four spiralling columns, and faces

[65] Not including the Floriana parade ground which is in a fortress town.
[66] NLM 142d, ff.456v. - 457.

Fort Ricasoli's Main Gate as reconstructed in 1958. The spiral columns have five instead of the original six twists.

Rinella Creek and the Grand Harbour.[67] A flight of steps leads from the shore to this gate. The normal way to and from the fort was by boat.[68]

During the building of Fort Ricasoli's foundations, the military engineer Valperga frequently visited the site. On 15 October 1670 he submitted a report to the Commission

---

[67] Hughes, (1969), 131.
[68] AOM 1016, f. 259v.

of War and Fortifications on the progress of work, together with his suggestions on the methods of construction. He strongly advised against any alteration to his plans because this would cause great errors in angles and defences, the only remedy for which would be expensive demolition and rebuilding. Such caution was needed for the measurements of all the ramparts, fausse-braye, the ditches, covert-ways and ravelins. He urged good lime and sand to be used all around the walls. He instructed the masons on the building of level fortifications by means of boulders and soil. For an example he showed them the new walls which were being erected between St John and St Nicholas Bastions of the Cottonera Lines. He insisted that the parapets should be at least as high as a man's breast in order to forestall any accidental fall. He wanted the ground outside the Main Gate to be levelled to create a road to render possible the movement of carts and soldiers from Rinella Creek. The walls of the fausse-braye were about 22 metres high. By the time Valperga wrote his report in October 1670, they had reached the height of two metres.[69]

Valperga's final instructions and departure

Before leaving Malta, Valperga also commented on other works. He was of the opinion that the fortifications then being planned to envelop Fort St Elmo and thus complete the walls of Valletta were not urgent and could be taken in hand when the Order had enough money because these works served more for decoration and grandeur than for the actual defence of the mouth of Grand Harbour, it being already well defended by Forts St Elmo, St Angelo, Valletta and the new Fort Ricasoli.[70] Valperga also designed a fort for Marsamxett Island, with ramparts similar in dimensions to those of Fort Ricasoli.[71] This latter fort was built after 1725 by another military engineer and was called Fort Manoel.

By 17 November 1670 Valperga had finished the foundations of all the fortifications he designed and submitted all the plans to the Grand Master. He left for Naples on the *Sant' Antonio* galley, also escorted by the *San Luigi*. He was granted an allowance of 1,000 doubloons by the Council of the Order.[72] However, he had to pay for the expense of the journey.[73]

A critical appreciation of the plan

During the seventeenth century, the universally accepted method of defence was the bastioned fortification, that is a fort whose walls are all defended by one another and as a result of which there is no dead ground, which is land outside the fort that could not

---

[69] AOM 6551, ff. 48 - 48v.
[70] Ibid., 49. The lower Fort St Elmo bastions of Valletta were subsequently built by the military engineer Don Carlos de Grunenbergh after 1684.
[71] AOM 6554, ff. 131v. - 132v.
[72] One doubloon was roughly equivalent to four *scudi*.
[73] AOM 261, f. 171v.

General view of Fort Ricasoli from above the mouth of Grand Harbour looking towards the east. Note the circular moat of Orsi Tower, lower right, as well as an expense gunpowder magazine on the bastion above it. Note the difference between the bastioned trace of the Open Sea Front (left) and the tenaille trace of the Grand Harbour Front (right). The Ricasoli arm of the breakwater is in the foreground. Fort St Rocco lies on the slope in the background.   (Courtesy: DOI)

be seen (and therefore shot at) by means of flanking fire from any part of the fortifications. In Ricasoli, all the component parts of the fortifications could defend each other, and in this regard, Valperga's trace is laudable. But Ricasoli is also a coastal fort and for this reason it is at an advantage because the two fronts which flank the sea do not need major works such as bastions, but a tenaille[74] trace is sufficient, as was actually

---

[74] NLM 34, f. 214.

carried out in the Grand Harbour south-east front. The open sea (or north-east) front, however, was built in the form of a bastioned trace which added to the strength of that side. When another military engineer criticised Valperga for having constructed such an unnecessarily strong fortress, he was probably referring to the open sea front; surely not the land front which was at once heavily criticised for the smallness of its bastions.

In two reports submitted to the Council of the Order dated December 1670 and April 1671, the Maltese engineer Gaspare Beretta approved of Valperga's design of Fort Ricasoli, but he wished to see further and more substantial fortifications built on the fort's land front. His comments were similar to what he had already reiterated about the Cottonera Lines, that is, Ricasoli needed more ravelins and greater bastions and curtains.[75] One of the most important defects which subsequent military engineers attributed to the fort was the smallness of its land front.[76] Both the French Republican spies operating in Malta in 1798, and the Maltese insurgents and British strategists during the blockade of the French troops in 1798 to 1800, thought that Ricasoli could be assaulted at the small bastions especially in the left flank of the land front.[77] Valperga himself in his report said that he wanted a "small fort" to be built and Beretta at once objected to this idea.

It is true that Fort Ricasoli does not cover the whole length of the promontory, and the subsequent projects on the outworks were in consequence of this defect. The bastions are also very small when compared to those of Cottonera which were designed by the same engineer. The faces of the bastions of Cottonera are about 100 metres compared to 75 metres (upper wall) or 86 metres (fausse-braye) for those of Ricasoli. The flanks of Cottonera are 40 metres long; those of Ricasoli are 13 metres or 25 metres. Cottonera's curtains are each 150 metres long; those at Ricasoli land front are 38 metres or 65 metres.[78] One has to keep in mind, however, that the land front of Ricasoli had to defend a much smaller region than the approaches to Cottonera. Because of this major defect most subsequent military engineers considered Fort Ricasoli a small and weak fort. This is why outworks and retrenchments were added to the land front down to the 1830s. The slow building and re-building of Fort Ricasoli continued through the following two centuries.

---

[75] AOM 6402, f.307.
[76] Hoppen, 92.
[77] See Chapter 7.
[78] NLM Plans C 20.

3

The Building of the Fort, 1670 - 1798

One of the gravest mistakes made by the builders of Fort Ricasoli was that the land front was constructed with bastions and curtains which were too small not only for the fort, which was the largest on the island, but also for the area which they had to cover and defend. Even after the completion of the major parts, many of the military engineers who came to Malta to comment on the state of the fortifications criticised Valperga's work and often proposed alterations to the fort. But these changes to the original designs compounded the problem. By 1693, the fort had cost the Common Treasury of the Order about 100,000 *scudi*,[1] and by 1798, a similar sum was yet again spent on repairs and additions.

Supervising Engineer Fra Mederico Blondel

The task of seeing to the building of Fort Ricasoli once Valperga had sailed, fell on the chief military architect of the Order of St John, who in 1670 was Fra Mederico Blondel. On 25 June 1670 the Grand Master and Council of the Order granted permission to Blondel to exchange the compulsory one year's caravan duty on the galleys of the Order with two years' service at the site of the fort.[2]

Criticism of Valperga's Project

Beretta's opinion

Even before Fort Ricasoli approached completion in 1674, criticism of Valperga was already forthcoming from other military engineers. It was customary for the Order to ask various military engineers to examine and comment on some new project. Their reports were distributed among all those interested, be they military engineers or

---

[1] Hoppen, 92.
[2] AOM 124, no pag.

common, but trusted, knights. Valperga's reports were criticised by Lieutenant General Gaspare Beretta on 4 December 1670 and on 1 April 1671.[3] He was the first to suggest that the site needed a larger fortress, with longer curtains at the land front. This would render unnecessary Valperga's project for joining Cottonera to Ricasoli with three large bastions across Kalkara valley which would have entailed a large expenditure.[4] Beretta advocated great care in the alignment of the bastions so that the strength which the fort lacked due to its size, would be remedied by accuracy of fire.[5]

Verneda's comments

At times, the plans and reports for proposed fortifications were sent to military circles in Europe for inspection by foreign engineers. This was done partly to guarantee expert opinion, but also in order that princes might take interest and promise contributions for the works. Malta was regarded as a bulwark of Christendom. Fort Ricasoli was no exception. On 31 July 1671 Count Verneda, an engineer in the service of the Republic of Venice commented on the fortifications of the Cottonera after that he had attended a meeting held for this purpose in the residence of a certain General Grimaldi.[6] Verneda at once agreed with Beretta that Ricasoli was too small. He argued that the boats of communication could be fired upon from Salvatore Hill which, he said in the light of experience gained at Crete, could be occupied.[7] The siege of Candia had taught the Venetians many lessons in the art of siege warfare and Verneda was continuously referring to what had happened in the East when he warned that the Turks could occupy the ditch of Ricasoli because the fausse-braye had produced bastions which were too small, same as the ravelins; all being ominously similar to those of Candia. Verneda opted for a radical solution to the defence of the south east shores of Grand Harbour and the three cities by the construction of one continuous line of defence made up of eight great bastions starting from Ras Hanzir and ending at a point on the open sea roughly 1000 metres to the south east of Ricasoli where Fort St Rocco now stands.[8] The shores between the front of Fort Ricasoli and the terminating point of the new line would be secured by a trench of coast defence.[9] The Turks would not be able to see, much less occupy any part of the coast of Grand Harbour with this scheme. But it was not all that simple to construct such a line. There were four valleys to cross. It is true that the number of bastions would have been the same as in the Cottonera, but Verneda's bastions would each have been double the size of any of Cottonera's bastions. The scheme was prohibitively expensive and manning the walls would have created problems. The Marsa would still have been liable to enemy occupation. Presumably because of these reasons Verneda's proposals were never carried out.

---

[3] AOM 6402, f. 303.
[4] AOM 6551, f. 54 v.
[5] AOM 6554, ff. 139-140.
[6] AOM 6551 f. 55 v.
[7] Tregellas, 187.
[8] AOM 6551 ff. 55 v-56.
[9] Tregellas, 207.

Blondel's defence

Verneda's arguments were subsequently taken up by Blondel. The fact that Blondel, the engineer who had supervised the works at Ricasoli after Valperga's departure was the one who criticised him is disturbing. He denied any responsibility for all faults which were later noticed by other engineers.

In 1681 Blondel advocated Verneda's proposals for a larger Cottonera, and criticised Valperga's plans to join Ricasoli to Cottonera. He regretted the fact that Verneda's proposals could not be put into effect since Cottonera was already in an advanced stage of construction, with parapets completed in some parts. He commented on Ricasoli regretfully, and thought that it was a pity that such an important site was occupied with such a small and defective work. The fausse-braye added to its cost but not its strength. In carrying out the works, Blondel was compelled to make some alterations in the design, especially on the sea front. Blondel suggested the building of a sea battery *a fleur d'eau*; for the removal of Orsi Tower; and for the widening of the ditch. He was against the building of the barracks in the casemate of the land front. He was highly critical of Valperga's use of the composite Italian and Dutch system of defence.[10]

Grunembergh' contribution

One of the most famous military engineers who reported on Fort Ricasoli was Don Carlos de Grunembergh, who was a colonel and engineer in the service of the King of Spain in Sicily.[11] Grunembergh came to Malta in 1681 at the invitation of Grand Master Gregorio Caraffa in order to give his advice *'per regolar alcune difficoltà che s'incontrano'*.[12] He was shown around Floriana Lines and Fort Ricasoli by the Commissioners of War and Fortifications, who put their difficulties.[13] Grunembergh did not suggest any extensive alterations so as not to burden the Order with undue expenditure.[14]

Grunembergh mentioned the fact that Ricasoli had always been considered as the weakest fort, so he proposed to lengthen the fausse-braye by twenty-six metres so that the enemy might not venture near the fort at Wied Ghammieq, being dominated by his proposed works. He also proposed a covert way to the prolonged fausse-braye which was inclined towards the sea in such a manner that the ravelin should dominate the glacis more thoroughly. Grunembergh did not think that the enemy could post any battery on Salvatore Hill. He also thought that St John half bastion was too high to successfully defend the Grand Harbour (tenaille) front, and therefore he suggested lowering the bastion to six metres higher than the Main Gate curtain. He also wanted to lower the covert way

---

[10] Ibid., 206, 209.
[11] Hughes, (1967), 215.
[12] AOM 262, f. 124.
[13] Ibid., f.127.
[14] dal Pozzo, ii, 482.

and the glacis in front of the middle bastion of the land front so that they would be more fully dominated by the latter front.[15]

These recommendations by Grunembergh were approved by the Council on 16 March 1681. In payment he was given a medal costing 400 doubloons with the effigy of St John on one side and the coat of arms of the Grand Master on the other.[16] The Council also decided that all works of fortification should stop until the Floriana Lines were completed.[17] A knight, Fra Ugo de Vauvilliers was entrusted with the execution of Grunembergh's designs on 16 April 1681.[18] Notwithstanding the latter order, some of the alterations suggested by Grunembergh were started immediately. In July 1683, the former landowners of land at Rinella which had been requisitioned for the building of the fort were paid from the tax for the fortifications.[19] However that year difficulties arose again and once again Grunembergh was invited to come to Malta.[20] He could only come to the island in January 1687.[21] Although this time Grunembergh did not comment specifically about Ricasoli, he still showed his greatest interest in the defence of the mouth of Grand Harbour and advised the Order that batteries *a fleur d'eau* or simple parapets should be built on the rocky foreshores of Fort St Angelo and Fort St Elmo in order to assist Ricasoli in the defence of the harbour mouth. His other contribution was the design of the surrounding bastions of lower Fort St Elmo which not only completed the Valletta walls, but added greater strength to the mouths of both harbours.[22]

The Governor's House

Before Grunembergh's arrival in 1687, the house of the Governor and Lieutenant Governor was built at Fort Ricasoli. Blondel's plan for this house was approved by the Council on 18 November 1686.[23] The House was situated just behind and above the Main Gate. At ground floor level was a guard room which faced the parade ground and which had four arcades. Agius de Soldanis[24] writing in the 1750s described this house as a very beautiful gubernatorial palace, access to which had previously been by means of a round flight of steps the ruins of which were still discernable on the pavement of the third arcade of the guard house. The palace suffered extensive damage during a thunderstorm and whirlwind on 6 November 1757.[25] In this house was an armoury; a portrait of Grand Master Nicholas Cotoner; and painted on the walls were the coat of arms of the

---

[15] AOM 6551, ff. 64v.-65. Also in AOM 6554, ff. 176-179. Tregellas, 196, attributes these alterations to Blondel.

[16] AOM 262, f.128v.

[17] Ibid.

[18] Ibid., f. 129v.

[19] Ibid., f. 157v.

[20] Ibid., f. 160.

[21] Ibid., f. 289v.

[22] Ibid., ff. 292v., 293v.-294v.; Also AOM 6551, ff. 66v.-67 and AOM 6554, ff. 190v.-192v.

[23] AOM 262, f. 279v.

[24] NLM 142 d, f. 458.

[25] Faurè, iv, 1041.

The fausse-braye at lower left and the left flank of Saint Francis Bastion at upper right.

The left flank of Saint Francis Bastion showing four embrasures at the top and two other at the (lower) fausse-braye.

Governors of the fort with relative inscriptions underneath each one.[26] Over the years, and probably in the early nineteenth century, the coat of arms were painted over and their memory was forgotten. On 14 November 1901 the frieze was re-discovered by some British Officers who had meanwhile turned the room into an Officers' Mess. It is not known whether they had been led by de Soldanis' manuscript or whether the discovery was accidental. The coats of paint were scraped by Captain Butcher of the Royal Artillery. Butcher himself, together with a certain Mr Portelli Carbone filled up the blanks in the inscriptions where the letters had been obliterated. The commander of the fort, Major General D. O'Callaghan of the Royal Artillery requested further instructions from the Governor since the cost of restoration would amount to £20, according to architect L. Gatt. The restoration was carried out in December 1901 from the funds in excess of the vote for the Restoration of Antiquities of the Civil Government.[27] Unfortunately the house was destroyed by a bomb in 1942.[28]

The state of the fort in 1693

All the necessary buildings inside Fort Ricasoli were nearing completion in 1693, and the Commission of War and Fortifications was trying to find means of establishing a permanent garrison. For this reason on 22 November, the Grand Master Fra Adrien de Wignacourt, the Grand Prior of the Order (that is the head of the knights' chaplains), and engineer Blondel were invited by the Commission for a tour of inspection at the fort. The visit took place on 4 December.[29] Blondel gave a running commentary to the Grand Master and his retinue as they walked about. This provides a picture of the state of the fort in 1693.

On disembarking from the boat, the Commissioners inspected and approved of the ramp which lead to the Main Gate for it was built appropriately for the transport of material and was provided against denudation by rain water and sea spray. Blondel explained that Valperga was responsible for the major parts of the walls including the bastions, curtains, fausse-braye, ravelins, counter-scarps and for the ditches, but neither Valperga nor Blondel himself were responsible for the internal casemated barracks in the land front, since they both were on the continent when the works were planned and executed. The casemate was not contemplated in Valperga's plans. It was already collapsing since it was weak and could not support the terreplain. The internal walls of the bastions were eroded, as also the masonry of the parapets, because the stone quarried from the same site was not good enough.[30] Blondel proposed that the steps leading to St Francis Bastion should be widened. The visitors also inspected St John's Half Bastion, where it was noticed that the curtain joining it to St Francis Bastion was also giving way, and that all

---

[26] Ibid., f.459.

[27] National Archives of Malta (NAM), Public Works 143, ff. 92v.-93, 112v.

[28] H. Braun, *Works of Art in Malta; Losses and Survivals in the War*, (London 1946), 7.

[29] AOM 1016, ff. 258-263.

[30] The site of Ricasoli is composed of globigerina limestone, which provides the golden building stone commonly known as *tal-franka*. It normally weathers well (Bowen Jones, 24,26,28), but this particular type could have been of an inferior quality.

the land front was made up of parts which were too small for effective defence. Blondel defended his position by reminding the Commissioners that he had noticed these defects when the flanks of the scarps and counterscarps of the ditch near the open sea were nearing completion, but he insisted that his remarks had been ignored by them. The Grand Master and the Commissioners praised both the Governor and the Lieutenant Governor's houses, as also both sets of barracks.[31] In 1681 Blondel had criticised these barracks due to their proximity to the bastions.[32] The Grand Master and the Commissioners decided that repair works and alterations at Ricasoli should be taken in hand immediately.

The building continues

During the next five years, further works were carried out at the fort. In 1697 the vedette or sentry box at Ricasoli Point was restored and a guard was stationed there in order to give the alarm when ships approached.[33] A year later, all the parapets on the two sea fronts were restored with the use of lower coralline limestone (*zonqor*) stone, which is much harder than globigerina limestone.[34] On the shore at the furthest north-east corner of the fort, where the land front ditch and the glacis meet the open sea, the rock was cut so that there would be no possibility of encircling the fort by way of the shore from Wied Ghammieq.[35] In 1698 the fort was permanently garrisoned by Grand Master Ramon Perellos y Rocaful. Therefore the coats of arms of the Order of St John, and of Grand Masters Nicola Cotoner and Perellos were sculptured over a commemorative inscription above the Main Gate of the fort. The inscription recorded the foundation of the fort by Fra Giovanni Francesco Ricasoli, Nicola Cotoner's contributions for its erection, and the stationing of a permanent garrison in the fort by Grand Master Perellos.[36] The inscription reads as follows:[37]

FORTALITIUM A FUNDATORIS NOMINE RICASOLUM
EMIN. NICOLAUS COTONER AUXIT,
DEFENSORIBUS ANNUO STIPENDIO
LIBERALITER CONSTITUTO:
EMIN. RAYMUNDUS DE PERELLOS Y ROCCAFULL
PERFECIT
AD ARCENDIAS HOSTIUM INSIDIAS,
AD TUTANDAM NAVIUM STATIONEM,
MILITE INTRODUCTO,
ILLAESAM IN POSTERUM
PUBLICAM SECURITATEM
SERVAVIT.
ANNO REPARATAE SALUTIS 1698

---

[31] AOM 1016, ff. 258-263.

[32] Tregellas, 209.

[33] AOM 1016, f.425.

[34] Ibid. The contract for the provision of the stone was given by tender and was won by Giovanni Maria Saliba of Luqa who later sub-contracted the work in February 1698. Ibid., f. 426.

[35] Ibid.

[36] Ibid.

[37] NLM 372, no pag.

Grand Master Fra Ramon Perellos y Roccaful under whose magistracy Fort Ricasoli was permanently garrisoned.

In 1703, the French military engineer and knight Chevalier Claude de Colongues presented the Council with his plans for Ricasoli. It seems certain that the tenaille Grand Harbour front was not yet completed. It was Colongues who proposed a battery with battlements in this front, as well as the traverses and the caponniers in the ditch. He also proposed a small fort at San Salvatore. Plans for more outworks started to take shape.[38]

Fort Ricasoli was furnished with large cisterns[39] which continued to be used until quite late in the nineteenth century. On 24 March 1708 Romano Carapecchia, a famous architect who was employed as *fontaniere* or water supply general manager with the Order, reported about all the cisterns in the fortresses of Malta. Compared to the other fortified places, Ricasoli had enough water. There were ten cisterns, which at the time contained 946 cubic *canne*, or 7568 cubic metres of water. The largest three cisterns were in the place of arms or parade ground near the barracks.[40] The Commission of War and Fortifications kept custody of the keys of these cisterns after 1755.[41]

The additions of 1714 by the French military engineers

In 1714 a huge Turkish naval armada, composed of thirty soltanas, seventeen Barbary men-of- war, twenty galleys and forty galliots were preparing for war.[42] Fortunately for the Maltese, the fleet was directed against the Venetian Republic's possessions of Morea (the Peloponnesus) and Corfu. But the Order could never be sure before the attack materialised and an added impetus was given towards the perfection of the fortifications. In the six months starting 1 October 1714, no less than 46,262 *scudi* were spent on defence.[43]

An anonymous report suggested more batteries be placed at Ricasoli, since it was invaluable for securing the mouth of Grand Harbour in view of relief forces coming to Malta in case of siege. It mentioned the shortcomings of the left flank of the land front, which was still incomplete. The writer thought that it was necessary to build a counterguard there, and to lengthen the fausse-braye to the sea. He was optimist about the outcome of an eventual siege if these works, together with a fort on Bighi (San Salvatore Hill), were taken in hand.[44] Some work on the glacis was undertaken in consequence to this report.[45]

In reply to the above report, the second engineer of the Order, Fra Francois Bachelieu started by criticising Valperga's choice of the site of the land front. If it had been

[38] AOM 6551, ff. 74v.-77; AOM 6554, ff. 218-225.
[39] NLM 142 d., f. 466v.
[40] AOM 6551, ff. 80v.-83v.; AOM 6554, ff. 237-242.
[41] AOM 1015, f. 134.
[42] R. Cavaliero, *The Last of the Crusaders*, (London 1960), 112.
[43] AOM 6545, f. 3.
[44] AOM 6552, ff. 40v-41v.; NLM 290, 9-13. These proposals match those outlined in the plan attached to the backpage of NLM 290 manuscript.
[45] NLM 290 backpage plan.

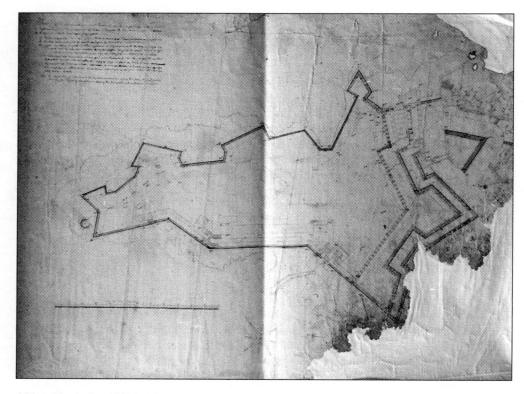

Old archival plan of Fort Ricasoli. Note the moat of Orsi Tower on the left and the countermines on the right.

(Courtesy: NLM)

constructed further afield, it would have defended a larger area towards Cottonera. He agreed that Valletta and Fort St Elmo should dominate Ricasoli and Dragut Point. Bachelieu suspected that the anonymous writer had been merely reporting hearsay and grievances from within the fort itself, and calculated that the cost of building the counterguard and other outworks suggested by the previous writer on the left flank of the land front would be prohibitively expensive at about 38,000 *scudi*. He conceded that a fort at Bighi was necessary.[46]

The countermines[47] of Fort Ricasoli must be attributed to a certain engineer Boulè.[48] The mines were completed after 1715 by digging shafts at certain points in the ditch. Four main tunnels protruding from these shafts then by-passed the ravelins from

---

[46] AOM 6552, ff 50v.-52v.; NLM 290, 9-13.

[47] Countermines were tunnels excavated beneath the glacis through the counterscarp wall, terminating in a small shallow pit designed to house an explosive charge which was fired by the defenders when the enemy occupied the ground directly above the mine, or when they would be heard digging a mine nearby. Spiteri, (1994), 639.

[48] NLM, Plan R 19.

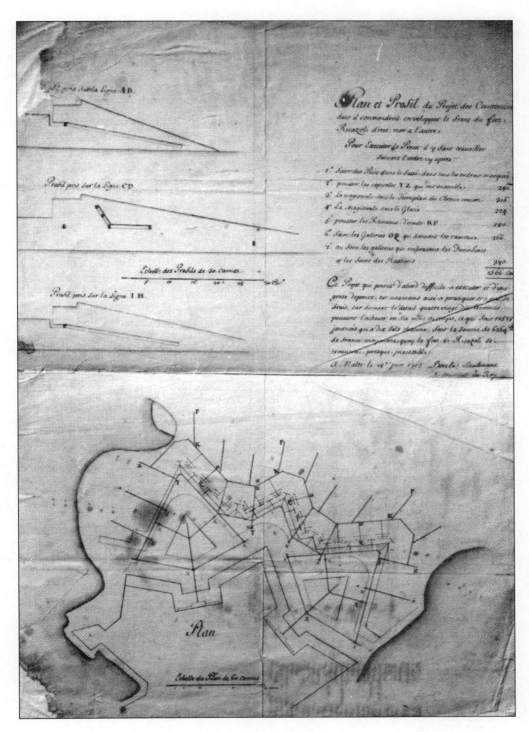

Old archival plan of the countermines of Fort Ricasoli. (Courtesy: NLM)

underneath the ditch with central mines right under the centre of each ravelin. The other mines were cut beneath the ditch and glacis. According to Boulès scheme, 3,112 cubic metres of mines were dug. According to his plan, ninety men worked on the project for six months for a total 12,528 working man-days costing 6,254 French *livres*.[49] Only the 1761 report by the engineer Pontleroy ever mentions the countermines again.

The three most notable engineers who came to Malta in this period were Jacob de Puigiraud de Tignè, Francois Charles de Mondion, and Philippe de Vendosme. They were all French. The art of military architecture had been the domain of Italian and Spanish engineers in the sixteenth and seventeenth century. The French engineers of the eighteenth century followed in the footsteps of the great Sebastian la Prestre de Vauban, who had developed three systems of fortification, and the French school became master.

De Tignè

De Tignè made two visits to Malta, one in 1715[50] and one in 1716.[51] He was a knight of the Order of St Louis and the highest ranking engineer in the French army. Later he was given the honour of wearing the Cross of the Order as a reward for his devotion to the knights and for services rendered.[52] De Tignè carried on a number of minor, but very necessary works in most fortifications of Malta. True to the reputation of the French military engineers of the time, de Tignè concentrated on the need for perfecting the land front of Fort Ricasoli by adding outworks. He reported to Council on 25 September 1715.[53]

According to de Tignè, Fort Ricasoli was important for the defence of the Grand Harbour, especially in view of protection for relieving forces. He could not understand how Valperga had built such large bastions at Cottonera and much smaller ones at Ricasoli. He proposed the following alterations and additions to Ricasoli: forty metre traverses and a retreat passage for ten musketeers; the removal of the gentle scarp and stairs in the ditch; the widening of the places of arms on the curtains; the repair of the covert way to which a small banchette should be added on top of the parapet; the elongation by twenty metres of the covert way in front of the left bastion using hard wearing stone, mortar, and a mixture of quicklime and iron and lead; the reinforcement of the glacis and building of two caponniers of communication joining the curtains of the fausses-braye to the counterscarp at the centre of the two ravelins; the closure of the two extremities of the ditch with walls; the repair of many internal parts of defence such as banchettes, parapets and embrasures.

Even if all these additions and alterations were carried out, the fort would still be weak, and therefore de Tignè suggested that Ricasoli should be divided into two by the building

---

[49] Ibid.
[50] Porter, 168.
[51] Ibid., 175.
[52] AOM 627, f. 218.
[53] NLM 1301, ff. 97-104.

The rock hewn ditch in front of Bastion and Curtain number 2. St Emo arm of the breakwater is in the distance.

of a retrenchment composed of two half bastions, one curtain, one ravelin and ditch exactly half way between the land front and Ricasoli Point roughly at the height of the barracks behind St Nicholas Chapel. This would have turned Ricasoli Point into a keep.[54]

On 17 July 1715, the Commission of War and Fortifications approved de Tignè's suggestions, and most of them were subsequently carried out.[55] The retrenchment as proposed by de Tignè, however, never materialised, probably because the land front lies at higher level than Ricasoli Point and therefore the latter would not hold if the land front was occupied. Vauban himself commented on de Tignè's suggestions. On 15 February 1716 he recommended what had been proposed. Ricasoli, he noted, enjoyed an excellent position. However, its successful defence also depended on the other forts which dominate it, such as Valletta and Cottonera.[56]

In 1716 de Tignè came to Malta for a second visit and submitted a further report to the Commission of War and Fortifications on what still had to be done in most fortresses in

---

[54] As appears in NLM Plan R. 9, and R. 17.
[55] AOM 6552, f. 39.
[56] NLM 1301, f. 133.

Malta. He also presented an estimate of the cost of the works he was proposing. With regard to Ricasoli, he proposed an expenditure as follows:[57]

1000 *scudi* to modify the covert way, to construct places of arms and traverses;
2000 *scudi* for the construction of a counterguard;
  200 *scudi* to do away with the steps in the salient angles of the covert way;
  400 *scudi* to construct two caponniers of communication from the curtains to the ravelins, and six traverses in the ditch;
  150 *scudi* to construct one large traverse under St John's Bastion;
  200 *scudi* to repair the parapets and banchettes;
6000 *scudi* to construct a retrenchment from Wied Ghammieq to Rinella Creek; and
1000 *scudi* to construct a large circular battery to defend the entrance of the Grand Harbour.[58]

In other words, de Tignè proposed to spend 10,950 *scudi* on Ricasoli alone, out of a total 246,150 *scudi* he thought necessary for all the fortifications. The most interesting works he proposed were the caponniers which were constructed later, and then reconstructed under British occupation. The counterguard Tignè proposed was subsequently also suggested by Vendosme. It was only finished between 1788 and 1795.

Vendosme's suggestions

Although Philippe de Vendosme's greatest contribution towards the defence of Malta were his projects for the coastal batteries and redoubts towards which he also contributed financially, he also produced a report on Fort Ricasoli, dated 25 September 1715, in which he was highly critical of the measurements of the points, faces, flanks the covert ways, as well as the position of the barracks. Indeed he only praised some repairs which had been done after an earlier visit of his.[59] Vendosme argued that if the enemy captured a ravelin, they could easily fill the ditch with its own rubble and scale both the fausse-braye and the bastions on the land front. He contended that the parts of the fortress did not defend each other effectively, and brought as an example the tenaille front which had few flanks. Vendosme suggested that the counterguard, which the anonymous writer of 1715 had proposed, be built at the earliest possible occasion.[60] Vendosme thought that if Ricasoli was taken in a siege, the rest would fall within five days. It was therefore necessary for the fort to be further strengthened, especially by lowering the ditch in order to let sea water in and thus turning it into a sea filled moat. The fort would thus be isolated and invulnerable.[61]

After all these suggestions had been put to the Commission of War and Fortifications, the latter advised Grand Master Perellos that the damage which had been caused by the

---

[57] NLM 1301, ff. 175-177; Porter, 173-174.
[58] By 1761, this battery was again advocated by another engineer, AOM 1054, f. 18.
[59] No evidence of Vendosme's earlier visit is tracable.
[60] AOM 6560, no pag.
[61] AOM 6552, ff. 39v.-40.

The left ravelin in front of Curtain number 5 between Saint Dominic and Saint Francis Bastions. The caponnier of communication is also visible.

The caponnier of communication showing the doors leading to the left ravelin and the rifle gun-ports.

various conflicting schemes and counter schemes of all these military engineers was great and confusing. Some defective works needed demolition and rebuilding. The Council of the Order therefore decided to adopt de Tignès works only and not to allow alterations, since those were the bare minimum for effective defence.[62] De Tignès proposals for Ricasoli were therefore considered as final. It is true that other engineers commented on repairs needed at Ricasoli, but in the main these latter engineers of the Hospitaller period stuck to de Tignès proposals.

Engineer de Mondion and Ricasoli

The third military engineer to comment about Fort Ricasoli in this period was Charles Francois de Mondion. He had studied under Vauban and came to Malta in 1715 as de Tignès deputy.[63] Mondion later became the resident engineer to the Order of St John and contributed greatly towards the building of baroque Malta in the 1720s by designing Fort Manoel, which is considered as the most perfectly planned fort in Malta, and by re-shaping Mdina with his town planning and magnificently ornate palaces there. For services rendered, he too was made an honorary knight of St John.[64] Mondion did not belie de Tignès suggestions when he commented on Ricasoli in September 1719. He too was of the opinion that the strategic position of the fort was crucial for the successful defence of the whole harbour area. He proposed the building of more covert ways, even though the completion of the Floriana Lines took precedence.[65]

Repairs carried out between 1722 and 1761

Most of the alterations as suggested by the three French engineers of the 1715-1719 period were only carried out because of a further war scare in 1722. For the period between 22 November 1721 to 27 March 1723, Pietro Mallia, the contractor, was paid 3,376 *scudi* 0 *tari* 18 *grani* by the Commission of War and Fortifications. His masons had repaired the covert way and glacis.[66] Palissades were erected in the covert way soon afterwards. The caponniers were ready by 8 July 1722.[67] Although the Commission of War and Fortifications had a very lean budget for all works of defence to be carried out, more money was forthcoming for the payment of children and galley slaves who were employed in carrying the material needed.[68] All the repairs envisaged for the minimum state of defence were completed by 1722.[69] However, Pietro Mallia was still paid a further 70 *scudi* for work done at Ricasoli between 1722 and 1728.[70]

[62] NLM 1301, ff. 111-112.
[63] D. de Lucca, 'Baroque Town Planning in 18th Century Mdina', in *Sunday Times of Malta*, 1 August 1976.
[64] AOM 627, f. 162v.
[65] AOM 1011, ff. 22-23v.
[66] AOM 1019, ff. 109-110.
[67] AOM 1011, f. 43v.
[68] Ibid., ff. 45, 45v.
[69] AOM 267, f. 114v.
[70] AOM 1019, ff. 109-110.

Workmen were employed to repair the damage done by the natural elements on the open sea flank of the fort which suffered greatly from its exposure to the sea. In 1752, it was restored by the use of more durable stone at the expense of the Cotoner Foundation.[71] By that time salt pans had been cut on the foreshore of the fort. The Lieutenant Governor employed people to gather the salt. Each person inside the fort was allowed a ration of 3/20 *tummoli*[72] of free salt. The chaplain's ration was 1 *tummolo*, while the commanders received a larger share.[73]

The 1761 war scare

In the early 1760s added incentives were created for improvements in the defence of the island because of another war scare. This was as a result of the capture by the Christian slaves of a Turkish sailing warship called the *Ottoman Crown*, which reached Malta on 6 October 1760. The ship was taken over by the Hospitaller Navy and re-named *San Salvatore*. Grand Master Emanuel Pinto de Fonseca was concerned about the possibility of reprisal by the Ottomans, and preparations for a siege were made.[74] The Order once again invited a number of French military engineers to Malta. Francois Charles Bourlemaque was head engineer[75], the others being Pontleroy, Desandrouin, Fournier, and Decuire. On 18 October 1761 they presented their views and proposals to the Commission of War and Fortifications.[76] They agreed with what de Tignè had suggested almost half a century earlier. Fort Ricasoli was important for the defence of the Grand Harbour, therefore urgent repairs had to be approved immediately.[77] Earlier that year some outworks which would have made investment of Ricasoli easy were demolished.[78]

During the French engineers' visit, the resident engineer of the Order, Francesco Marandon defended his position by asserting that he had already noticed some defects in the bastions during de Tignès visit. He was suggesting demolishing the fausse-braye in order to enlarge the bastions proper, and that St Dominic Half Bastion, which was rather small, weak and isolated, should be made more secure by building a retrenchment at its neck. This was quite an interesting proposal which was only carried out more than sixty years later under British rule. Another interesting proposal made by Marandon was that should Gozo be occupied by the enemy, the Gozitan refugees could be housed at Fort Ricasoli.[79]

---

[71] Hoppen, 94.

[72] One *tummolo* was equivalent to 0.1818 hectolitres.

[73] NLM 142 d., f. 465v.

[74] C. Testa, *The Life and Times of Grand Master Pinto*, (Malta 1989), 126.

[75] Bourlemaque was a knight of the Order of St Louis. He was brigadier in the army of France, and came to Malta at his own expense.

[76] Porter, 179.

[77] AOM 6557, f. 89.

[78] AOM 271, f. 176; AOM 6558, f. 13v.

[79] AOM 6558, ff. 97v.-98v.

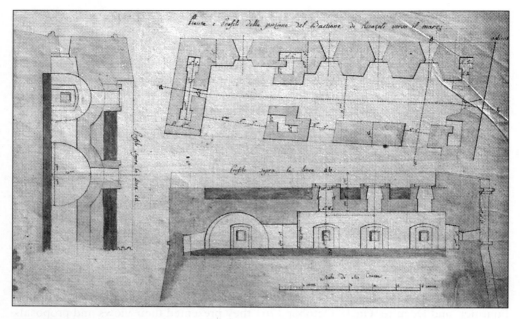

Old archival plan showing embrasures and casemated gun emplacements in bastion number 2 on the Open Sea Front.

(Courtesy: NLM)

Bourlemaque's deputy, the engineer Pontleroy rejected Marandon's idea for the demolition of the fausse-braye, since the enlarged bastions would still not be large enough for an effective defence, and therefore the money spent would be merely thrown down the drain. He was in favour of de Tignès proposals for building the much needed outworks on the left of the land front. Attention had to be paid there in order to eliminate any dead ground near the outworks. Pontleroy also proposed some alterations to the countermine system.[80] The opinions of the visiting Frenchmen were heeded more by the Council of the Order, and in fact little was done immediately after 1761.[81] The fausse-braye was extended and the covert ways were enlarged under the direction of the knight-bailiff and engineer Rene Jacques de Tignè, until the funds which were forthcoming from the Cotoner Foundation were exhausted.[82] The owners of land requisitioned for these works were only paid in 1771.[83]

The building of the outworks on the left flank, 1788-1795

The last major works carried out at Fort Ricasoli by the Hospitallers were those undertaken between 1788 and 1795 by means of which the greater part of the suggestions

---

[80] AOM 6557, ff. 117-119.
[81] Hoppen, 94.
[82] AOM 1054, f. 18.
[83] AOM 1015, f. 94.

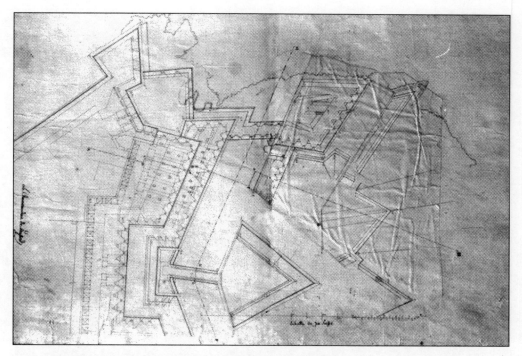

Old archival plan of the outworks to the left (open sea) flank of the Land Front of Ricasoli which were subtantially completed between 1788 and 1795.   (Courtesy: NLM)

made by earlier engineers were put into effect. Because of its exposed position and earlier neglect, the fort was in a very bad state of repair in 1788, and a full scale programme of renovation and maintenance had to be undertaken. By 1789, under the direction of bailiff de Tignè the repairs to the sea flank were complete, a small tenaille had been added to the left flank of the land front, and work had begun on repairing and improving the covert way. Work ceased because of lack of funds. However in 1788 bailiff engineer de Tignè managed to obtain modest additional funds which could be directed towards the outworks of Fort Ricasoli.[84]

The money needed amounted to 116,000 *scudi*, according to an estimate by the bailiff engineer.[85] They were to be paid by the Common Treasury of the Order, and work started in May 1788,[86] although the plans were only ready the following 11 December. This time the walls were not built of the soft globigerina limestone, but of hard lower coralline limestone, right up to the cordon. The parapets were to be three metres wide, two metres over the terreplain and about 1.2 metres over the banchettes. They were constructed of

---

[84] Hoppen, 94.
[85] AOM 1015, ff. 322, 323.
[86] AOM 1054, f. 18.

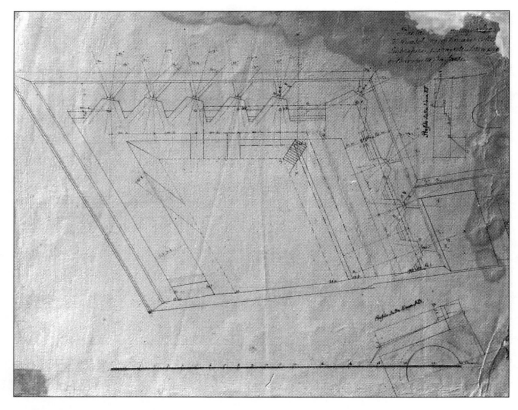

Old archival plan showing the St Dominic counterguard, built between 1788 and 1795.

stone, although the banchettes were made of earth. A platform covered the upper part of the opposite counterscarp. No embrasures were allowed in the new works, since these could be dangerous where stonework was used for the parapets.[87]

After one year's work, the gangs of bricklayers and children were still occupied with the walls of the right ravelin, and much of the funds would be exhausted when only the work on the two ravelins was completed.[88] Further plans for the outworks on the left flank of Fort Ricasoli were drawn by the resident French knight engineer Fra Etienne de Tousard on 25 August 1792.[89] Both the bailiff de Tignè and Fra de Tousard worked hard for the securing of the mouth of Marsamxett Harbour. In 1792, the latter drew up the plans for the last fort built by the knights in Malta at Dragut Point in the entrance of Marsamxett Harbour. The bailiff de Tignè donated the first 1,000 *scudi* for its

---

[87] AOM 1015, ff. 331-332.
[88] AOM 1054, f. 18.
[89] AOM 1015, f. 352.

Pre 1976 aerial photograph of the open sea front of Ricasoli from above Wied Ghammieq, looking towards Valletta and Sliema in the background to the north-west. Note the left flank of the Land Front, including the covertway; ditch with shed on the left; St Dominic counterguard; the fausse-braye; St Dominic (Number 5) half-bastion to the right and Bastion Number 4 to the left by the open sea. Beyond the retrenchment lies the parade ground. The viaduct of Fort St Elmo arm of the breakwater, destroyed by the Italian E-boats on 26 July 1941 is visible in the upper right. This part of the ditch was infilled and Curtain No. 5 was breached in 1976 when a road was built for the passage of container trailers into the parade ground of the fort.　　　　　(Courtesy: DOI)

construction, and same as had happened at Ricasoli and Chambray in Gozo, the fort was named after its founder. It is interesting to note that Fort Tignè has an analogous site to that of Ricasoli when the Malta harbours are viewed together. According to de Tousard's plans, St Dominic Half Bastion had to be completely restored; the fausse-braye beneath it was elongated to the shore; and traverses would link the small bastion on the open sea front to the counterguard. About 650 cubic metres of walls were planned, but only about 500 cubic metres were subsequently completed.[90]

The money for the new repair works was forthcoming by way of the customs duties called *Nuovo Imposto*, which had been collected since the building of the Cottonera Lines to finance defence works. On the 20 October 1794, Salvatore Gatt, the contractor of works, was paid 1,827 *scudi* 10 *tari* 10 *grani* due to him for one year's work,[91] although he was paid an average 1,200 *scudi* yearly.[92] Between 21 May 1788 and 12 August 1795, the Common Treasury spent 78,193 *scudi* on the outworks of Ricasoli, mainly on weekly wages for the workers and in the provision of materials especially lime and palissades. These latter materials determined the extent of the expenditure since outlay on wages was almost always the same. This happened for example during the week ending 1 May 1793 when 1,172 *scudi* were forwarded to Giuseppe Portanier for six months' provision of lime. Out of the figures one gets an idea of the extent of activity at Ricasoli.[93]

Table I			
Expenditure in repairs on Fort Ricasoli by the Common Treasury, 1788-1795			
Year	scudi	tari	grani ·
1788	7,072	3	1
1789	13,857	10	13
1790	6,109	9	0
1791	6,755	8	3
1792	11,729	4	6
1793	25,633	10	15
1794	3,883	0	16
1795	1,243	0	8
total	76,284	11	2

With the total figure above one must add 14,214 *scudi* 7 *tari* 13 *grani* spent by the Cotoner Foundation during the same period, as well as 2,541 *scudi* 7 *tari* 18 *grani* spent

---

[90] NLM Plan R. 18.
[91] AOM 1015, f. 427.
[92] Ibid., f. 432.
[93] AOM 1013, passim.

by the Foundation in 1769-1770, which would bring a total of 92,949 *scudi* 3 *tari* 11 *grani*.[94]

The peak period of work was reached in 1793 when 25,633 *scudi* were spent. 1789 and 1792 were other peak years in which 13,857 and 11,722 *scudi* were spent respectively. The two months which mark the peak of activity were May and June 1793. During these two months no less than 9,766 *scudi* were spent, mainly for the provision of lime and other materials.[95] Another 9,749 *scudi* were spent by the Common Treasury on repair works at Ricasoli between April 1796 and February 1797.[96] When the French Republican troops occupied Fort Ricasoli in 1798, the construction on the outworks was not yet fully completed.

As can be seen above, the knights were ready to spend huge sums of money for the repair works at Fort Ricasoli, even when as a consequence of the French Revolution the Order was receiving less than half the money it used to get from its commanderies in Europe. The building of Fort Ricasoli only stopped whenever funds were exhausted. Obviously the earlier mistakes of Valperga and other engineers; the location of the fort which was too exposed and vulnerable to the elements of nature; and the important strategic situation of the place itself, made the knights quite oblivious of the great amount of money the fort had cost them.

---

[94] AOM Treasury Series A 48.
[95] AOM 1013, passim.
[96] AOM 1015, f. 562.

4

The Arming and Working of the Fort

The Cotoner Foundation

By 12 June 1674, Fort Ricasoli was in such an advanced state of construction that an enemy could occupy it to their own advantage and presumably a skeleton garrison was posted there, although the official establishment of the garrison occurred only twenty-four years later. This can be ascertained by the fact that on that day, Grand Master Cotoner donated 15,000 *scudi* to the Treasury so that some warehouses might be built at Valletta wharf and at a place called the Polverista, so that the resulting rents would be devolved for the wages of the garrison of Fort Ricasoli. He also gave 150 *scudi* monthly for the same purpose until the said buildings were completed.[1] This was really the start of a series of endowments by the same Grand Master which led to the Cotoner Foundation nineteen years later.

The garrison of Fort Ricasoli, as well as the endowment of the chair of Surgery and Anatomy at the Hospital of the Order, were paid by the Cotoner Foundation, which was founded by Grand Master Cotoner on 13 August 1693.[2] The Foundation was composed of three knight commissioners nominated by the Grand Master. One of them had to be Aragonese, the other two of different nationalities. They had no fixed term of office. The first three commissioners were Fra Arnaldo Moix, Fra Charles Felix Doraison, and Fra Cristoforo Balbiani.[3] The Foundation was sometimes also referred to as Ricasoli Foundation. The estates of the Foundation were divided into urban and country. By 27 February 1676, Grand Master Cotoner had already acquired or built the following estates which were later administered by the *Fondazione*, and which earned the sums as shown in the following table II:

---

[1] AOM 262, f. 30v.
[2] AOM 131, ff. 38-40. The Foundation also paid annual allowances to members of the Order who were related to Cotoner.
[3] AOM 6430, f.126. A partial list of the commissioners may be seen in Appendix V.

Table II

Property administered by the Cotoner Foundation[1]

2 houses over arches in a Valletta Square rented @ 232 *scudi* per annum;
other houses near the old abattoir of Valletta @ 30 *scudi* per annum each;
10 newly-built warehouses at Marsamxett, Valletta (5 ground-floor and 5 first storey);
12 warehouses outside the Customs House at Valletta;
4 warehouses near Salvatore Church at Valletta Marina @ 120 *scudi* per annum;
4 warehouses and 2 houses near Porta della Marina @ 220 *scudi* per annum;
4 warehouses at St Theresa quay, Cospicua, rented @ 80 *scudi* per annum;
Windmills: 2 at St Margaret place, Cospicua @ 300 *scudi* per annum;
1 near the Capuchin Monastery at Floriana @ 130 *scudi* per annum;
1 near the gunpowder magazine at Floriana @ 130 *scudi* per annum;
1 at Zebbug and 1 at Zurrieq, both @ 150 *scudi* per annum;
1 at Naxxar @ 150 *scudi* per annum;
1 at Lija which was still under construction.

[1] AOM Treasury Series A 37, ff. 1-9.

By 1690, the Foundation was earning 2,441 *scudi* annually from its one-hundred and eighty different urban properties.[4] It was also earning 2,387 *scudi* from its twenty-one country estates. Meanwhile the Common Treasury of the Order assumed the burden of maintenance and restoration works in the same properties, as well as costs of transport, and publication of notices for gabelles.[5] By 1798, the country estates of the Cotoner Foundation also included lands near or at Wied Znuber; Mriehel; Bingemma; tal-Blata; and tal-Qala; Hal Muxi, ta' Laurenti, St Blase Chapel, and at Gisari ta' Gallesia near St Martin's (the last four at Zebbug); at tal-Handaq; ta' Gxisa at Attard; Irdum Masesa at Madliena; and ta' Bonport; Wied Zebbug near St Julian's; Xghajra; ta' Forn il-Gir at Zebbiegh; ta' Braxia (Pietà); and at Fiddien; the gardens at tal-Hareb at Attard; and three other windmills at Zejtun, Gudja and Zebbug.[6] The annual income of the Foundation for the financial year May 1790 through April 1791 accrued to 27,505 *scudi* 3 *tari* 3

[4] AOM Treasury Series A 45 (1).

[5] AOM Treasury Series A 45 (3), 112.

[6] AOM Treasury Series A 48.

grani, of which only 4,902 *scudi* 0 *tari* 15 *grani* from the country estates. The expenditure on the urban property was of 20,830 *scudi* 5 *tari* 8 *grani* leaving a balance of 1,772 *scudi* 8 *tari* 19 *grani*, since there was a balance in the country account.[7]

The Foundation was responsible for the maintenance of the garrison in Fort Ricasoli, whilst the fortifications were the responsibility of the Commission of War and Fortifications and the Common Treasury. However, there were provisions for reciprocal contributions if the need arose.[8] Though the fort was lightly manned in 1674, the garrison of the fort was only established on 13 June 1698 by Grand Master Ramon Perellos when Fra Ramon Despuig was appointed first Governor.[9] The delay was caused by a jurisdictional quarrel with the Bishop. A solution was found by means of a Papal Brief of 1693 granted in favour of the Order.[10]

The Maltese-Hospitaller Garrison

The garrison consisted of the Governor, who was the commander of the fort, and the following officers and men in order of rank: the Lieutenant to the Governor (these highest two ranks were reserved for knights); Major; Sergeant; Lieutenant Sergeant; corporals and common soldiers. Maltese soldiers could reach the rank of Sergeant at the least.[11] Although no evidence has been traced as to whether they had to be Aragonese or not, all known Governors were Aragonese.[12] Two of these Governors, Ramon Despuig and Francisco Ximenes de Texada later became Grand Masters. The position of Governor in Fort Ricasoli was considered as a post which offered good training ground for the Magistracy. The second-in-command was the Lieutenant Governor. The person chosen for this position had to have all the best qualities to impart military discipline. The letters of appointment of the Lieutenant Governors invited their colleagues to treat them as equals, and their subordinates to obey and respect them.[13]

A case history of the career progression of a Governor is that of the Aragonese knight Fra Giorgio Montaner. On 11 June 1712 he was appointed Captain of the Valletta regiment.[14] Four days later he was granted leave in order to visit Spain.[15] A fortnight later, however, he was appointed Lieutenant Governor of Fort Ricasoli, which suggests that he did not proceed to his native country after all.[16] His successor, Fra

---

[7] AOM Treasury Series A 46 (18), and A 48 (19).

[8] AOM 653, f.202.

[9] AOM 264, f. 166v., and AOM 133 f. 3v. Despuig was elected by the Council of the Order on 10 April 1698.

[10] The problem of spiritual jurisdiction is dealt with in Chapter V.

[11] A(rchiepiscopal) A(rchives) F(loriana), L(iber de) S(tatus) A(nimarum), Vittoriosa, 1797, ff. 39-40.

[12] See Appendix VI for a partial list of Governors.

[13] AOM 1051, f. 242. See Appendix VII for a partial list of Lieutenant Governors.

[14] AOM 616, f. 112v.

[15] Ibid., f.54.

[16] AOM 6430, f. 127.

Matteo Duretta was appointed on 1 April 1713, making Montaner's term at Ricasoli of less than ten months.[17] Montaner's connection with Fort Ricasoli resumed on 17 December 1736 when he became Governor.[18] Two years later he transferred back to Valletta without severing his ties with the fort as Commissioner of the Cotoner Foundation.[19]

The great majority of soldiers inside the fort were Maltese, and many lived there in Married Quarters together with their families. The social history of the fort, including details about the structure of the population are treated in Chapter 6. Suffice to say here that the garrison averaged sixty to seventy troops[20], but the total inhabitants averaged about 140 persons. These could be supplemented though by a troop of fifty men from the sailing ships battalion in case of siege. In 1777 the Regiment of Malta was raised by the Chapter General of the Order. It was recruited from foreign lands, but most of its 1,203 soldiers turned out to be incompetent. 2,988 *scudi* of the Cotoner Foundation were henceforth redirected for the regiment, which needed a yearly total of 84,240 *scudi*. As compensation, the regiment had to detach 111 men as reinforcement for Fort Ricasoli, as well as 87 to Fort Manoel.[21]

The garrison included men with special duties. There was a sentry in the sentry-box overlooking the harbour, whose duty it was to signal the guard boats.[22] The Grand Hospitaller had to send a surgeon to Fort Ricasoli in case of emergency,[23] although normally there was a salaried resident doctor inside the fort.[24] A boatman regularly connected the fort with Valletta and the other harbour towns, such as Battista Debono of Vittoriosa who dutifully performed his daily trips for sixteen years between 1689 and 1705, when he finally took up the post of guard of the Cospicua *Manderacchio*, or lighters' pen.[25]

Armament and other Ordnance

In its visit to Fort Ricasoli on 2 October 1697, the Commission of War and Fortifications decided the exact position and amount of guns to be posted inside the fort. The members suggested that the platforms should be made of hard lower coralline limestone,[26] but no details are available as to the number or calibre. On 17 March 1708, some naval guns

---

[17] Ibid.
[18] AOM 145, f.275v.
[19] AOM 6430, f.126.
[20] NLM 142d, f.466v.
[21] J.M. Wismayer, *The History of the K.O.M.R. and the Armed Forces of the Order of St John*, (Malta 1989), 30-33.
[22] AOM 1016, f.465.
[23] AOM 1015, f.386.
[24] AOM Treasury Series A 48.
[25] AOM 1186, f.124.
[26] AOM 1016, f.425.

of the sailing ship *San Giovanni Battista* were transferred to Ricasoli.[27] It being also a coastal fort, Ricasoli could use guns interchangeably with the squadron of sailing ships-of-the-line of the Order which was established in 1701. In 1714 most of the guns in the fort were reported to be in good working order, and the shot was near the platforms ready for use.[28] Two years later the Commission of War, acting upon the advice of the military engineer Mondion, sent a consignment of shot to Fort Ricasoli, which was enough to cater for one hundred light guns. Mondion suggested that the defenders had to have a superiority of 3:1 in ammunition against the besiegers in order to be safe. Also following his advice, 800 cubic metres of stone balls and 9,000 palissades which could cover 180 metres of ground were also sent there.[29] During the war scare of 1722, the guns of all calibres were increased to thirty. On 29 June eighty gunpowder barrels were sent to the fort although proper storage had not as yet been found for them.[30] Gunpowder magazines were surely in existence though by the 1750s. They were also used to manufacture ropes therein,[31] and to store palissades.[32] On 1 May 1723, it was deemed necessary to arm the fort with six cannon to defend the Grand Harbour flank alone.[33]

Whenever there was a war scare, all the artillery was mounted. This happened for example in December 1746, when such frantic action was noticed in the fort by the chaplain Gaetano Reboul.[34] Occasional repairs and provision for ornaments were made by the Commission of War. In 1758 cartridges were provided for the cannon to be loaded.[35] For the later half of the eighteenth century, information about the exact number of guns in the fort is available, as shown in Table III below.[36]

The Order attached great importance to the defence of the Grand Harbour. The defence planners had amassed the greatest concentrations of artillery existing in Malta at Fort Ricasoli and Fort St Elmo, both at the mouth of the harbour. In 1785, Fort Ricasoli alone was armed with 70 guns, which included thirty-one 24-pounders, ten 12-inch mortars, and two 12-inch shell firing mortars. In comparison, Fort St Angelo had the next biggest concentration of ordnance with sixty guns; Fort Manoel fifty, and Fort St Elmo's St Raymond Post at the mouth of the Grand Harbour, forty-two. These out of a total of 1,127 cannon and mortars in the three islands.[37] Table IV gives a break down of the ammunition at Ricasoli in September 1785.[38]

---

[27] AOM 265, f.261.
[28] AOM 266, f.125v.
[29] AOM 6565, ff. 6,8,28, and AOM 6547 ff. 8,10,32.
[30] AOM 1011, ff. 37,37v.,46,57.
[31] NLM 142d, f.466.
[32] AOM 1015, ff. 418-419.
[33] NLM 1219, f.136.
[34] NLM 20, f.103.
[35] AOM 271, f. 92v.
[36] derived from AOM 1061, ff.48-52; AOM 1062, ff. 48-59; and AOM 6549, no pag.
[37] Wismayer, 55, 64.
[38] Ibid., 57-58.

Table III Guns in Fort Ricasoli (1761-1790)			
	1761	1783-1787	1790
Bronze Guns			
24-pounder cannon	1	1	1
colombrines:			
18-pounder	2	2	2
12-pounder	10	10	10
9-pounder	11	7	7
8-pounder	4	2	2
4-pounder	2	2	2
½-pounder	2	2	2
bomb mortars	2	2	2
Iron Guns:			
Cannon:			
24-pounder	0	30[1]	30
12-pounder (naval)	12	12	12
1-pounder (naval)	0	2	1
stone mortars	10	10	10

[1] Of which 6 were naval.

Table IV Ammunition at Fort Ricasoli, 1785
1260 x 24-pounder round shot; and 270 x 24-pounder grape shot;
140 x 18-pounder round shot; and 30 x 18-pounder grape shot;
1550 x 12-pounder round shot; and 330 x 12-pounder grape shot;
630 x 8-pounder round shot; and 37 x 8-pounder grape shot;
141 x 4-pounder round shot; and 30 x 4-pounder grape shot;
2 x 6-ounce round shot;
1598 paper cartridges.

In Orsi Tower there were 4 x 6-pounders iron guns; 280 x 6-pounder round shot; and 60 x 6-pounder grape shot.

Heavy rearmament was undertaken in March 1777 when, following the advice of engineer Bourlemaque, who had coastal defence at heart, seventeen of the above 24-pounder guns were transferred to Ricasoli from Mistra, Lembi, Ahrax and Comino Batteries, as well as from St Lucian's Tower.[39] Other cannon were posted at Ricasoli, part of fifty newly arrived in August 1778.[40] If Bourlemaque's advice was upheld by the Commission of War and engineer Fra de Tignè, (who visited the fort early in 1762[41] following a report that the gun carriages had been corroded to such an extent that they had become unserviceable), then the new cannon were distributed in the following manner:[42] twelve 24-pounders were posted on the sea front; four 12-pounders defended the mouth of Grand Harbour; and twenty-three other guns of divers calibre defended the land front.[43] Throughout the 1780s, the Grand Harbour front was defended by no less than six 24-pounder guns; twelve 12-pounders; and two 1-pounders.[44] Moreover in 1787, eight 24-pounders were ordered. In 1792, the Commission of War reported that Ricasoli needed at least sixty-four cannon: thirty-one 24-pounders; two 18-pounders; twenty-two 12-pounders; seven 8-pounders; and two 4-pounders.[45] Not all of these guns were serviceable at once. In June 1789, only twelve out of twenty-four 24-pounders of the sea front were mounted. The others were being refitted. Meanwhile, all the iron cannon were being varnished.[46] Both Fort Ricasoli and Orsi Tower had an infinite amount of divers articles and tools needed in a fort, such as incendiaries, funnels, scales, spades, hammers and other. In the inventories that are still extant,[47] no mention is made of musical instruments or articles associated with cavalry.

The function of Orsi Tower

In the 1750s, Orsi Tower was armed with four bronze guns.[48] By 1761 the tower still had two 6-pounder and two 8-pounder guns,[49] one gun short of the five 8-pounders which were considered necessary for it by Bourlemaque.[50] The extra cannon was never delivered. Orsi Tower had to make do with four 6-pounder iron guns until the 1790s. There were eighty-nine round shot for use in 1770.[51] The gunpowder for the tower was

---

[39] AOM 1015, f. 155.
[40] Ibid., f. 30.
[41] Ibid., f.18.
[42] AOM 6557, f. 222.
[43] Ibid., f. 225.
[44] AOM 1015, f.316.
[45] Ibid., ff. 354, 356, 361.
[46] Ibid., ff. 330, 340.
[47] AOM 1061 and AOM 1062 passim.
[48] NLM 142d, f. 458.
[49] AOM 6549 no pag.
[50] AOM 6557, f. 225.
[51] AOM 6543, bundle 15.

The circular moat at the site on Ricasoli Point where Orsi Tower stood between 1629 and 1821.

provided according to need from the fort. Orsi Tower was provided with a tin loudhailer for communication with vessels.[52]

The primary function of Orsi Tower was its role in the prevention of the escape of slaves, since they usually took possession of a boat in rough weather and tried to sail out of harbour and on to the North African coast. Whenever there was a large number of slaves on the island, orders were accordingly given and measures taken for added security.[53] During wintry days, that is between 9 November and 7 May, there were only two gunners on service, but by night there were no less than four soldiers and two gunners. In summer there were three gunners during daytime, and three soldiers and two gunners at night time. Oil for the night was provided by the Cotoner Foundation.

The resident head in Orsi Tower had to live there at all times except in very bad weather when he could leave the tower with the permission of the Governor of the fort or his lieutenant. He was responsible for the good maintenance of its four small cannon. He had to make sure that both the gunpowder and the cannon were not wet or humid. The drawbridge had to be kept closed at all time. He was also responsible for signalling to

---

[52] AOM 1061, f. 52.
[53] AOM 270, f. 50.

the hospital and Santa Lucia in Valletta across the Grand Harbour with a lamp or musket shots. Great penalties threatened whoever opened either the tower's gate or the northern gate of the fort, or whoever left them open without permission.[54] On the point bastion of Ricasoli, just behind the tower, six gunners took charge of the numerous artillery every day,[55] two during daytime, and four during night time. The sergeant or corporal of Ricasoli regularly checked whether the muskets and cartridges of the gunners posted at Ricasoli Point were in good condition or not.[56]

Whenever the guards saw a vessel leaving harbour at night without the company of a guard boat, they had to fire two musket shots, and by means of loudhailers request the captain to stop. If the vessel went ahead, the gunners were to open fire on her. During daytime all shipping was allowed out except when the guard-boats signalled to the contrary. As from February 1747, one of the guard-boats was detailed to just behind Ricasoli Point near the tower at all times, ready to stop any suspect vessel. The other guard-boat was berthed below the Upper Barracca in Valletta ready to accompany any friendly vessel by night. During night-time, the Barracca guard-boat had to reply to the signals of the one near Orsi Tower. This was not necessary during daytime. Meanwhile Fort St Elmo had to open fire whenever Orsi Tower or any guard-boat fired at a vessel.[57]

Fort Ricasoli's role in case of invasion

In case of the sighting of an enemy fleet, Fort St Elmo spread the alarm by hoisting the flag of the Order.[58] In 1774, this regulation was changed and a bonfire was to be the signal during daytime. At night-time flares would be used. Fort Ricasoli was to reply at once in the same manner. If it did not, then a mortar shot would be fired for the same purpose from Fort St Elmo.[59] The commander of artillery was to send all gunners at his disposal at Fort Ricasoli and the other forts, as soon as the alarm was given. The Governor of Fort Ricasoli could ask for reinforcements from the Cospicua regiment, numbering three hundred men, and if the sailing ships were at harbour, fifty more men, together with twelve gunners and twelve sailors of the sailing ships' battalion could be requested from the navy.[60] The commander of artillery had to ensure that in all forts there were sufficient weapons for the reinforcements.[61]

In case of an attack on Malta, Fort Ricasoli's batteries had to protect the mouth of both harbours by firing at any enemy vessels who tried to force their way in or who got near to the shore. The 24-pounders firing at an elevation of 45 degrees could protect the coast

---

[54] Ibid.
[55] NLM 142d., f.466.
[56] AOM 270, f. 50.
[57] Ibid., ff. 51-51v.
[58] AOM 1015, f. 88.
[59] Ibid., ff. 123-124.
[60] Ibid., f. 124.
[61] Ibid., f. 125.

down to 2,500 metres to the south, roughly to San Leonardo, according to the estimated range of cannon tested in 1747.[62] Until 1715, the coast between Ricasoli and Marsascala was not considered in danger of invasion, because of the rough shoreline. Since 1620, it was defended by Santa Maria delle Grazie Tower, which was erected by Grand Master Alof de Wignacourt at an expense of 4,948 *scudi*, four kilometres to the south-east of Ricasoli. The garrison was composed of a commander, two bombardiers and eight men, although these could be increased to one hundred in an emergency, while the artillery consisted of two 6-pounder iron guns.[63] If an invasion in this sector did occur, it was up to sorties organised from Cottonera and Ricasoli to repel the invading force if its size was limited.[64] Next to no material is extant regarding the deployment of the artillery in the various forts around Grand Harbour, and the zones each battery was intended to control, or how cross-fire could be concerted.

During the eighteenth century, and more especially in the 1760s, following recommendations by teams of French military engineers such as Bourlemaque, Pontleroy and Louvicour, a system of coast defence was adopted by the Order to defend the whole island and not merely the harbour areas. Pontleroy opted for the building of an entrenchment, that is a line of low defensive walls, for the entire south-east coast of the island.[65] The entrenchment which was made up of nineteen bastions linked by seventeen curtain walls, spanned six kilometres from Wied Ghammieq near Ricasoli, down to Zonqor Point. They were crudely built with rubble stone of the *pietra a secco* type by three hundred men under the direction of Bailiff de Tigne and took about ten years to complete.[66] The three military engineers also suggested that three coastal batteries be built between Ricasoli and Zonqor Point for a total thirty-two guns,[67] but this project never materialised.

This defensive system of Malta's south-east coast depended on the mobility of the Maltese Militia regiment of the village of Zejtun, which numbered 476 men in 1716;[68] and 600 in 1761. One thousand other men defended the coast between Fort Ricasoli and Zonqor.[69] As a back-up reserve force, the Zejtun regiment had to rush to the exact spot on the coast where a landing took place while Ricasoli's men had to stay inside the fort. If Marsascirocco Bay was occupied, The Zejtun regiment would meet the enemy south of Zejtun village itself.[70] It was very important for the defenders that the land around the village of Zabbar be held for as long a time as possible since any retreat into the fortified cities had to pass from its limits.[71] Once the retreating regiments were past

[62] AOM 6543, no pag.
[63] Spiteri, (1994), 488. This tower was demolished by the British military authorities to make room for a large coastal battery.
[64] AOM 6552, f. 6v. and AOM 6554, f. 4.
[65] NLM 140, f. 153.
[66] Spiteri, (1994), 565. Only a few courses in detached parts remain as evidence of such defensive work.
[67] AOM 6557, f. 184.
[68] AOM 1011, f. 82v.
[69] AOM 6557, f. 163.
[70] Ibid., ff. 168-169.
[71] Ibid., f. 181.

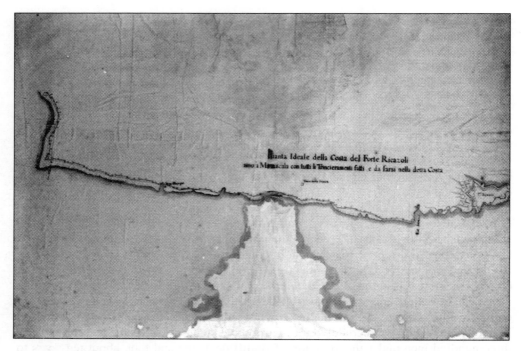

Old archival plan showing the coastal entrenchments built between Fort Ricasoli and Zonqor Point.
(Courtesy: NLM)

Zabbar, they would be protected by Cottonera's or Ricasoli's fire. 300 of them were to take cover in each place, 60 were to retreat into Senglea, and the rest would cross the harbour and join Valletta's garrison.[72]

From the moment the retreat was completed the normal siege type of warfare would be resorted to. It is unfortunate that no documentation is extant about the role Fort Ricasoli would have in such a siege. The three 24-pounders; three 16-pounders; three 12-pounders and the ten 8-pounder guns which were posted on the land front of Ricasoli[73] were more than enough to dominate and control the enemies' moves as far south as Saint Rocco, distant one kilometre. Saint Rocco incline could present some problems to the fort because it reaches an altitude of about thirty-five metres above sea level. However, one cannot see inside the fort from Saint Rocco, and any threat was expected to be countered by means of cross-fire with St Salvatore and St Louis bastions of the Cottonera Lines, which were also more favourably placed to control Xghajra and the approaches from Zabbar.

[72] AOM 271, f. 85.
[73] AOM 6557, f. 225.

90

5

Saint Nicholas Chapel

The building of the chapel

Since Fort Ricasoli was a large fort with a sizeable garrison, many of whose members lived there with their families, and also since the religious Hospitaller Order obviously cared for the ecclesiastical needs of its members and dependants, Grand Master Nicola Cotoner obliged the Cotoner Foundation to provide the funds needed for a chapel to be built inside the fort. For this purpose, Cotoner instructed the resident engineer of the Order Fra Mederico Blondel to set out plans.[1]

Blondel's original idea was to erect the chapel to the right of the Main Gate and guard room, at the neck of St John demi-bastion at the end of the great land-front barracks, which by 1674 had already been built. A chapel there would have the choir-stalls right at the neck of the bastion and the nave would form part of the first arcade of the barracks themselves, thus adding to safety from bombing. Undermining during a siege was impossible there because of the protection afforded by the bastion.[2] The site as first planned by Blondel would be practically identical to that of St Anne's Chapel in Fort St Elmo. The engineer might have been influenced by that plan. However, the churches in Fort St Angelo, and the eighteenth century Fort Manoel were both built in a more central position.

The chapel at Ricasoli, however, was only started soon after 31 March 1696[3] and was completed by 15 May 1698[4]. By then, the site had been changed to the present position that is more central to the fort and to the left, rather than to the right of the Main Gate, after advice by the Conventual Prior[5] and the Commissioners of War. This place was chosen because it was nearer to the Governor's House; more accessible from the place of

---

[1] AOM 1016, ff. 259v.-260.

[2] Ibid., f. 260.

[3] AOM 264, f. 97.

[4] Ibid., ff. 166v.-167.

[5] The Conventual Prior was the head priest serving the members of the Order. His seat was the Conventual Church of St John in Valletta, presently Malta's co-cathedral.

Saint Nicholas Chapel (1698).

arms (parade ground); it was not humid; it was sheltered from the bitter wintry *Gregale* wind, and still secure against bombing. Moreover, the chaplain and vice-chaplain were housed in the first quarters of the Grand Harbour Front barracks, that is next door to their church. It had also been decided that the church should be detached from other buildings. Beneath the chapel a crypt was dug as a measure against rising damp and to provide for burials. To it a hatchway and flight of steps was dug from the sacristy that is behind the choir of the chapel, being accessible from the epistle (left) side of the chapel.[6]

The chapel was dedicated to St Nicholas of Mira, Bishop of Bari, in memory of Grand Master Nicola Cotoner whose namesake Foundation paid for its construction and maintenance.[7] The church was consecrated on 15 May 1698. That day, Grand Master Ramon Perellos, accompanied by many dignitaries of the Order, purposely crossed over from Valletta to attend personally. The Conventual Prior blessed the chapel and said Mass.[8] On 19 May 1698 the church was formally raised to the dignity of parish chapel, though with some reservations.[9]

---

[6]AOM 1016, f. 260-262v.
[7] A. Ferris, *Memorie dell'Inclito Ordine Gerosolimitano*, (Malta 1881), 52. Also AOM 502, ff. 110v.-111.
[8] AOM 264, ff. 166v.-167v.
[9] AOM 502, ff. 110v., 111.

Saint Nicholas Chapel – Main Altar.

Saint Nicholas Chapel – Side Altar.

By a Papal Brief[10] dated 29 September 1693, Pope Innocent XII, acting on the recommendations of four Cardinals, declared the chapel to be built in Fort Ricasoli as a parish church under the jurisdiction of the Order.[11] The Brief also specified certain conditions. The parish priest or chaplain of the fort had to be a chaplain of the Order.[12] However, he was not totally independent of the Bishop. In order to hear confessions and to administer the viaticum and extreme unction, the chaplain had to receive permission both from the Bishop in ordinary in Malta and from the Prior of the Conventual Church. Although one of the reasons for the granting of this Brief was that the church was quite distant from any other, it stood in the limits of the parish of Vittoriosa. Hence the people of the fort had to go to Vittoriosa for the celebration of the sacraments of baptism, matrimony, paschal communion, and also for burials.[13] The parish priest of Vittoriosa would take over once the funeral procession was outside the gates of the fort.[14] It is to be noted that similar conditions governed the ecclesiastical affairs of the Order's chapels in other forts. Fort St Angelo too for example, lay within the limits of Vittoriosa. Since Kalkara became a parish in 1898, Fort Ricasoli formed part of the newer parish.

The chaplains of St Nicholas Chapel were presented by the trustees of the Cotoner Foundation.[15] They were also paid by the Foundation. The chaplain received 80 *scudi* annually; the vice-chaplain received 50 *scudi*.[16]

Other buildings attached to the chapel were the chaplain and vice-chaplain's houses. The latter dates from the early 1720s. On 28 July 1722, Reverend Carlo Refalo, the vice-chaplain asked for permission by the Commission of War to build a new house for himself since the one he had was too damp. He had already cut and procured the necessary stone-bricks, but still needed the go-ahead by the Commission.[17]

Description of the chapel

The chapel is rectangular in shape, about eighteen metres long and nine metres wide. Its architecture is simple and austere, reflecting the military style. The facade is simple to screen the unitary space inside. The light decoration is basically Mannerist with Baroque echoes and touches as evidenced by the leather-thin decoration around the portal. At floor level the door is flanked by barred openings to provide ventilation for the crypt.

---

[10] A Papal Brief is a letter of instructions sent by the Roman Curia.

[11] See Appedix VIII for a copy of the Brief.

[12] The chaplains of the Order officiated in various churches and chapels of the Order both inside and outside Valletta. These churches, such as the one at Ricasoli, were under the jurisdiction of the Order and were visited by the Prior of the Conventual Church and not by the Bishop of Malta. W.L. Zammit, *The Chaplains of the Order of St John in Malta, 1631-1798*, (B.A.Hons Dissertation, University of Malta 1971), 171.

[13] AOM 264, f. 21v. The present author was quite fortunate in this regard, since the Parish Archives in Vittoriosa could be consulted in order to extrapolate interesting information regarding the demographic history of eighteenth-century Ricasoli, as can be appreciated in Chapter 6.

[14] NLM 142d, f. 465v.

[15] AOM 6535, f. 67v. For a list of chaplains and vice-chaplains see Appendix IX.

[16] AOM 390, no pag.

[17] AOM 1018, f. 1.

The austere features are emphasised by regular stone-dressed courses. Above the lateral dados stand engaged pilasters surmounted with Tuscan capitals. The facade is broken by an entablature which arrests the sudden upward lift of the eye. The decoration is enhanced by a cornice and two finials at both ends. A typically Mannerist central elliptical window between the cornice and entablature projects morning sunlight onto the main altar of the chapel. The sides of the chapel are divided into three bays, each perforated by a window. Engaged pilasters create pattern and rhythm to the side elevation.

Inside the chapel there were three altars, the main altar at the choir, and two others at the sides. The main altar was dedicated to St Nicholas. By order of the Cotoner Foundation, a daily Mass was said for the repose of the soul of Grand Master Cotoner. Both chaplain and vice-chaplain were given 30 *scudi* each annually for saying this Mass.[18] Twelve extra Masses every month and other Masses early in the morning before the changing of the guards were also said on each feast day and Sunday. Alms for each Mass amounted to 3 *tari*. The second altar was dedicated to Our Lady of Pilar. It was founded by the Reverend Fra Tommaso Ondeano, chaplain of the Langue of Aragon on 10 September 1749 having given 50 *scudi* to the Cotoner Foundation.[19] In 1760 Ondeano gave another 83 *scudi* to the *Massa Frumentaria,* of the Valletta Commune, which imported wheat in bulk, so that the interest could be devolved to the celebration of the Vespers, as well as one solemn and two other ordinary Masses on 12 October which was the feast day of the patron saint. Two years later Ondeano increased his contribution by a further 133 *scudi* with 3 per cent interest directed for the same celebrations.[20] The third altar was dedicated to St John the Evangelist. It was founded by Pietro Pulis on 20 December 1750 who deposited 50 *scudi* with the Cotoner Foundation on condition that a Mass be celebrated on all feast days.[21]

In the crypt, an old wooden statue of Our Lady of Sorrows was venerated. This statue had been on one of the Order's galleys during the Rhodian period before 1523.[22] So great was the veneration of the people inside the fort towards it, that most of them used to visit this icon daily. The Cotoner Foundation therefore erected an altar in honour of the icon. There were two other altars in the crypt. One was dedicated to the Holy Cross. It was founded by Arcangelo Chetcuti on 21 April 1751, who had deposited 50 *scudi* with the Cotoner Foundation with the obligation of a Mass on the titular feast day. The other altar was dedicated to the Scourging of Christ. It was founded by Reverend Paolo Piscopo on 4 March 1757 in the same circumstances as the other altar.

The chapel was rich in ornaments, icons and relics. The most venerated relics were placed in a large box bound with velvet and crystal under the main altar.[23] There were about seventy-seven relics of various saints including Saints Nicholas, John the Baptist, Peter

---

[18] AOM 1953, iv, 289.
[19] Ibid., ff. 287-288.
[20] AOM 154, f. 134.
[21] AOM 1953, iv, f. 288.
[22] Ferris, 53.
[23] NLM 142d, f. 460v.

Crypt of Saint Nicholas Chapel - Altar dedicated to Our Lady of Sorrows.

Crypt of Saint Nicholas Chapel - Altar dedicated to the Holy Cross.

Crypt of Saint Nicholas Chapel - Altar dedicated to the Scourging of Christ.

and Joseph, as well as of the Holy Cross, and others.[24] Among the icons venerated in the church, three deserve mention. Hanging above the main altar was a painting of St Nicholas by the famous Italian knight and painter Mattia Preti. As was customary, it anachronistically but significantly featured Grand Master Nicola Cotoner in it.[25] Another painting was that representing Our Lady of Victories, which was probably a copy of the one hanging in the conventual church of St John in Valletta.[26] The third painting was another representing a half-length portrait of St Nicholas,[27] which had been brought over from Rhodes in 1530 by the family Tolossenti together with other icons. This portrait was highly venerated by the family, but after two centuries, on 5 December 1744, being the eve of the saint's feast, Reverend Giovanni Battista Tolossenti, who was their last descendant, donated it to the church of Fort Ricasoli for public exposition and veneration. It was blessed by the chaplain Reverend Gaetano Reboul, and he also inscribed its story on the back of the frame.[28] Another portrait in the church was one representing Giovanni Battista Bosa, who had formerly been chaplain of the fort. This portrait was acquired by Gaetano Reboul in 1753 from Reverend Filippo Grech. At that time Bosa was still alive, being referred to as 'the retired chaplain of the fort'.[29]

The furniture of the chapel came from four distinct sources. There was the furniture released by the conventual church of St John; the Cotoner Foundation donated some other furniture; some ornaments and furniture were left by chaplains or devotees; and lastly there were ornaments which belonged to the Confraternity of Our lady of the Victories that was canonically established in the chapel. These included sacred relics; silver ware; vestments; books and missals; flowers; candles; flags and other objects.[30]

Reverend Gaetano Reboul was also responsible for the founding of a library at the fort. This contained manuscripts and memoirs relating to both the church and the fort.[31] Reboul was indefatigable in his efforts to exchange favours in order to acquire books or other articles needed for the church, sometimes with his friend, the well known Maltese author Reverend Ignazio Saverio Mifsud acting as go between.[32] About 1752, Reboul was writing notes about the fort and its church.[33] Reboul was instrumental in acquiring a second hand choir for the church in an underhanded and unusual way, also showing how ingenious he was. On 31 July 1752 he wrote to his cousin, Reverend Carlo Reboul so that the latter may contact Reverend Francesco Castiglio, the chaplain of the church of Our Lady of Victories in Valletta, so that his cousin might request the choir from Castiglio, since it came to be known that a Spanish knight was going to pay for a new

---

[24] AOM 1953, iv, f. 290, gives the whole list.

[25] NLM 142d, f. 468.

[26] Ibid., f. 462.

[27] Ibid.

[28] NLM 20, ff. 74, 75.

[29] NLM 1029, no pag.

[30] NLM 142d, ff. 467-484. Agius de Soldanis gives an inventory of all the articles found in the church in the mid-eighteenth century.

[31] NLM 142d, f. 464.

[32] NLM 1029, no pag.

[33] Ibid. More about Reboul's diary later on in the chapter.

one at the Valletta church. However, Gaetano insisted with his cousin that the latter should not mention him with Castiglio, since they were on bad terms because of some malicious talk by Castiglio's own vice chaplain.[34] There is no doubt that St Nicholas church benefited from Reboul's term as chaplain.[35] Incidentally, three years later we find Reboul, together with the chaplain of Fort Manoel, Reverend Fra Luigi Delucia still in dispute with Castiglio, since the latter was taking the 14 *tari* which the deceased relatives paid as funerary duty of accompaniment for the journey he made from the hospital to Valletta quay, before they were ferried for interment at Ricasoli or Manoel. The two chaplains in the forts pretended at least 10 *tari* for their service at the interment.[36]

Just inside the Main Gate of Fort Ricasoli, in the Guard Room, there was a niche dedicated to Our Lady of Graces. It was taken care of by the chaplain, as well as by two procurators nominated by the same chaplain. On the feast day of the Blessed Name of Mary, an altar was erected beneath this niche and the congregation used to hear Mass after a very short procession from the church to the Guard Room. Everyday the holy rosary was recited in front of this niche for the repose of the soul of Fra Giovanni Francesco Ricasoli.

Dispute over ecclesiastical jurisdiction

The papal brief of 29 September 1693, turning the chapel in Fort Ricasoli into a parish church of the Order was only valid for seven years. Hence every seventh year, a renewal of the Brief was sought and gained. This happened for example on 27 March 1763 when, together with the privileges granted in 1693, Pope Clement XIII granted perpetual indulgencies to all those who visited the church and any altar therein,[37] especially the privileged altar of St Nicholas.[38] Indulgencies for the repose of the dead were also received whenever the congregation heard Requiem Mass. The papal briefs of 24 April 1770,[39] 23 October 1781,[40] and 17 March 1791,[41] all confirmed these privileges. Moreover on 23 November 1784, a further Brief issued by Pope Pius VI granted to the church the privileged sung vespers and High Mass on the feasts of St Nicholas and St Anne.[42]

The papal brief of 1693 expressly declared the church inside Fort Ricasoli to be independent of the jurisdiction of the local diocesan and was under the Order's jurisdiction instead.[43] During the 1690s, relations between the Order and the Bishop of

---

[34] Ibid.
[35] NLM 142d, f. 466.
[36] AOM 152, ff. 37v.-38. It is not known what the Council of the Order decided in this regard.
[37] AOM 271, f. 243.
[38] Ibid., f. 255v.
[39] AOM 272, f. 206v.
[40] AOM 273, ff. 263v-266.
[41] AOM 274, ff. 190, 190v.
[42] Ibid., ff. 47, 47v.
[43] AOM 264, f. 21v.

Burial place in the Crypt of Saint Nicholas Chapel.

Malta, Monsignor Davide Cocco Palmieri, were strained because of the question of jurisdiction over the administration of the Sacraments.[44] The Bishop found new ground for action against the Order in the brief of 1693, since it stated that Ricasoli's chaplain could not administer the Sacraments nor hear the confessions of the inhabitants of the fort without permission from both the Bishop and the Prior.[45] Seeing that he had certain powers over the church of St Nicholas, the Bishop tried to take over control. For this purpose he informed the chaplain that he intended to visit this parish church as an Apostolic Delegate and that he would assess the functions of the church regardless of the Order's privileges. The chaplain informed the Grand Master and Council of the Bishop's intention, and on 6 July 1700 the latter appointed a Commission of three senior knights who together with the secretaries of the Grand Master were to examine the matter, give adequate advice, and act accordingly.[46]

By 8 July 1700, the commissioners had already sent the Order's advocate to the Bishop's Curia, claiming that the latter's intent went contrary to the privileges of the Order as expressly written in the Pope's Brief.[47] The Bishop's claims were based on the universal practice by which all the Order's churches could be visited by the Bishop as Apostolic Delegate if the Sacraments were administered therein, according to the disposition of the Council and the Papal Bull[48] *Exposcit* by Pope Pius V. The Commission of three knights, however, noted that in the Brief of 1693, the church was declared in full right *pleno iure* under the jurisdiction of the Order as a member of the conventual church, and so the universal practice did not hold in this case. The Bishop, however, still went to Ricasoli to carry out his pastoral visit, but he was refused entrance. Therefore both the Bishop and the Order decided to refer the matter to the Holy See. The Order confirmed the commissioners with their responsibilities until further orders from the Council.[49]

The dealings with the Holy See protracted for a long time as was usual at that time. Until July 1701 for example, the Pope had not as yet received the Order's reasons for exemption from episcopal visits to St Nicholas' church.[50] It is not clear how the dispute ended. However, three years later the Bishop still claimed jurisdiction over the parish. In 1703 Mgr Cocco Palmieri held a diocesan synod at the cathedral church for the publication of which he ordered Fra Domenico Gambigallo, the chaplain, and Fra Giovanni Bosa, the vice chaplain of Ricasoli to be present. They refused to attend. In a statement of protest registered in the chancery of the Order on 23 April 1703, they declared that they were not bound to participate in the publication of this synod since they were not subject to the jurisdiction of the Bishop.[51]

---

[44] S. Caruana, *Jurisdictional Quarrels Among the Three Authorities in Malta, 1695-1701*, (B.A.[Hons] Dissertation, University of Malta, 1976), 87.

[45] AOM 264, f. 21v.

[46] AOM 265, f. 16.

[47] Ibid., f. 17.

[48] A Bull is a letter of important and binding instruction or intent by the Pope.

[49] AOM 265, f. 17.

[50] AAF, Corrispondenza, Cardinal Paulucci to Mgr Cocco Palmieri, July 1701, f. 348.

[51] AOM 265, f. 93.

The most important feasts celebrated

The most important religious feast celebrated in Fort Ricasoli was that of St Nicholas, the patron saint, on 6 December. It was celebrated by the singing of Vespers, High Mass with panegyric, and a procession around the fort.[52] On 6 December 1746 Reverend Gaetano Reboul celebrated this feast and carried the box of sacred relics around the fort. To mark the occasion he set various inscriptions both inside and outside the church.[53] In 1731 the chaplain Fra Carlo Refalo lay a small garden outside the fort, the income from which was then directed for the celebration of the nine days' devotions (*novena*) of the feast of St Nicholas.[54] The income from this garden was 31 *tari* per annum in 1791, which by then was short of the expense needed for the nine days' devotions. Therefore the chaplain Fra Andrea Fenech enlarged the garden and thus secured a larger income.[55]

Other important feasts celebrated in Fort Ricasoli included the feast of Our Lady of the Victories on 8 September.[56] This day was held in high regard by both the knights and the Maltese since it marked the anniversary of the victory of the Great Siege of 1565. That day a procession was held around the fort. Saint John of God was also particularly venerated by the inhabitants of the fort. On 8 September 1745, after the singing of the Vespers, the relics of this saint were carried in the above-mentioned procession.[57] Similar celebrations were also held on 24 June, the feast day of Saint John the Baptist, and the Sunday after Corpus Christi, which was also celebrated in High Mass.[58] On 24 December 1739, Christmas Eve functions were celebrated both in Fort Ricasoli and in Fort Manoel for the first time.[59] Particularly interesting was the fifth Christmas Eve function held in the fort's chapel in 1743 when Reboul was chaplain.

In fact Reboul invited the Reverend Ignazio Saverio Mifsud, then still a twenty-one year old seminarian, to recite the Christmas sermon at a quarter to midnight.[60] The youthful Mifsud wrote down the extended notes of his panegyric and later inserted them in a manuscript which is full of such early Maltese writing, much studied by scholars of the Maltese language.[61] It may be argued that Ricasoli gave its fair contribution to the history of the Maltese language too, since Mifsud's sermons are still considered among the earliest prose in Maltese. Reboul and Mifsud kept close friendship throughout their lives. The latter's edited version of Reboul's diary is the only part which survives.[62] That day,

---

[52] NLM 142d, f. 463v.
[53] NLM 20, f. 100.
[54] AOM 1018, ff. 385-386.
[55] AOM 1023, ff. 285-286.
[56] NLM 142d, f. 463.
[57] NLM 20, f. 75.
[58] NLM 142d, f. 463.
[59] NLM 20, f. 52.
[60] J. Zammit Ciantar, "Priedka tal-Milied tas-Sena 1743," in *il-Mument*, 12 December 1993, (supplement), 9-15.
[61] NLM 48.
[62] G. Reboul, *Giornale de Successi dell'Isole di Malta e Gozo*, compendiato da Ignazio Saverio Mifsud. Pubblicato a cura di Vincenzo Laurenza, (Malta 1936), 5-6.

the Ricasoli Christmas congregation heard the young seminarian introduce his sermon with the joyful tidings in Latin ... *Annuntio vobis gaudium magnum*..., and later they were given examples from their daily life in order to press on the need for repentance in preparation for the coming of Christ that same evening.[63]

Some of the chaplains

The first chaplain of Fort Ricasoli was Reverend Fra Matteo lo Castro,[64] whilst the first vice-chaplain was Reverend Fra Geronimo Signorino.[65] It is doubtful, however, if lo Castro ever performed duty in the fort, since he was already substituted by Reverend Fra Domenico Gambigallo of Senglea in 1692, six years before the present church was finished and the official establishment of the garrison. Gambigallo died in 1730.[66] The second chaplain was Reverend Fra Giovanni Battista Bosa, also of Senglea.[67] By 1743 Bosa had already retired, and he died in 1753.

A chaplain of Fort Ricasoli who made a name for himself was Reverend Fra Gaetano Reboul. He was already chaplain in 1743 when Ignazio Saverio Mifsud delivered his Christmas sermon there, and until June 1755 he was still chaplain there. Reboul was born in Valletta in 1707 and he died on 14 April 1759, probably at Ricasoli. He was buried in St John's conventual church.

He became chaplain of obedience of the Order in 1733, and his first appointment was that of chaplain of the Crucifix in the first hall of the *Lazzaretto* or quarantine hospital. Two years later he was appointed vice-chaplain of St Nicholas church in Ricasoli after the death of the former vice-chaplain Reverend Fra Carlo Refalo.[68] As already noted, Reboul took great personal interest in the religious well-being of the inhabitants, and he also wrote a diary of all the important events which were taking place in Malta in the middle part of the eighteenth century. Many facts mentioned have contributed to reconstruct the social environment of Malta at that time. Much of the original diary has been lost,[69] but Ignazio Saverio Mifsud's abridgement of this journal survives.[70]

The chapel of St Nicholas and the chaplains therein served their purpose well, that of catering for the religious and moral needs of the inhabitants of Fort Ricasoli. The fort had a resident population with its social ethos which was predominantly, but not exclusively military. The next chapter deals with the demographic and social history of the fort.

---

[63] Zammit Ciantar, 9.
[64] AOM 495, f. 105v.
[65] AOM 497, ff. 133v., 81v.
[66] AOM 533, f. 184v.-185.
[67] AOM 502, f. 108v.
[68] AOM 539, f. 126.
[69] NLM 428.
[70] NLM 20, vi, *Stromati*.

6

Demographic and Social History

Population Structure

Fort Ricasoli was only permanently garrisoned in 1698. After that date, there were soldiers living in the fort together with their families. Before the establishment of the parish of Kalkara in 1898, all the inhabitants of the fort were subject to the parish priest of Vittoriosa for baptism, Easter obligations, marriage and burials. Much can be said about the social and demographic history of the fort since the parish records at Birgu (Vittoriosa) or their original copies at the Archbishop's Curia in Floriana are still extant. Up to the French Revolution, the parish records were practically the only ones kept for births, deaths and marriages. But there was another book of records concerning the Eucharist, called *Liber de Statu Animarum*, literally "state of the souls", in which the parish priest recorded the marital status of each and every member of the flock and whether the precept of yearly confession and communion during Eastertide was adhered to.[1] Moreover, the parish priest used to draw a line between every household and sometimes the number of the room is also indicated. This could give an indication regarding accommodation in single, double, multiple, and married quarters. Important information about the totals, age and sex structure of the population at Ricasoli can also be gleaned from these important archives. It is evident, judging by the surnames of the inhabitants, that the great majority of the soldiers and their families were Maltese.

The baptism registers of Vittoriosa do not specify the exact place where babies were born, but surely by 1 July 1699 a baby girl had been born in Fort Ricasoli, the daughter of Clement and Theresa Vella. Unfortunately the girl died that same day soon after she was urgently baptised by the midwife.[2] Infant mortality must have been high. Barely one year later on 11 June 1700, Gatinuzza Galea, the one month old daughter of Luca and Caterina Galea died there.[3] Neither were these the first inhabitants of Ricasoli to die there. The first one to die in the fort was Pasquale Xeberras on 8 April 1699, barely ten

---

[1] S. Fiorini, "Status Animarum I: A Unique Source for 17th and 18th Century Maltese Demography," in *Melita Historica*, viii, 4, (Malta 1983), 327.

[2] A(rchivum) C(ollegii) C(anonicorum) V(ittoriosae), L(iber) M(ortuorum) III, 1690-1755, f.29v.

[3] Ibid., f. 34.

Table V
Population Structure of Fort Ricasoli, 1702 - 1801[1]

	1702[2]	*1715*[3]	*1727*[4]	*1738*[5]	*1754*[6]	*1765*[7]	*1779*[8]	*1797*[9]	*1801*[10]	*Average means*
men over 18	38	53	63	54	43	31	9	11	5	38
of whom over 60	9	26	32	27	22	14	1	3	-	17
men undisclosed age	-	4	-	-	11	18	40	23	-	12
wives and widows	32	44	45	36	27	34	33	31	2	35
boys under 18	17	24	26	18	17	16	21	47	5	23
daughters	34	33	38	17	11	23	38	37	2	29
remain from previous	-	25	28	58	25	28	16	11	7	
remain from previous two years	-	-	7	7	5	4	6	2	3	
TOTAL	121	158	172	125	109	122	141	149	14	137

[1] Exclusive of knights and chaplains.
[2] AAF, LSA, Vittoriosa 1702, ff. 38v-40.
[3] Ibid., 1715, ff. 52-53v.
[4] ACCV, LSA 1727-1738, ff. 21v-22v.
[5] Ibid., ff. 263v-264.
[6] Ibid., 1746-1764, no pag.
[7] Ibid., 1765-1805, no pag.
[8] Ibid., 1777-1786, no pag.
[9] AAF, LSA, Vittoriosa, 1797, ff. 39-40.
[10] ACCV, LSA, 1765-1805, no pag.

months after the garrison was established. He was interred in St Lawrence church at Vittoriosa.[4] The second death, that of Francesco Pullicino, occurred on 30 May 1699.[5] A total of nine deaths occurred in the first three years of the garrison in the fort, for a death rate of about 25 per thousand per annum.[6]

[4] Ibid., f. 28v.
[5] Ibid., f. 29.
[6] This is calculated at the total population rate of 121 in 1702.

The total population of Fort Ricasoli, not including the knights, chaplains, and the gunners of warships who were only transferred there during a war-scare, averaged about 137 in the eighteenth century, of which only about 60 were regular officers and soldiers. Table V attempts to survey the eighteenth century population structure of the fort, taking systematically nine sample years of which the *Status Animarum* are still extant.

As can be seen in Table V, the average mean population of Fort Ricasoli was 137. The median average is 133 for the years 1738 and 1779, while the range is 63, since the highest number of persons was in 1727 with 172 (or a Z score of +1.74), and the least number was in 1754 with 109 (or a Z score of -1.39). The standard deviation from mean was 20.1. This proves that throughout the century, the population of Ricasoli was closely grouped around the mean, and did not deviate much. Men capable of arms were considered those between the ages of sixteen and sixty-five. The table above proves that the garrison was often composed of about sixty men of all ranks.[7] In 1786 the garrison was made up of sixty-one men, compared to seventy-two men in Fort Manoel.[8] One can also compare Ricasoli's population and garrison with those of Fort St Angelo, which also defended the Grand Harbour, but which is smaller and forms a final keep behind the successive fortifications of Cottonera and Vittoriosa, necessitating fewer men. The total inhabitants of St Angelo averaged seventy-eight in the years shown in the above table, compared to 137 for Ricasoli, while the total number of troops averaged twenty-six, compared to sixty in Ricasoli. The dependency ratio of St Angelo, with 200 per cent, was appreciably higher than that of Ricasoli at 124 per cent.

Sometimes, the parish priest of Vittoriosa did not note the age of some of the persons inside Fort Ricasoli. This happened mostly in 1765, 1779 and 1797, resulting in partial information available regarding age as can be seen above. There was an appreciable number of wives and widows in the fort. Widows of soldiers and even sailors of the sailing-ships squadron of the Order could avail themselves of continued use of their habitation or rooms in the fort.

Home for the foundlings

The number of children in the fort might seem to have been exaggerated in comparison with the grown ups. This is because the fort had a curious function: that of acting as home for the illegitimate children from the Holy Infirmary, that was the hospital of the Order.[9] If foundlings were judged to be unbaptised, the Hospitaller, or knight-director of the hospital, sent these babies to St Dominic's parish church in Valletta for baptism. They stayed there until they were eight when these children were put in a charitable

---

[7] NLM 142d., f. 464. The manuscript gives the total number of inhabitants as eighty. In fact in 1754 there were about 109.

[8] AOM 163, f.324.

[9] P. Cassar, *Medical History of Malta*, (London 1961), 353.

institution. The boys were later sent to Fort Ricasoli.[10] They took leave from the fort when they were sixteen. They were taught Christian doctrine and any trade they chose.[11] Many of them, however, were taught navigation and were later employed in the Order's navy.[12] The foundlings were taken care of by the chaplain and vice chaplain of the fort. On 28 July 1777, the chaplain started to receive an extra allowance of 5 *scudi* per month, while the vice chaplain got 1 *scudo* 6 *tari* per month extra for this work.[13] In 1784, this payment was increased to 6 *scudi* per month.[14]

Giovanni Francesco went to Fort Ricasoli on 5 March 1783 and was apprenticed to the barber. Another foundling, Giovanni, had been working as a rope maker having learnt this trade in the house of a master craftsman who lived at Marsa. He was later employed as a servant at the hospital in 1769. Domenico Cachia, who was a legitimate child, was sent into Ricasoli in 1759 by decree of Grand Master Emanuel Pinto for having caused trouble to his parents. Giuseppe Mallia, born in 1762, was sent to the fort after his father died in the service of the Order, and by special decree of the Grand Master, he was allowed to stay there even after he was sixteen years of age. Giuseppe was sent to Ricasoli on 3 November 1782 and there learned carpentry. Giovanni Francesco Laugier went to the fort in 1782 but later sailed to Sicily with Dottor Antonio Polizzi, a student of Surgery.[15]

Mobility

The soldiers and other inhabitants of Fort Ricasoli were subject to the exigencies of the military. They therefore could be transferred by the Commission of War. The death rate was high as compared to nowadays, though surely not higher than Malta's average for the time. It therefore follows that mobility was quite high. Of the 121 people who inhabited the fort in 1702, only twenty-five were left thirteen years later. Most were transferred; moved to another place; or died. Of the 158 people who lived in the fort in 1715, thirty-one were still there twelve years later in 1727, and nine of them had been living there since 1702. Some exceptionally long stays at the fort are those of Stefano and Fiorenza Russo[16], from 1702 to 1738; Eugenia Mallia, from 1727 to 1765; Giuseppe Grech, who was posted at Ricasoli before 1754 and who was still there in 1797; and Nicola Farrugia who was born at Ricasoli in 1725, son of Giovanni Maria and Rose. He was married to Graziella and in 1765 he had a four-year old son named Giuseppe.[17]

---

[10] AOM 309, f. 75.
[11] AOM 308, f. 185v.
[12] AOM 1714, f. 38.
[13] AOM 1715, f. 8.
[14] Ibid., f. 16.
[15] NLM 375, no pag.
[16] In 1715 they feature as Rossi, and in 1727 the parish priest referred to them as Russi.
[17] ACCV and AAF, LSA Vittoriosa, passim.

The person who could lay the best claim to Fort Ricasoli as his home was Michele Mallia. Michele was born at Ricasoli in 1718, second son of Gregorio and Eugenia Mallia. By 1754 at age thirty-six, he was living by himself in a room at Ricasoli, presumably since he had already become an officer there. At age seventy-nine in 1797, on the eve of the French occupation of Malta, he was Sergeant of the fort. He did not survive the French occupation of the fort. Most of the Maltese soldiers and other inhabitants of Fort Ricasoli were replaced or evicted by the French troops in September 1798, soon after the Maltese rose in rebellion against the French.[18] By Easter 1801, only fourteen Maltese persons lived there. The seven members of the Mamo family were the only survivors of the French period. In fact the parents, fifty year old Antonio and Giuseppa, and their oldest son Vincenzo, aged twenty-four, had been living in the fort since 1779.[19]

Wages and the standard of living

Before discussing the lists of wages and salaries of the men working at Fort Ricasoli, it would be appropriate to give a rough estimate of the purchasing power of money in the eighteenth century. For this purpose the present author makes use of a bill for various foodstuffs dated 1760.[20]

Table VI					
Prices of foodstuffs, 1760					
per rotolo				apples	1 *t*. 4 *gr*.;
bread	8 *gr(ani)*;	beef	2 *t(ari)* 8 *gr*.;	pork	2 *t*. 4 *gr*.;
mutton	2 *t*.;	sugar	9 *t*.;	cheese	2 *t*. 3 *gr*.;
maccaroni	1 *t*. 10 *gr*.;	honey	2 *t*. 12 *gr*.;	green peas	12 *gr*.;
coffee	14 *t*.;	strawberry	2 *t*.;	chestnut	16 *gr*.
Per dozen					
artichoke	1 *t*.;	eggs	1 *t*. 8 *gr*.;	oranges	1 *t*. 10 *gr*.

---

[18] See Chapter VII.
[19] ACCV, LSA Vittoriosa, 1765-1805, no pag.
[20] AOM 6574, no pag.

Out of these prices one could formulate one meal for five persons together with bread needed for further subsistence for the rest of the day – table VII.

Table VII	
Meals for five persons	
meal	*cost*
pork	5 *t(ari)* 1 *gr(ani)*
mutton	3 *t.* 9 *gr.*
Five eggs with cheese and peas	2 *t.* 3 *gr.*
chestnuts	2 *t.* 8 *gr.*
maccaroni	2 *t.* 6 *gr.*
artichokes	1 *t.* 17 *gr.*
5 rotolos of bread	2 *t.*

One can deduce that a family of five normally needed 2 *tari* daily to subsist on one main meal. The average pay of a soldier at many towers or coastal batteries was 2 *scudi* per month.[21] In 1784, the soldiers at Ricasoli were paid 3 *scudi* per month salary.[22] Actually there are three lists of salaries for the men working both inside and around the fort as shown in the table VIII

There were occasional increases in wages, such as the chaplain's, on 1 July 1790, or the boatman's on 15 September 1779. The baker's wage too was increased on 1 May 1789. With the above salary, the common soldiers' life was far from comfortable. If his family of five decided to eat only bread, needing five rotolos a day, he would spend half his salary on food. If his family decided to eat pork, eight meals costing about five *tari* each would leave him with nothing. If his family opted for maccaroni, twenty meals at 2 *tari* 6 *grani* each would again exhaust his salary. Bread must have been the staple food of the soldiers of Ricasoli. As for the other ranks one notices that the boatmen and corporals had the same pay. The vice-chaplain had a salary only slightly higher than that of the soldiers, and less than that of the boatmen. The highest wages were given to the officer knights. It can be safely asserted that only those having a wage of 5 *scudi* or more could secure a comfortable living if their family was not large. At first glance one is surprised at the higher rates of pay of the workers on the fortifications. The master-mason, the bricklayer, the labourers, and the pickaxe diggers all had a pay equal or greater than that of the Lieutenant-Governor.

---

[21] AOM 1057, no pag.
[22] AOM 1014, loose folio at end of manuscript.

Table VIII — Wages of officers, troops and workers at Fort Ricasoli, 1750s - 1790s[1]			
Post	1750s	1780s	1790s
Governor	25 sc(udi)		
Lieutenant-Governor	10 sc.		
Sergeant	8 sc.		
Lieutenant-Sergeant	6 sc.		
Corporal	5 sc.		
Soldiers	4 sc.		
Chaplain	6 sc. 8 t(ari)	6 sc. 8 t.	7 sc.
Vice-Chaplain	4 sc. 2 t.	4 sc. 2 t.	5 sc.
Doctor	5 sc. 6 t.	5 sc. 6 t.	
Boatman	5 sc.	6sc. 6 t. / 10 sc.	
Bursar of Cotoner Foundation		6 sc. 6 t.	
Baker		2 sc.	
Artillery fitters		1 sc.	
Foreman		3 sc.	
Master mason		2 sc.	14 sc.
Watchman of stores			17 sc.
Bricklayer			16 sc.
labourer			10 sc.
Pickaxe digger			10 sc.
clerk			9sc 4 t.
children			3 / 6 sc.

[1] Derived from NLM 142d, f. 465; AOM Treasury Series A48; AOM 1013, no pag.

However one must consider certain facts. The soldiers' work was guaranteed and had an Invalid's Fund in case of illness. On the other hand, the workers at the walls of the fort worked day and night with only a few hours' sleep, if any. They were paid weekly according to days of work. While the garrison's employment was permanent, the workers' employment was only temporary and was terminated in 1795.

The wages of the men at Ricasoli were slightly lower than those of the employees of the Order's Navy. The first class sailors on the sailing-ships of the line had a salary of 3 *scudi* while a second class sailor received 2 *scudi* 6 *tari*, which are equal or less than what a soldier got at Ricasoli. However, the sailors also received a daily supply service of 1 *taro*, amounting to 2 *scudi* 6 *tari* monthly. The Captain received 45 *scudi*, twenty more than the Governor of the fort, while the first officer that is the second in command of a ship, received 20 *scudi*, double the pay of the lieutenant-governor of Ricasoli, whose salary of 10 *scudi* was the same as that of a lieutenant, who was third in command of a ship. It must be noted that the Captain of ship had to maintain the Captain's table for the highest ranking officers and passengers on his ship, and also had to pay the rent of his quarters at Galley Creek. The chaplains' salaries were quite similar; at 6 *scudi* 8 *tari* for that of the fort, and 6 *scudi* for that of the ships. The doctor at Ricasoli received 5 *scudi* 6 *tari* monthly while the surgeon on a ship received 15 *scudi*. The ships had a militia or battalion made up of soldiers. Here the comparative analysis is more transparent, as shown in the following table:[23]

Table IX Comparative monthly wages of Militia ranks		
rank	*Fort Ricasoli*	*Sailing-Ships Militia + supply service*
Sergeant	8 *scudi*	6 *scudi* + 5 *scudi*
Lieutenant-Sergeant	6 *scudi*	5 *scudi* + 3 *scudi* 9 *tari*
Corporal	5 *scudi*	3 *sc.* 6 *t.* + 1 *sc.* 10 *t.* 10 *gr.*
soldier	3 *scudi*	2 *sc.* 6 *t.* + 1 *sc.* 10 *t.* 10 *gr.*

The wages for the two classes of militia men correlate well, although the ones at sea could avail themselves of the supply service when aboard or on call at base. In fact the latter were slightly better-off. However, one must keep in mind that the work on the sailing-ships was much harder than that in the fort.

Pensions

An important social service provided by the Order of St John for its employees and their dependants was the Invalids' or Sick Fund. This was a contributory pension scheme administered by the Cotoner Foundation. Some money was held back from the wages of the soldiers of the fort in order to be deposited into the fund. Each invalid in the fort was given about 1 *scudo* 6 *tari* a month.[24] In the 1770s, the average monthly amount paid by

---

[23] AOM 1928, passim, for the salaries of the sailing-ships militia.
[24] AOM Treasury Series, A48.

the Fund was 5 *scudi*, while in 1780 the average monthly deposit was 56 *scudi*.[25] Ten years later, the Fund was giving 20 *scudi* monthly on average. The Invalids' Fund of Ricasoli was not unique for the time. The sailing-ships squadron of the same Order of St John too had a similar pension scheme. 2 *grani* were withheld daily from each crewman's daily ration of bread by the Commission of Sailing Ships. Similarly, 10 *grani* per *scudo* or 1/24 of the officer knights' allowances were also withheld for this pension. From this sailing-ships Invalids' Fund were paid the pensioners and sailors who were on secondment at base, as well as the running of the Nautical School; bread for the sick; and the salary of the surgeon.[26] This latter pension reflected the *Caisse des Invalids* of the French Royal Navy and the "smart money" of the British Royal Navy`s Chatham Chest. It must be stressed that the number of pensions was very limited. Those who retired or the dependants of the deceased had to petition the Grand Master for such a pension and this was only forthcoming if available, generally after the demise of another pension holder.

The secondment to base of the older or invalid sailors afforded another link between Fort Ricasoli and the Order's Navy. Very often the dependants of those who died in the service of the navy, or those dismissed, received a secondment or pension called *piazza morta*.[27] This type of pension was given as a pay to servicemen who were on secondment or not present in the ranks.[28] Some ageing or partly disabled sailors were sometimes transferred to Fort Ricasoli, as also to Forts St Elmo or St Angelo, or were pensioned off.[29] Anyone applying for the easier job in the fort and who had previously served for a long stretch on the ships, was generally preferred.[30] After 23 July 1773, pensioners of the galleys or sailing ships-of-the-line had henceforth to be over 50 or permanently disabled while performing their duty. The cases were individually assessed by the Commission of the Galleys or of Sailing Ships, and referred to the Grand Master. The pensioners would later be granted a *piazza morta* in one of the above mentioned forts.[31]

In 1740 Margherita Falzon begged for a counterfort in the Cottonera Lines in order to live in. Her father had served the Order as a soldier and later as sergeant on the galleys, the ships-of-the-line squadron and later at Ricasoli. Even her husband had served for sixteen years on the galleys. After five months of waiting, she was granted permission to occupy counterfort[32] 202 of Cottonera. In October 1777, Giovanni Formosa, after having served the Order for twenty-eight years as gunner on the ships, was transferred as *piazzante* to Fort Ricasoli.[33] He claimed a rise in his 1 *scudo* monthly wage since he was still active, but this was refused by the Commission of War.

---

[25] AOM 1014, no pag.

[26] AOM 1763, 83; AOM 1987, f. 10; and AOM 1890, f. 211 bis.

[27] V. Mallia-Milanes, *Descrittione di Malta, Anno 1716, A Venetian Account*, (Malta 1988), 76.

[28] A. Guglielmotti, *Vocabolario Marino e Militare*, (Rome 1889), 1211.

[29] AOM 1897, ff. 26, 18, 27.

[30] AOM 1189, ff. 173-174v.

[31] AOM 158, f. 28v.

[32] A buttress built behind a scarp wall for the purpose of strengthening the latter. Spiteri, (1994), 639. Many counterforts of the Cottonera lines contain large rooms which could be occupied for habitation, some of them to the present day.

[33] AOM 1021, ff. 475-476.

Petitions reflecting daily conditions of life

Interesting records that throw light on life around the fort are those registers of petitions from various people to the Commissioners of War and Fortifications.[34] Whoever wanted to build a house or a wall or in any way alter the land around Fort Ricasoli had firstly to ask for permission from the Commission lest any alteration prejudice the defence. As shall be seen later, this permission from the military was needed until quite recent times when the fort was evacuated by the British troops. The Commission reserved the right to demolish such works in case of need against adequate compensation. For example on 10 July 1734 Gregorio Abela asked for permission to build a wall around his land near Ricasoli. Permission on these conditions was granted two weeks later.[35] Twelve years later Abela wanted to rebuild this wall and to extend it to match with other walls in his estate. Permission was again granted to him.[36] In 1750 this same Gregorio Abela bought a garden with a house outside Ricasoli. The northern point of the property was only about 100 metres distant from the salient point of the middle bastion of the fort. He was granted permission to enlarge the house and to build a balcony.[37] In April 1798 Teresa Abela wanted to rebuild a room of 14 courses height, or about four metres near the fort.[38] Teresa may have been a relative of Gregorio Abela. In December 1747 permission was granted to Benedetto Attard, a priest from Senglea, who wanted to dig a well in a field near Fort Ricasoli.[39] In 1755 the reverend Dottor Giuseppe Zammit was also granted permission to erect a wall around his garden at Rinella.[40] In 1788 Michele Mifsud wanted to rebuild his two rooms near Ricasoli and to add a first floor to each, as well as a cistern. Permission was also granted.[41] Three years later permission was also granted to Paolo Bugeja who wanted to build a room between St Rocco and Wied Ghammieq.[42]

Another type of petition was similar to that of Margherita Falzon, that is of needy people who in any way had to do with Fort Ricasoli and who begged for rooms in which to live. On 3 December 1735, the widow of Maurizio Fiteni, an ex-Sergeant of the fort, being destitute, asked for a room to live in. On 3 January 1736 she was given a room under the steps which lead to the platform at the Main Gate of Vittoriosa.[43] In 1770 Maria and Vincenza Formosa were permitted to occupy counterfort 30 of the Cottonera which had been recently vacated by their grandmother. Their father Ignazio had served for

---

[34] AOM 6571, f. 90.
[35] AOM 1019, ff. 30, 35.
[36] AOM 1020, ff. 99-100.
[37] AOM 1024, ff. 185-186.
[38] AOM 1022, ff. 483-484.
[39] AOM 1024, ff. 164-165.
[40] AOM 1020, f 449.
[41] AOM 1022, ff. 423-424.
[42] AOM 1023, ff. 252-253.
[43] AOM 1019, f. 72.
[44] AOM 1021, ff. 285-286.

twenty years on the ships of the Order, and was serving in Ricasoli at the time.[44] In 1793, Gioacchino Mizzi, a soldier in Fort Ricasoli, who had also served on the ships, was allowed to cede counterfort 495 of the Cottonera Lines to his daughters.[45]

One last type of petition was that sent by soldiers or other inhabitants inside the fort who requested specific favours or who made some claims to the Commission of War. On 11 August 1736, the sisters Maria and Rosaria Mallia, daughters of Pietro, asked for the cancellation of a rent they were paying for a place that had been accorded to them as payment for the works done by their father as contractor at Fort Ricasoli. They claimed that their father had not been paid the full due. On 19 January 1737, the Commission replied that Pietro Mallia had been paid 3,376 *scudi* 0 *tari* 18 *grani* for the period starting 22 November 1721 and ending on 27 March 1723, as well as 70 *scudi* on 24 January 1728. Therefore their petition was dismissed.[46] On the 5 May 1778, Giuseppe de Martines, first Sergeant was granted leave and emoluments for four months.[47] On 6 February 1762, Gaetano Caruana was appointed foreman of works at Fort Ricasoli. He was a resident at the fort and had already acted as foreman when his predecessor had been taken ill. Caruana had been serving the Order since 1748 as gunner, both on the ships and on land.[48]

Life inside Fort Ricasoli was simple and the daily monotonous routine of drills and military preparation was only broken by the aforesaid religious feasts. There was a tavern inside the fort. The Governor had the power to let it.[49] There was also a bakery which was used by a salaried baker,[50] and finally there was also a cell or prison, in fact Mikiel Anton Vassalli was condemned to life imprisonment in the fort.[51] During the British period, the cell rooms were situated in the casemate to the right of the Main Gate curtain. It is not certain whether this was the same place used for detention in the earlier Hospitaller period.[52] The stores at Ricasoli were taken care of by a store-keeper. In 1728 Salvatore Curmi of Senglea was appointed store-keeper there. He was entrusted with the reorganisation of the stores since most of the materials had been lying about in the open and had deteriorated. His father had already been employed at the fort and Salvatore had lived there since childhood. Curmi was allowed to retain any stores judged to be unserviceable by the Governor.[53] Inside the fort there were workshops, especially the rope-makers', since the ropes could be strung open in the large parade ground or place of arms. The ropes manufactured at Ricasoli as well as at Vittoriosa were later used by the navy of the Order.[54] Abuses were reported, such as in 1739 when the tools at Ricasoli's workshops were being used for private work,[55] but this was a rare occurrence.

---

[45] AOM 1023, ff. 352-353.
[46] AOM 1019, ff. 109-110.
[47] AOM 1021, ff. 475-476.
[48] AOM 653, f. 118.
[49] NLM 142d, f. 465.
[50] Ibid., f. 466v.
[51] A. Cremona, *Mikiel Anton Vassalli u Zminijietu*, (Malta 1975), 18, 28.
[52] C. Testa, *The French in Malta: 1798-1800*, (Malta 1997), 7, specifically describes the prison as a dungeon.
[53] AOM 1019, f. 263.
[54] AOM 1187, ff. 109-109v.
[55] AOM 635, f. 2.

Passtimes

It is quite difficult to tell how the inhabitants spent their spare time. During the summer months, tournaments on boats were organised at Rinella Creek for entertainment.[56] Fishing was popular. It was free during daytime around the fortifications. But at night time, those who had permit to fish had to keep a distance of about forty metres from shore. Fishing from the shore was permitted during daytime.[57] On 2 July 1737, a certain Father Celso of the Theresian Order was drowned behind Ricasoli presumably while fishing.[58] Slaves were not permitted to go near the fort or anywhere near the mouth of the harbour for fear of their escape.[59]

Vassalli's detention and the shift towards French rule

On 12 June 1797, Mikiel Anton Vassalli, the father of Maltese literature, was found guilty of treason against the Government of the Order. He was at first condemned to death, but his sentence was later commuted to life imprisonment in Fort Ricasoli for revealing the identity of his co-conspirators.[60] Vassalli wanted the Maltese people to be more conscious about their civic rights; he wanted a code of law in the Maltese language and advocated free instruction for children. He wanted to educate the people. Vassalli was all out for innovations in the Order of St John. He suggested that the Order reach an agreement for a truce with the Turk; that Malta be more open for trade with the East; and that the Maltese language be formulated and established.[61]

In 1797, Vassalli joined the French party, also known as the Jacobin party, and soon after becoming the leader, he devised a plan to overthrow the Government of the Order by means of armed rebellion.[62] He was in league with General Napoleon Bonaparte, and had been in constant correspondence with Chevalier Barras, brother of a member of the Directory. When Fra Ferdinand von Hompesch became Grand Master in June 1797, Vassalli was allowed to roam about Fort Ricasoli at will.[63] After some time Vassalli was transferred to a Greek ship heading for Salerno,[64] probably upon the initiative of some French and other republican knights who wanted to get rid of Vassalli for fear that he would expose them as members of the republican party.[65]

The French military successes in Italy and the propaganda of republican ideas had no

---

[56] NLM 647, f. 29.
[57] AOM 1015, f. 532.
[58] NLM 20, f. 44.
[59] AOM 6571, f. 90.
[60] Testa, 7-8.
[61] F. Panzavecchia, *Ultimo Periodo della Storia di Malta sotto il Governo dell' Ordine*, (Malta 1835), 345.
[62] Ibid., 344.
[63] Testa, 7.
[64] J. Schembri, "The fortifications of Malta - Fort Ricasoli", in *Malta Land Force Journal*, (July 1971), 71.
[65] G. Cardona, "Mikiel Anton Vassalli (1764-1829)", in *Pronostku Malti*, 1976, 147.

slight influence in directing political affairs in Malta, where the absolute majority of the knights and merchants were French, culminating at last in sedition and intrigue. During the early months of 1797, the republican party in Malta which for some time had been in existence, acquired additional strength both in number and influence of its adherents. Traitorous knights and disaffected Maltese joined the conspiracy. Among these were two knights who had been involved in the repair works at Fort Ricasoli between 1788 and 1795. These were Engineer Fra Antoine Etienne de Tousard,[66] who had drawn the plans of the left flank of the outworks in 1792,[67] and the Commissioner of War and Fortifications Fra Philippe Jean Charles de Fay,[68] who audited the accounts of the expenditure during the same repair works on the fort.[69] Moreover even an officer-knight inside the fort itself, Fra Emanuel Cotoner, declared that he would never fight the French troops. Thus the Order faced Bonaparte in June 1798 with some high dignitaries, directly responsible for works or direction at Fort Ricasoli loyal to the Republic of France rather than to their own Sovereign Hospitaller and Military Order.

---

[66] Vassallo, 728.
[67] NLM plan R. 18.
[68] Vassallo, 728.
[69] AOM 1013, no pag.

7

The French Occupation, 1798 - 1800

The French occupation

Between 10 and 12 June 1798, the garrison of Fort Ricasoli, together with the whole Maltese population, witnessed the almost incredible take-over of the Islands by the French republican army led by General Napoleon Bonaparte. The dramatic events of the two years that followed constitute a most momentous period in the fort's history.

The invasion

At dawn on Saturday 9 June, the French fleet with a total of about 50,000 troops on thirteen ships-of-the-line, a number of frigates, and nearly four hundred transport approached Malta from the West. Although Bonaparte's intention was to occupy Malta, he requested permission to enter the harbours for replenishment as an excuse. The Grand Master could not permit such a breach of the neutrality of the Order of St John during a period of belligerancy between Christian powers. When he refused entry to the French fleet, the invasion began at dawn on 10 June.[1] The French troops disembarked at four different points of the coast: at Gozo; at St Paul's Bay to overrun the north; and at Bahar ic-Caghak area and at Marsaxlokk Bay to effect a pincer movement around the towns of the Grand Harbour and lay siege to them, if not take them by surprise.[2]

The defence

Malta was defended by a total 17,282 men.[3] Fort Ricasoli was garrisoned by an undisclosed part of 700 *Cacciatori* (Maltese) troops deployed also in Forts Tignè and Manoel.[4]

---

[1] C. Testa, *The French in Malta: 1798-1800*, (Malta 1997), 90.
[2] Ibid., "The French in Malta, 1798-1800", in *Mid-Med Bank Report and Accounts, 1989*, (Malta 1990), 34.
[3] F.G. Terrinoni, *Memorie Storiche della Resa di Malta ai Francesi nel 1798*, (Rome 1867), 19.
[4] A. Zarb, *Storia di Malta dalla Caduta dell' Ordine Gerosolimitano sino alla resa della Repubblica Francese*, (Malta 1856), 14.

Moreover some of the 1000 soldiers of the Malta Regiment, backed up by about fifty gunners of the sailing ships captained by Hospitaller navy officers would retreat from the coasts of the south-east into Ricasoli if matters came to the worse.[5] The Governor (or Knight commander) was Bailiff de Clugny. He did not reside in the fort since he also commanded the Zejtun militia. On the fateful 9 June Fra Charles Louis Odouarde de Tillet[6] was sent from Valletta to Ricasoli to substitute for de Clugny, but he was soon faced with insubordination by francophile knights. He ordered Fra Emanuel Cotoner to be sent prisoner in Fort St Elmo when the latter stated that he would never fight the French.[7] During the evening of 10 June the French ships came close to the fort. When the gunners tried to charge their guns, the cartridges were found filled with wet charcoal and just a little gunpowder. Others were found without fuses or rods. Some cannon had balls of different calibre prepared near them. De Tillet was shaken but he still sent for fresh ammunition from aboard the *San Zaccaria* warship, while he arrested and replaced the master in charge of gunpowder. This kind of sabotage also happened in other forts.[8] The guns at Ricasoli could only fire ineffective shots at the French ships since these kept at a safe distance.

The attack

By noon of Sunday 10 June, the column of General Desaix, who had landed at Marsaxlokk, advanced to within reach of Cottonera and Ricasoli, to where the Zejtun militia under Chevalier Tommasi had retreated.[9] The column even joined General Vaubois' troops who had marched from the north.[10] Fort Ricasoli had to suspend fire for a while since the Maltese militia was in a disorganised retreat.[11] The French soldiers routed the local militias for two reasons: the French were more disciplined and experienced; and the Maltese were sometimes betrayed by their officer-knights who went over to the other side. All through the day the confused situation within the encircled cities steadily deteriorated. French agents were openly discouraging any loyal knights and Maltese troops to fight.[12] This was the case both in Valletta and Fort Ricasoli. Since Grand Master Ferdinand von Hompesch and Council of the Order could no longer count on the support of many knights, and after realising that there was a total breakdown in communications, they decided to seek an armistice in view of capitulation.[13] By 6.00 a.m. on Monday 11 June, the white flag was flying over Forts Ricasoli and St Elmo.[14] A delegation was sent to Bonaparte at 11.00 a.m. and the armistice was signed.

---

[5] G. Faurè, *Storia ta' Malta u Ghawdex*, (Malta 1913), iii, 1169.

[6] Terrinoni, 16.

[7] NLM 1130, f. 78.

[8] G.V. Ellul, "The French invasion of Malta: an unpublished account", in *Hyphen*, No 3 Spring 1978, (Malta 1978), 11.

[9] Faurè, iii, 1174.

[10] H.P. Scicluna, *Documents relating to the French Occupation of Malta in 1798-1800*, (Malta 1923), 117.

[11] Ibid., 1175.

[12] Testa, (1990), 35-36.

[13] Zarb, 49.

[14] Testa, (1997), 71.

Capitulation

During the afternoon, however, while a delegation sent by Bonaparte was formulating the terms of capitulation in Valletta, the tide again turned in favour of the troops loyal to the Order, mostly Cospicuans in Cottonera, Fort Ricasoli, and Fort St Angelo. Even after that the Convention between the French Republic and the Order of St John decreeing the surrender of the Maltese Islands was signed at 1.00 a.m. on Tuesday 12 June,[15] the garrisons of the above mentioned fortresses would not let go, but since Valletta had capitulated, they would have braught great damage and punishment upon themselves had they resisted further. The Bishop, Mgr Vincenzo Labini sent a holy priest, Father Salvatore Casha, rector of the church of the souls of Purgatory in Valletta, to Ricasoli and finally convinced the Maltese to surrender.[16] At 9.00 p.m. Forts Ricasoli and St Elmo hoisted the French flag.[17]

Bonaparte at Ricasoli

At about 10.30 p.m. General Bonaparte entered harbour on a fleet of launches. He first set foot on Maltese soil at Ricasoli steps and made a one hour tour of inspection inside the fort. He stationed a troop of soldiers who had escorted him on other launches. Later he proceeded to Valletta marina in order to take possession of the island.[18]

Fort Ricasoli had not been tested at war. The Hospitaller Order collapsed and the defenders there could do nothing but abide by what common sense dictated in the circumstances. One can only imagine what might have happened had the central Government of the Order decided to withstand a siege. According to pro-French spies in Malta reporting to the French Directory in 1797, Fort Ricasoli or the Cottonera could easily be invested and occupied as a preliminary to Valletta's capitulation.[19] Although most military engineers of the eighteenth century had observed that Ricasoli's defences were small and weak, extensive repairs and additions to the outworks had been carried out in the 1790s, and the French spies in Malta might have purposely exaggerated the weakness of the defence to hasten French preparations for a take-over, since they stood to gain.

The French in Ricasoli

The Maltese population of the fort

The Maltese garrison were allowed to sail to Valletta or Cottonera unmolested by the French. Most of the gunners of the Hospitaller sailing ships squadron who had been

---

[15] Ibid., 70.
[16] F. Panzavecchia, *L'Ultimo Periodo della Storia di Malta sotto il Governo dell'Ordine Gerosolimitano*, (Malta 1835), 475-476.
[17] F. Sammut, *Bonaparti f'Malta*, (Malta 1997), 139.
[18] Ibid.
[19] W. Hardman, *History of Malta During the French and British Occupation*, (London 1909), 24-25.

posted at Ricasoli were recruited by the French fleet which sailed to Egypt. Many perished there fighting the British Royal Navy at Aboukir Bay. Thus ended the knights' rule at Ricasoli. Henceforth, the fort was no longer inhabited by a majority of Maltese persons. In 1797 there had been a total of 151 persons in Ricasoli, excluding knights[20] and the occasional reinforcement of 50 gunners of the ships. The overwhelming majority of the former were Maltese, of which eleven men of over 18 years of age; 23 men of undisclosed age; 31 wives and widows; 47 boys under eighteen years; 37 daughters, and two chaplains. Most of these persons were evacuated from the fort after 12 June 1798. Throughout 1798, there was only one death recorded at Ricasoli. This was that of one year old Marianna Zammit on 28 July.[21] The evacuation of the Maltese must have taken place in stages between 1798 and 1800. The only death registered in 1799 was that of Giovanni Antonio Gruppi, aged 75.[22] He was a newcomer to the fort. By 1801, only fourteen Maltese inhabitants were left in Ricasoli. These were 38 year old Giuseppe Ellul, 30 year old Antonio Falzon, the five members of Saverio Pace's family and seven members of Antonio Mamo's family.[23] Only five members of the Mamo family were survivors of the Hospitaller era. Of these fourteen persons, only five were men over 18 years of age. It should be noted that the population of Fort St Angelo went through the same upheaval. By 1801, only fourteen Maltese persons were left inside the fort out of 65 in 1779.[24]

The Maltese insurrection

The peaceful rule of Malta by the French was very short-lived. The expectations of the population, especially the rural part, were dashed to the ground in the summer of 1798. Bonaparte first, and the Commission of Government that acted in concert with the French Commissioner of Government, later promulgated laws which could have helped the Maltese emerge from feudal submission into an enlightened rule. But the Maltese were not prepared for sudden changes. On 2 September 1798, the Maltese rose up in rebellion against the French because the French troops despoiled many churches of their riches; anti-clerical laws were put into effect; the lack of hard cash could not keep the population and the government provided with the basic necessities; food supplies from Sicily were curtailed; many workers formerly employed by the Order and paupers depending on the knights' charity could no longer be maintained and were left destitute; prices were rising and Maltese merchantmen flying the French flag were subjected to harassment by allied warships.[25] Five days after the news of the French defeat at Aboukir Bay reached Malta, the people of Rabat chased back to Valletta some Maltese government officials who had been sent there to sell gold and silver articles that had been confiscated in Rabat and

---

[20]AAF, LSA, Vittoriosa, 1797, ff.39-40.
[21]ACCV, Liber Mortuorum V, 1736-1837, 82.
[22] Ibid., 100.
[23]ACCV, LSA, 1765-1805, no pag.
[24] Ibid., 1777-1779.
[25] Testa, (1997), 38-39.

Mdina. In the afternoon the Mdina commandant who had bullied a hostile crowd was murdered. The rebels sent word to all other villages for help. The general uprising of the Maltese was on.[26]

General Claude Henri Vaubois had been appointed French commander in chief of the Maltese Islands. Rear Admiral Denis Decres, who was Captain of the ship *La Diane* was appointed Governor of the outlying fortresses of Cottonera, Ricasoli, Manoel and Tignè, and part of the crews of these ships were stationed at Ricasoli too.[27] More particularly, Fort Ricasoli was entrusted to the command of Captain Lecite.[28] On 2 September, Major Seit was appointed new commander of Fort Ricasoli in lieu of Lecite who was transferred to Cottonera to reinforce Predier's garrison there. Lecite was ordered to disburse 200 *scudi* in order to furnish adequately the Governor's Quarters at Ricasoli for Seit. One day later, Predier and Lecite sallied out towards Zabbar from Cottonera. Lecite was killed there.[29] In October 1798, Pierre Bastè an officer of *La Diane*, escaped to Valletta from Fort Chambrey in Gozo which capitulated that month, and was posted at Ricasoli to command the ships' gunners inside the fort.[30]

On 3 September, people from Birkirkara routed a French relieving force which had sallied out of Valletta towards Mdina. By 4 September the French forces in Malta together with nearly 40,000 city-dwellers (about a third of the total population), were besieged by the rural Maltese insurgents inside Valletta, Floriana, Cottonera, and Forts Tignè, Manoel and Ricasoli. Mdina, the coastal towers, and the Castello and Fort Chambrey in Gozo were soon occupied by the Maltese. They brought whatever cannon they found in these forts or towers to entrenchments which they erected around the harbour area to effectively besiege the harbourside towns.[31] The Maltese insurgents organised themselves into battalions according to their village under the command of local notables. They established their headquarters at San Anton Palace, and sent for help to Ferdinand of Sicily; to Portugal; to Great Britain and to Russia.[32]

The French garrison left at Malta totalled 3,053 men.[33] These were augmented though by the gunners and sailors of the three aforementioned ships. They alternated one day alert and one day rest. Still they were exhausted. Vaubois' intention was to hold on to the cities until help would arrive from France. At Ricasoli there were about 300 men of the 6th half brigade navy battalion, some of whom were Maltese who were not trusted.[34] Many were substituted by fresh naval troops who arrived on 26 September 1798.[35] Out

---

[26] Ibid., (1990), 39-40.
[27] Hardman, 563.
[28] Faurè, iv, 44-45.
[29] Testa, (1997), 281, 287-288.
[30] Ibid., 761.
[31] Ibid., 40.
[32] Ibid., 40-41.
[33] Hardman, 76.
[34] C. Testa, *Maz-Zewg Nahat tas-Swar*, (Malta 1980),ii, 273.
[35] Testa (1997), 320-321, 361.

of a total of 1,143,000 cartridges in the cities, 24,300 were in Ricasoli. On 27 September thirty-five Maltese soldiers tried to escape from Cottonera and Ricasoli, but they were discovered by an innkeeper and a baker.[36] On 21 December the distrusted Maltese soldiers and gunners inside the forts were put under lock and key, and were henceforth only given minimum food rations.[37] This was the first time that Fort Ricasoli withstood a siege, although the Maltese rebels could not be likened to a proper disciplined military force. Again, the part played by the fort was that of an outlying post defending Valletta and Cottonera. The besiegers hoped that if Fort Ricasoli was captured, the surrender of Valletta would follow easily.[38]

The Maltese battery of cannon nearest to Fort Ricasoli was the one at Zabbar, commanded by Augustine Said. It was made up of four cannon,[39] and 338 men at all time.[40] By 1800, the Maltese battalions totalled 2,503 men, of which 248 of the Zabbar battalion under Clement Ellul, Joseph Cachia and Joseph Ellul; and 469 of the Zejtun battalion under Francis Miceu at St Rocco Battery, and Giovanni Battista Rebull of the assault parties.[41] In February 1799, the Maltese erected another battery of 32 pounder cannon at St Rocco, about one kilometre on the coast to the south-east of Ricasoli.[42] Shot from this battery could not only reach the fort, but also Valletta and Fort St Elmo.[43] After firing inside the fort, the St Rocco battery did a great deal of damage. The French were continuously on guard at Ricasoli fearing an assault, and reinforcements that had been sent there from Valletta early in 1799 were discontented and in great consternation.[44]

Most of the Maltese people who still remained in Fort Ricasoli were expelled. They were useless mouths to feed. By 1800 in fact, only about 700, out of the original 40,000 Maltese living in the harbour towns remained.[45] The Maltese who were expelled had to pass through an interrogation by Maltese judges in order to check whether they were bona fide refugees or spies. On 29 September 1798, judge Giuseppe Calcedonio Debono interrogated Gregorio Scicluna and Salvatore Cassar who had fled from Ricasoli with some animals and bundles of clothes and goods. He found them to be both in good faith and in good health.[46] Both Scicluna and Cassar had come to live inside the fort after 1797.[47]

[36] F. Cutajar, *L'Occupazione Francese di Malta nel 1798*, (Malta 1933), 60.

[37] NLM 1238, f.36v.

[38] Ibid., f.41v.

[39] Faurè, iv, 30-31.

[40] NLM 1096, no pag.

[41] Testa (1997), 831-832.

[42] Hardman, 200; and A.G. Chesney, *Historical Records of the Maltese Corps of the British Army*, (London 1897), 10.

[43] Hardman, 210.

[44] Ibid., 200.

[45] Testa, (1990), 41.

[46] NLM 1238, 1.

[47] AAF, LSA, Vittoriosa, 1797, ff.39-40.

The course of the blockade

The blockade of the French inside the harbour towns took the form of a regular siege. Some Royal Navy ships were dispatched by Admiral Horatio Nelson to blockade the entrances to the harbours. The French organised occasional sorties and both warring sides frequently indulged in artillery duels, none with any tangible result. Stalemate ensued for two whole years. The only time that the French tried to defeat the Maltese by a well organised sortie of considerable size was early in the siege on 6 October 1798. It partly originated at Ricasoli and partly at Cottonera. The intent was for the French main body to march on Zabbar from Vittoriosa in order to pillage it. Another French troop sortied from Ricasoli to encircle the Zabbar men from the east and the south (that is from the Zabbar-Xghajra Road) and cut their communications with Zejtun. When the Ricasoli troops reached St Clement chapel in the limits of Zejtun, the latter's battalion met them in force.[48] The French column which had sortied from Cottonera found Zabbar deserted, but when they broke ranks and entered the narrow streets, they were met by fierce villagers firing point blank at them. Two small cannon which had been brought over secretly to the centre of the village were fixed on the French who retreated in disorder.[49] The French commander at Cottonera, Predier, died at Zabbar together with another eight soldiers. Thirty-two others were wounded.[50]

Since it was obvious that the siege would be long, Vaubois ordered that rations be cut. The troops had only enough food for seven months, but they ultimately resisted for two years. Life inside Fort Ricasoli must have been squalid and quite miserable mostly for lack of adequate victuals. The French used to sortie out of Ricasoli to find fresh vegetables or to capture any Maltese person who could inform them on what was happening.[51] When on 15 November 1798, they sortied out of Cottonera under cover of fire from Vittoriosa and Ricasoli, they suffered casualties, but were very happy with their vegetable trophies.[52] Indeed they needed all sorts of commodities, even mattresses. On 11 October the Commission of Government requested 130 libani grass ropes to be used for mattresses at Ricasoli, since hay was being fed to the animals that were left alive.[53] One particularly curious episode tells on the lack of necessities inside the fort and the angry state of the Maltese. One day in February 1799, a French officer climbed out of Ricasoli in order to find some figs at Rinella. An armed farmer saw the officer and shot him dead. Some other Zabbar farmers severed his right arm and head. They piked the latter on an alabard with a fig in his mouth, and proceeded with it to Zabbar, Zejtun, Ghaxaq, Gudja and then on to San Anton Palace at Attard where the Maltese leaders used to meet.[54] In early 1800 the French were trying to get nourishment from the sea by fishing. The battery at St Rocco fired on French soldiers who had sailed from Ricasoli to fish.[55]

---

[48] Faurè, iv, 44-45.
[49] Testa, (1990), 42.
[50] Faurè, iv, 44-45.
[51] C. Testa, *Maż-Żewġ Naħat tas-Swar*, (Malta 1982), iii, 572.
[52] Cutajar, 71.
[53] Testa, (1980), 317.
[54] Faurè, iv, 66-67.
[55] B. Ransijat, *Assedio e Blocco di Malta*, (Malta 1843), 156.

British intervention

Both Captain Alexander John Ball, Captain of the British ships blockading the harbours, and Colonel Thomas Graham, the British general officer commanding troops in Malta, were certain that if Admiral Nelson could spare about 1000 to 1200 troops, Fort Ricasoli could be scaled and occupied. There would then be no hope at all for the French to be relieved by their navy.[56] On 28 August 1799, Ball instigated the building of a new three-gun battery at St Rocco, closer to Ricasoli in order to further harass any movements in the harbour.[57] The battery only became operational on 22 October.[58] In concert with other batteries at Corradino and Tal-Borg (Paola), it fired for two consecutive days and the French could do nothing since Valletta was too exposed.[59] In December 1799, the Maltese dug up trenches even nearer to Ricasoli, to prevent French ships from entering or escaping Grand Harbour and to cover any assault that might be launched on the yet incomplete left flank of the Ricasoli land front (St Dominic Bastion). Therefore Vaubois sent 100 more men to Ricasoli on 12 December. The General ordered Decres to put a permanent guard on the left (St Dominic) bastion as a precaution. The parapets there were quite low and workmen could not be found. Therefore Decres was instructed to find the most advantageous posts if an attack was launched, especially if the British ships' cannon covered such assault. Fixed guards were also placed in the fausse-braye at the seaward (left) flank to cover any invasion of the ditch.[60] Large amounts of earth-filled sacks were delivered to Ricasoli from Valletta in order to add protection to the defenders and to repair the weak parapets of the fort.[61] Vaubois had been informed about the intentions of the Maltese regarding Ricasoli when three Irish soldiers defected from the British.[62]

The Maltese did come close to the bastions of Fort Ricasoli on more than one occasion. On the 25 and 26 June 1799, a Maltese battalion came close to attack the Cottonera Lines, under cover of British ships' cannon shot. However, Forts St Elmo and Ricasoli replied and the column retreated in disorder.[63] In November 1799, a company of Maltese soldiers from Zejtun and Zabbar occupied Bighi Palace, right across Rinella Creek from Ricasoli, by night. They made noises while pulling down wooden doors. A company of French soldiers was sent from Valletta but the latter were discovered by the Maltese and were annihilated.[64] In December 1799, a detachment of British troops arrived, and two weeks later, over 1000 men from the Kingdom of Two Sicilies were brought over.[65]

---

[56] Hardman, 225.
[57] Ibid., 222.
[58] Faurè, iv, 80.
[59] Ransijat, 140.
[60] Hardman, 626.
[61] Ibid., 627.
[62] Testa, (1982), 624.
[63] Ibid., 569.
[64] Zarb, 332.
[65] B. Blouet, *The Story of Malta*, (Malta 1981), 139.

The final months

By 29 March 1800, the French were rapidly losing any hope of being reinforced from France. There was only one ship left in Grand Harbour, the *Guillaume Tell*. At 11.00 p.m. Rear Admiral Decres and Captain Soulnier ably evaded the blockade and sailed for France on the ship with 130 sick Frenchmen and another 50 passengers. Most of the crew had served for nineteen months at either Ricasoli, Manoel, or Tignè. They were captured at dawn near Sicily, suffering the loss of 50 men. Decres himself was wounded.[66] Two months later, the British Government finally decided to help the Maltese in a more tangible way. General Graham deployed two regiments, the 30th and the 89th outside Ricasoli and Cottonera, which were the two positions of greatest risk from where the French could organise surprise sorties, although all direct roads had been ploughed up. Some batteries had been too exposed but they had stone blockhouses for better protection at their rear.[67] Summer of 1800 wore on in much the same way as did the previous two years of siege. Whenever a British ship approached the harbour, she was fired upon from Forts St Elmo and Ricasoli, both of which were promptly answered by the battery at St Rocco.[68] August witnessed increased bombing by the Maltese into Ricasoli.[69] Although thousands of Maltese died of malnutrition and epidemics, the plight of the French was similar, or even worse. They finally consumed the produce of their vegetable gardens, the dogs, cats, and rats. On 5 September just after the second anniversary of the start of hostilities, General Vaubois capitulated to General Pigot who had just taken over from Graham as commander of the small force of British troops. In spite of the representations of Ball and the Maltese leaders, Pigot refused to allow a formal place for the latter at the surrender ceremony.[70]

By Article 1 of the Capitulation of the French garrison in Malta, Fort Ricasoli, together with Fort Tignè, was immediately surrendered to British troops so that the Royal Navy ships could enter the harbours in safety.[71] At 4.00 p.m. on 5 September 1800 the British soldiers of the 35th Foot Regiment under the general direction of Pigot entered Ricasoli. The French troops there evacuated at the same time[72] with full military honours.

---

[66] Testa, (1982), 675-677.
[67] Hardman, 297.
[68] Testa (1997), 797.
[69] Ransijat, 209.
[70] Blouet, 139.
[71] Ransijat, 218.
[72] Hardman, 319,322.

Part II

The British and Post-War Periods

8

Military History under British Rule

General Military and Strategic Development

The history of British Ricasoli (1800-1964) is devoid of any great military event since British Malta was never occupied. The only action which the Fort witnessed were the Froberg mutiny of Balkan soldiers in 1807, and the attack on the Harbour by an E-Boat flotilla of the Italian Navy on 26 July 1941. How Ricasoli, or indeed the whole of the island's fortifications would have performed if Malta was ever attacked by a determined enemy, is a matter of speculation.[1]

Malta was occupied by the British troops in 1800. However it was only after the end of the Napoleonic Wars in 1814 that Malta definitely became a British Colony by the First Treaty of Paris, and it even risked being returned to the Knights of St John when Britain and France concluded the Peace of Amiens in 1802, which was aborted, partly because of British intransigence in effecting the tenth article concerning Malta. Therefore it must be borne in mind that the strategic importance of Malta for the British Empire was only gradually appreciated by the British Military as events unfolded during the nineteenth century. Consequently, Fort Ricasoli was further built, altered and rearmed as military necessities dictated. Prior to the opening of the Suez Canal in 1869, Malta's strategic import for the British Royal Navy was that of sentinel in the Inland Sea.[2] It served British interests well during the Greek War of Independence between 1820 and 1822; during the various crises which engulfed the ailing Turkish Empire in the nineteenth century; and especially during the Crimean War of 1853-1856. It was from here that most regiments sailed for war in the Levant. After 1869, Malta became a very indispensable link in the sea-route towards the British Empire in India and East Africa.

This was not only because the newly invented steamships needed constant and abundant supplies of coal, but also because Malta was now needed to repair, refit and rearm the

---

[1] S. C. Spiteri, *British Military Architecture in Malta*, (Malta 1996), xi.
[2] Ibid., 8.

ships of the Navy. For this reason, the dockyard, which had originated at Vittoriosa as a galley-yard under the Knights, and which had expanded into a shipbuilding yard in the early eighteenth century at Cospicua and French Creek, was further developed into a modern dockyard starting from 1848 with the building of the first dry dock at Dockyard (ex-Galley) Creek, and later with the building of the other dry docks in French Creek after 1891. By the end of the eighteenth century, Grand Harbour had been turned into a great naval base. All these developments made the steamships and their bases interdependent. Admirals had nightmares about their bases being destroyed behind their backs.[3] It became increasingly important that the bases should be protected by fire heavier than that of any attacker.

But this was a very difficult task during the nineteenth century, because rifle muzzle loading (RML) guns started to be made with ever increasing range, accuracy, and penetrating power, especially after 1850. Between 1800 and 1860, it had been enough to simply change the ordnance on the gun emplacements of the existing old Knights' fortifications with only minor modifications. After 1860, the longer effective ranges meant that the arcs of fire of the existing batteries in the forts around the harbours left many "dead zones" which had to be filled by building new forts and batteries increasingly more distant from the harbours' mouths than Ricasoli or Tignè. Otherwise the dockyards and shipping in the harbours could be subjected to high velocity explosive shells fired from warships laying outside harbour with impunity. Worse still, very few, if any, of the powder and shell magazines were now bomb-proof and the old works were too exposed and quite incapable of resisting the fire of the new guns.[4] This is why between 1860 and 1900, a number of forts and batteries were built along the coast south-east of Ricasoli; or north-west of Tignè, often within a few hundred metres distance from each other. The adoption of different general strategic plans by the military authorities also contributed to the pile up of these batteries, which turned Malta into one impregnable fortress. In 1888, that a warships squadron would try to force the harbour's mouth and damage the facilities inside was considered very improbable by British military advisors Nicholson and Goodenough.[5] By the end of the nineteenth century, St Elmo, Ricasoli, and Tignè were no longer the only forts with the task of defending the harbours from sea-borne attack.

As shall be seen in the chapter about the Second World War, the invention of the aeroplane and its use for air-raids starting from 1911, brought about another revolution in strategic military thought. The existing forts had to be altered in order to cope with the new threat coming from above. From 1933 onwards, especially with the rise of the fascist threat from Italy, Great Britain was forced to invest in the fortification of Malta. New aerodromes, coastal batteries and infantry defences were built while the strength of its garrison forces and anti-aircraft defences was gradually increased. A network of anti-aircraft gun batteries deployed in concentric rings around the Grand Harbour and

---

[3] R. Vella Bonavita, "The 100-ton 17.72 inch R.M.L. Armstrong gun at Rinella Battery, Malta: A brief account and description," in *The Malta Year Book*, (Malta 1978), 431.
[4] Ibid., 433.
[5] Spiteri (1996), 143.

other naval and military installations were built. To these were added anti-aircraft searchlights and sound locators. By 1939 it was estimated that to take Malta by force would cost an aggressor 60,000 lives.[6]

The post war period saw the gradual dissolution of Britain's Colonial Empire, although Britain remained predominant in the Middle East until 1956, when Malta played her last significant role as a British base in the attack on Egypt during the Suez crises. During this same post-war period, missiles began increasingly to take over the role of both anti-aircraft and coastal guns, rendering obsolete the forts and heavy batteries such as Fort Ricasoli. By 1960 most forts and batteries in Malta including Ricasoli, were closed down and disarmed. The general strategic importance of the Island as a naval and military station diminished rapidly as Great Britain lost interest in policing the Mediterranean, and began a rundown of her stations that finally ended with the complete withdrawal of her forces from Malta in 1979.[7]

Fort Ricasoli and its strategic role in Malta's defence

Barely three months after that British troops occupied Malta, Fort Ricasoli was considered by the visiting forces' chronicler Anderson[8] as "a place of great strength, as it stands upon a rock, and... commands the entrance of the Grand Harbour from a variety of points", although it was realised by Claudius Shaw of the Royal Artillery in 1810[9] that Ricasoli was still dominated by Fort St Elmo and Valletta whose batteries stood higher and more central. But Ricasoli could defend a large stretch of the South East coast towards Xghajra and Zonqor Point. The land-ward side was strong and commanded the countryside for a considerable distance as well. These comments confirm the opinion that the British Military were more than satisfied with the state of the fortifications as left by the Knights. It is also thought that they had quite a headache in adequately manning all the forts of Malta.

By the time of the Crimean War, and more especially with the realisation that Malta could become an important naval station on the route to India when the Suez Canal would open, the strategic position of Malta became increasingly important and the British Military could spend more money on arming Malta. Concurrently, Ricasoli's position too obtained a boost. For example, in 1855 during the Crimean War, Maltese merchants pressed the authorities for permits to build warehouses along the Grand Harbour, including along Bighi Bay, underneath the Naval Hospital. Governor Reid supported the idea also because a new road around the shores of Bighi Bay would serve Fort Ricasoli in case of necessity during a siege.[10] The Admiralty felt the need for land suitable to install a naval practice rifle range. By July 1861, all the foreshore at Wied Ghammieq, just outside Ricasoli's

[6] Ibid., 11, 52.

[7] Ibid., 12, 88.

[8] A. Anderson, *A Journal of the Forces which sailed from the Downs in April 1800*, (London 1802), 117.

[9] C. Shaw, *Malta Sixty Years Ago*, (London 1875), 18.

[10] National Archives, Malta (NAM), Despatches, Governor Reid to Secretary of State (S.o.S.) Lord Newcastle, 1850-1855 Military, pp. 167-169.

Aerial photograph of the Rinella-Wied Għammieq - Ricasoli area. The fort is at the centre of the photograph. In the foreground is Fort St Rocco (now Rinella Movie Park), and the Mediterranean Film Studios. Valletta stretches in the background. Fort St Angelo is in the middle of Grand Harbour to the left.

(Courtesy: DOI)

outworks, was in possession of the Naval Authorities on long lease from the Civil Government.[11] The range was situated on the foreshore between Ricasoli and St Rocco Battery. The House was built shortly after 1867,[12] and new latrines were also constructed in May 1911.[13] In 1922 an electric generator was installed in a purposely built shed too.[14] The ranges included six 1st Class targets and Running Man with shelter sheds and butt.[15] The site of these ranges now form part of the Mediterranean Film Studios.

Fort Ricasoli and its neighbouring Forts

In 1866 and the 1872, acting on the suggestions of Colonel Jervois of the Royal Engineers, and of Brigadier General J. Adye respectively, the British Military authorities resuscitated the 1722 plan of the knights to defend only the populated part of Malta south-

---

[11] Ibid., Public Works Department (PWD) 145, ff. 259v.-260; 146, ff. 38v.-39. A further 99-year lease deed was signed by the two authorities on 14 August 1906. Ibid., 146, ff. 85v.-86.
[12] Ibid., Plans Ricasoli 248.
[13] Ibid., 316.
[14] Ibid., 316.
[15] Ibid., 312.

1945 perpendicular aerial photograph of the Rinella area, showing from left to right Fort Ricasoli; Fort Rinella (centre) and Fort St Rocco (right).   (Courtesy: NAM)

east of the Great (natural) Fault, by building a continuous 14 kilometre entrenchment, later called the Victoria Lines, from Fomm-ir-Rih to Madliena with four forts at Bingemma, Targa Gap, Mosta and Madliena; and of building coastal forts or batteries all along the low south-east coast.[16] Ricasoli's position was strengthened by the building of five forts or batteries to within five kilometres of its south-east coast in the relatively short period of fifteen years, between 1878 and 1893, as shown in table X.

Similarly to the north-west of Fort Ricasoli across the mouth of Grand Harbour the following eight forts or batteries were completed between 1874 and 1902. They too had the task, similar to that of Ricasoli, of defending both Grand Harbour and Marsamxett Harbour, more especially from any attack which might materialise from the north or east of the harbours (see table XI).

After the building of all these forts, the position of Fort Ricasoli changed from one which had always been somewhat peripheral when compared to that of Valletta or Fort St Elmo, to one which was more central in the general deployment of forces which defended the Malta harbours. Fort Ricasoli now had three neighbouring batteries which, owing to their close proximity and uniqueness, deserve a special mention. These are Tryon, St Rocco, and Rinella Batteries.

Table X
Coastal Forts south-east of Ricasoli

Fort / Battery	Distance from Ricasoli (in metres)	date when built	original armament
Ft Rinella	175	1883	one 17.72", 102.5 ton RML[1]
Ft St Rocco	800	1878/1905	three 12.5", 38 ton gun[2]
Delle Grazie Bty	2050	1893	two 10", 18 ton Breach-Loaders (BL) and two 6" BL[3]
Ft San Leonardo	3275	1878	four 11", 25 ton guns[4]
Zonqor Battery	4425	1886	three 7", 6.5 ton RML[5]

[1] J. Vella Bonavita, "Rinella Battery and one-hundred ton gun: Teenagers Din l-Art Helwa summer camp 1969" in *Teenagers' Din l-Art Helwa Quarterly*, vol. 1 No 1, Autumn 1969 (Malta), 25.
[2] Spiteri (1996), 241.
[3] J. Quentin Hughes, *Malta: A Guide to the Fortifications*, (Malta 1993), 119.
[4] Ibid., 199.
[5] Spiteri (1996), 439-440.

Table XI
Forts and Batteries north-west of Ricasoli:

Fort / Battery	distance from Ricasoli (in metres)	date when built	original armament
Tryon Battery	500	1900	six 12-pounder Quick Firing (QF) guns[1]
Garden Battery	1550	1894	one 9.2 BL gun and two 6" BL guns[2]
Cambridge Battery	1675	1886	one 17.72", 102.5 ton RML[3]
Sliema Fort	2300	1874	two 12.5", 38 ton RML and two 10", 18 ton RML[4]
Spinola Battery	3675	1894	two 9.2" and two 6"[5]
Pembroke Bty	4775	1902	two 9.2" BL[6]
Fort Pembroke	4925	1879	three 11", 25 ton RML[7]
Madliena Fort	6500	1880	one 11", 25 ton RML; four 64 pounders; two 40 pounders[8]

[1] Spiteri (1996), 445.
[2] Hughes (1993), 135.
[3] R. Vella Bonavita, (1978), 439.
[4] Spiteri (1993), 263-264.
[5] Hughes (1993), 227.
[6] Spiteri (1996), 475.
[7] Ibid., 325.
[8] Hughes (1993), 141.

Tryon Battery

Tryon Battery was located 500 metres across the Grand Harbour mouth from Ricasoli Point below St Lazarus Curtain on the rocky foreshore of Valletta. The Battery was built in 1900 because the British military authorities were never quite satisfied with whatever protection could be afforded to the harbour mouth. One important reason why Tryon Battery was built was that the Quick Firing guns on the high bastions of Forts St Elmo and Ricasoli could not be depressed down enough to engage any ship which might have slipped to the mouth of Grand Harbour. The battery included six 12-pounder Q/F guns.[17] These complemented the batteries at Ricasoli strongly enough.

St Rocco Battery

St Rocco Battery, lying 800 metres to the south-east of Fort Ricasoli, was originally built for three 38 ton guns between 1873 and 1875 at a place where the Maltese battalions had put up a battery during the French blockade. It formed part of an 1860s strategic plan to encircle the harbours area with detached forts, to include protection from possible attacks by way of the countryside. Since it was found defective and small by engineers Goodenough and Nicholson in 1888, it was totally rebuilt in 1900-1905. It firstly had three 9.2" Mark X breach-loading (BL) guns mounted *en barbette*, but by World War II, it mounted three 6" BL guns which proved effective during the Italian E-boat attack on Grand Harbour in 1941. After the war, St Rocco was installed with three 5.25" guns until disarmed in 1958. After 1888, Ricasoli's land front had to be rearmed with newly developed and highly effective Gotling machine guns so that larger calibre shot would not damage St Rocco.[18]

Rinella Battery and 100-ton gun

Fort Ricasoli's next door neighbour on the south-east coast barely 175 metres distant from the salient point of the central land front bastion (No 6 or St Francis Bastion) is Rinella Battery which is the epitome of the nineteenth century arms race fortification. As has already been pointed out, during the latter half of the nineteenth century, there were rapid improvements both in the defensive armour plate capacity of ships, and in the calibre of their offensive armament. So much so that in 1878, Sir W. G. Armstrong and Company of Newcastle were able to produce a RML gun of 102.25 tons of 17.72 " calibre. It could fire a one ton projectile at 500 metres per second, which could pierce 21" of wrought iron armour plate at about 1.6 kilometres. Its range, however, was over five kilometres and could fire a shot every four minutes. Only two such guns are still extant today: one of them next door to Ricasoli at Rinella Battery; the other at Napier of Magdala Battery in Gibraltar.[19]

---

[16] Spiteri, (1996), 383-400.
[17] Spiteri (1996), 445.
[18] Ibid., 241-252.
[19] R. Vella Bonavita, (1978), 439-440.

Although the Ordnance Board rejected Armstrong's design, the firm had a subsidiary company in Italy, and there eight such guns were cast at the order of the government of the newly united Italian Kingdom as armament for two of their battleships, the *Dandolo*, and the *Duilio*.[20] After Italy's annoyance at France's take-over of Tunisia in 1881, the former country joined the central powers of Germany and Austria-Hungary in alliance.[21] It suddenly occurred to the British Military that these two ships could obliterate all the coastal forts of Malta one by one before bombarding Valletta, since the island only had 38 ton, 12.5" RMLs, which were powerless to pierce those ships' armoured plate.[22]

Therefore between 1882 and 1886 two self defensible forts were constructed either side of Malta's harbours: Cambridge Battery at Sliema; and Rinella Battery, each to house a 100 ton gun.[23] The site was selected for more than one reason. It was not economical for extensive alterations to be carried out at Fort Ricasoli itself. The gun needed massive concrete bedding on its emplacement. The batteries were situated slightly further from the mouths of the harbours to intercept intruders at a distance, before the latter ships could lie within range of the harbour mouths. Between 1879 and 1882, twenty-one tummoli (2.35 hectares circa) of land between Fort Ricasoli and St Rocco Battery were requisitioned by the Military Government from private proprietors, for which the latter got £943. 13s. 10d. recompense, and a further £ 96 to farmers who lost their crops (not to mention their jobs!). These lands were taken to host the battery, and the roads connecting Ricasoli to St Rocco.[24]

Rinella Battery is almost square in shape; its seaward face slightly convex. It is surrounded by a vertically walled ditch into which musketry caponniers project. The approach lies over a drawbridge, through the gate, past the guardroom, and into the small place of arms (square). Barrack rooms stretch along the back wall, lit through shuttered windows which could be closed except for a thin slit for musketry defence.[25] The gun was entirely operated by machinery and hydraulic power, handled by eighteen men. Underground lie magazines, shell and cartridge stores and lifts and rammer-beams to convey both shell and cartridge to the muzzle; as well as passageways leading to the caponniers and the counterscarp gallery across the ditch.[26] Cambridge Battery at Qui-Si-Sana, Sliema (now part of a hotel complex), is a mirror image of Rinella Battery. With the completion of Rinella and St Rocco Batteries, Fort Ricasoli was provided with added protection from the Eastern sea and land approaches. Ricasoli's centrality in the strategic development of Malta's fortifications was now pronounced.

The two gargantuan guns at Rinella and Cambridge were struck off the approved armaments list in 1907.[27] The gun at Sliema was scrapped by the army in the 1950s.

---

[20] J. Vella Bonavita, 25.
[21] D. Thomson, *Europe Since Napoleon*, (Harmondsworth 1972), 526.
[22] Spiteri, (1996), 411.
[23] Hughes, (1993), 183.
[24] NAM PWD 580, N., 31-61.
[25] Ibid., 183.
[26] Spiteri (1996), 427.
[27] Ibid., 433.

Aerial photograph of Rinella 100-ton Battery (1884), with the ex-Naval rifle ranges (now Mediterranean Film Studios grounds) in the foreground.

(Courtesy: DOI)

The one at Rinella was saved by the Navy. Rinella Battery was handed over to the Malta Government on 2 March 1965. Between 1965 and July 1991 the battery formed part of the Malta (later Mediterranean) Film Facilities Studios. Since the *Dandolo* and the *Duilio* battleships have long been scrapped, the gun at Rinella is, together with the one at Gibraltar, unique in the world. Between 1969 and 1979, the Youth Section of the Maltese national trust *Din l-Art Helwa* organised summer camps at the battery to sandblast and paint the gun against corrosion.[28] Since July 1991, the national heritage foundation *Fondazzjoni Wirt Artna*, is trying to restore the battery to its former shape, it being entrusted with the battery by the government under a management agreement.[29]

---

[28] J. Vella Bonavita, 25.
[29] Fondazzjoni Wirt Artna, *Fort Rinella and the Armstrong 100 Ton Gun: A Brief History*, (leaflet, Malta, 1994), 4.

Armament

General considerations

Since Britain's tenure of Malta was not definite before 1814, and also since the total length of fortifications in Malta were greater than the British garrison could hope to man, the British Military authorities only re-sited the existing armament to suit their priorities. But in 1837, the French Navy introduced the Paixhans guns on its warships. These were the first guns which could fire explosive shell, instead of common round cannon balls. After 1842 grooved rifling for more accurate targeting was invented, and a little later warships started being steam-driven, becoming faster. In the 1860s then, iron-clad ships were built with armour capable of withstanding powerful shot.[30] Therefore both after 1837 and the 1860s, the armament in defensive fortification had to change. The architecture of the same forts had to change too, if entirely new forts or batteries were not built for the newer and more sophisticated guns. British strategy had to change, especially after 1840, to depend on garrisons first, rather than on naval might at sea alone.

The ensuing escalation in the gun versus armour race led towards larger and larger guns. The calibre and weight of guns increased enormously in a relatively short space of time. In 1866, 23 ton guns were the norm. By 1874 RML guns had reached the weight of 38 tons, and were being replaced by 16" RML guns of 81 tons, capable of smashing 23" of armour. Soon after, the 17.72" calibre, 102.25 ton RML gun, capable of penetrating 26" of armour, like the one at Rinella Battery, was developed.[31] Moreover in the 1870s, the Breach-Loading (BL) guns were perfected and the Admiralty adopted them too. It must be realised that ordnance at Fort Ricasoli had to be regularly changed, and the gun emplacements had to be continuously re-adapted and re-designed.

The saluting battery

Since Fort Ricasoli lies at the entrance to Grand Harbour, it always saluted very important visitors or special ships upon their entry, as well as on special festive occasions, same as the battery on Lascaris Bastion in Valletta. In this way, guns found a *raison d'etre* even during peaceful times. As early as 4 June 1812, for example, the saluting battery at Fort Ricasoli fired salvos on the occasion of King George III's seventy-fourth birthday.[32] On 22 June 1897, the battery celebrated Queen Victoria's Diamond Jubilee in the same manner, and six years later it also fired salvos on the occasion of King Edward VII's visit to Malta.[33] On 24 January 1911, the battery fired a gun salute when the royal yacht *Medina* with King George V on board, was entering Grand Harbour.[34]

---

[30] Spiteri, (1996), 25, 70.
[31] R. Vella Bonavita, (1978), 434, and Spiteri, (1996), 7.
[32] Faurè, iv, 163.
[33] Ibid., iv, 407, 556.

The guns in the Fort

In December 1800, three months after that the British troops occupied Fort Ricasoli, the armament consisted of a number of 24 to 42 pounder cannon. The battery of 24 pounders located on the eastern (No. 5, or St Dominic) bastion was considered very effective against any sea borne enemy attacking the Grand Harbour from the East.[35] After the development in armament considered above, new heavy cannon for the defence of the harbour was expected at Malta in 1853.[36] Some were surely destined for Ricasoli. As soon as the new guns arrived, the old obsolete iron guns were planted into the wharves of the harbour to act as bollards for fastening ships at berth.[37] Some of these guns are still visible by the moles.

In 1864, there was a total of 104 guns at Fort Ricasoli, some of which in casemates in No. 1 and No. 2 bastions at Ricasoli Point.[38] The number, type and calibre of the different guns was as follows in Table XII:

Table XII Guns in Fort Ricasoli, 1864		
Number	*calibre*	*type*
4	110 pounders	Armstrong BL
23	68 pounders	
1	10 inch (″)	
24	8″	
6	32 pounders	
10	24 pounders	
12		mortars
24		carronades
total 104		

---

[34] A. Samut Tagliaferro, *History of the Royal Malta Artillery,* (Malta 1976), 347.
[35] Anderson, 118.
[36] NAM, Despatches, 1850-1855, 34. Governor W. Reid to S.o.S. Newcastle.
[37] Ibid., 55.
[38] Hughes, (1993), 171.

The four 110 pounders and the twenty-three 68 pounders were among the heaviest of the total 770 guns in Malta at the time.[39] But the guns at Ricasoli were soon replaced after a report by Colonel Adye of the Royal Engineers in 1872. Casemates for three 11", 25 ton RML guns; two 10"; and two 9" guns were being built in No 1, 2 and 5 (St Dominic) bastions, that is, those most in command of the sea approaches.[40] By 1878, the works on the casemates were completed and the following ordnance was placed: one 38 ton; two 25 ton; two 18 ton; and two 12 ton guns.[41] That year Fort St Rocco was built, and in order not to place the new fort at risk, the heavier guns on the land front of Ricasoli were replaced by lighter Gotling guns.[42] Barely a year later, the RML guns at Ricasoli were only kept as auxiliary armament since they had been made obsolete by the newer breach-loading guns for which new emplacements were laid out at the Fort.[43] The old smooth bore guns were removed in 1885, although the 24 pounder carronades were retained in the fausse-braye as trophies.[44]

During this period of rapid change there was continuous debate about the best way to arm Fort Ricasoli. The greatest difficulty lay in the fact that the parade ground was too high and showed above the parapet from the sea. Even the bastions were too clearly defined, and therefore marked from the sea. According to engineers Nicholson and Goodenough, commenting in 1888, only the larger RML guns had to be kept,[45] although there was some minor rearmament in 1899.[46] By 1907, it was realised that the Victoria Lines could not be held in case of invasion in the north. The defence strategy changed again to include holding on to all the coast in such case. Therefore the coast defence of Malta were armed in 1914 with sixteen 9.2" guns of which none at Ricasoli; twenty 6" quick firing (QF) BLs Mark VII guns of which three at Ricasoli; and fourteen 12 pounder QF guns of which two at Ricasoli. This was the situation obtaining at the fort at the outbreak of the First World War in 1914.[47] After World War I, 6" BL guns were dismantled (as in other forts), but three anti motor-torpedo-boat 6 pounder QF double-barrelled guns were mounted.[48]

Before the Second World War, Fort Ricasoli was rearmed with three twin 6 pounder guns in metal turrets. The emplacements were located in bastions 2, 3, and 4, and each had a high concrete fire control tower. The rear of the gun turrets were protected by a concrete apron.[49] By 1939, the fort had two 12 pounder QF guns, and three 6 pounder twin QF guns.[50]

---

[39] Ibid., 288.

[40] Spiteri (1996), 184.

[41] Hughes (1993), 171.

[42] Spiteri (1996), 242.

[43] Ibid., 79.

[44] Ibid., 184-185.

[45] Ibid., 188-189.

[46] N. Samut Tagliaferro, *British Military Facilities in Malta*, B.E. & A., dissertation, (University of Malta, 1982), 55.

[47] Spiteri (1996), 48-49, 189.

[48] A. Samut Tagliaferro, "British fortification and defence," in *Archivum*, (1989), 87, 89..

[49] Spiteri (1996), 193.

[50] A. Samut Tagliaferro (1989), 89.

Between 1950 and 1960, missiles began to take over the role of both coastal and anti-aircraft guns, rendering obsolete all the forts and heavy batteries.[51] All the forts, including Ricasoli, were dismantled especially between 1956 and 1958. The guns were cut up and sold off for scrap, and therefore there is no trace of the later guns used in Malta's forts. Some RMLs have been saved and many smooth bore guns remain as witness to the nineteenth century armaments race and the decline of the gunpowder firing gun, but not at Ricasoli. Some of its earlier guns lie on the seabed, while others are planted into the wharves of Grand Harbour, serving as bollards.

Ricasoli torpedo station and defence system

The gun was not the only weapon which Fort Ricasoli housed in its long history. In the 1870s, the submarine mine was developed for coast defence, and the British Military Authorities were quick in installing two torpedo systems of the Brennan type: one at Ricasoli; and the other at Fort Tignè. Both were therefore intended to defend the harbour mouths against a fast approaching force. Ricasoli's torpedo station was installed on the harbour side of the salient of the Point (No. 1) bastion. The torpedo rooms and propulsion mechanisms were housed in rock-hewn chambers and the torpedoes were launched down tramways into the sea through tunnel openings. The station had a 30 metres long launching way with an 18 inch gauge tramway, engine room, store rooms and directing station. The inventor himself, Louis Brennan planned the station. The torpedoes were arranged in a row of nine tubes inside the position, ready for launching. The Brennan torpedo carried high explosives and travelled underwater toward the target to a range of 1830 metres, propelled by two unwinding fine steel wires within the torpedo. An engine on shore, connected to the wires, maintained the unwinding of the reels to provide the necessary motion to the torpedo, which was steered by varying the speed at which either wire was unwound. In 1904 the system was dismantled due to its obsolescence.[52]

Searchlight systems and emplacements

With the invention of electric light it became possible to light a large area to be defended by gunfire. After 1870 Coast Artillery Searchlights (CARL), were developed in Britain. Fixed lights illuminated a large fixed area, for example the immediate vicinity of the harbour mouths; while moving lights detected and tracked moving sea craft. Two fixed lights were installed at Fort Ricasoli, (another four at Fort St Elmo) in 1889 in order to create an illuminated area outside the harbour mouth. The emplacements were built into the seaward Nos. 1, 2, and 3 curtains of Ricasoli. They were protected with iron shutters. The latter one was placed in 1894, having an angle of aperture of only 10 degrees. It lighted a narrow area of the Grand Harbour mouth from St Elmo Point to about 250 metres to the North East. Additional lights were placed in 1906. By World War II, the illuminated area had been considerably expanded.[53]

---

[51] Spiteri (1996), 52.
[52] Ibid., 83, 189, 193.
[53] Ibid., 189, 192-193, 489, 491-493.

143

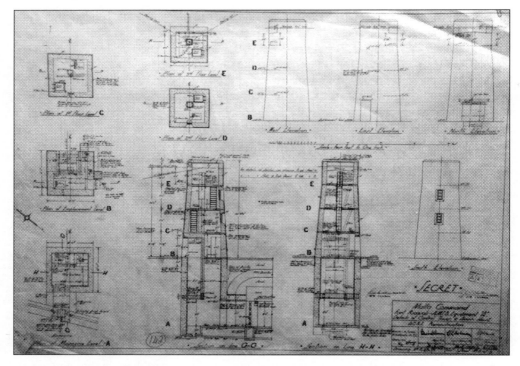

Plan of Anti-Motor Torpedo Boat equipment showing details of Central Tower and Amunition Hoist.

The generators of the petrol paraffin internal combustion type for the electricity were inside the fort. In 1904 three 25 horse power Ackroyd Engines were installed for this purpose. By 1942, most of these had been replaced by the compression-ignition engines using diesel-oil. The coastal searchlights of Ricasoli proved their worth during the Italian E-boat attack on Grand Harbour on 26 July 1941.[54]

Additions and alterations, 1800-1964

The Fortifications

Work on the fortifications had to be carried out mostly to adapt them to the continuously improving offensive and defence weapons in the nineteenth and twentieth centuries, and to the re-arrangement of artillery.[55] Especially after 1850, Fort Ricasoli changed into a heavy gun fort with powerful coastal batteries. The military engineers who designed and laid out these alterations were members of the Corps of Royal Engineers. The British

---

[54] Ibid., 494. For the story of the attack, see Chapter XV.
[55] Hardman, 337.

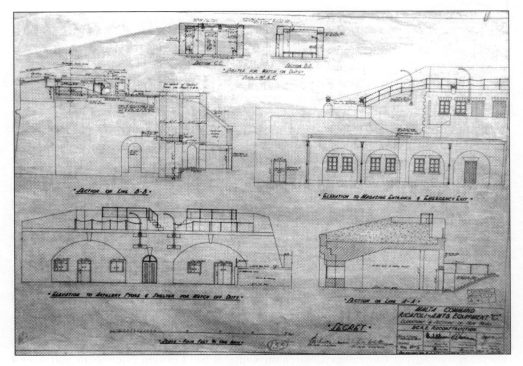

Plans of Anti-Motor Torpedo Boat equipment on Bastion No 2, showing artillery stores and shelters.

(Courtesy: NAM)

Military re-named the bastions of Ricasoli for their better convenience, by assigning numbers starting from Ricasoli Point bastion (No. 1). The open sea bastions were given Nos. 2 to 4; while St Dominic, St Francis and St John bastions were re-named Nos. 5,6, and 7 bastions respectively. The curtain flanking each bastion to its right was given the same number as that of the respective bastion.[56] The first works undertaken by the British inside the fort between September and December 1800 were improvements to the Governor's House and the parade ground.[57]

When the French troops took over Malta, the works on the left flank of the land front and outworks were not yet completed, in fact, General Vaubois was quite worried about a possible attack by the Maltese battalions on this part, and strengthened it with sacks filled with earth on 12 December 1799.[58] Although Anderson and the first British garrison in Malta were quite satisfied and impressed with Ricasoli's strength,[59] this flank was still considered weak by Captain Harry D. Jones of the Royal Engineers in 1831,

---

[56] NAM Plans, Ricasoli 6.
[57] Anderson, 118.
[58] Hardman, 626.
[59] Anderson, 117-118.

also because it was partly wrecked by the explosion of a gunpowder magazine during the Froberg mutiny of 1807. Hence Jones built a retrenchment with musketry loopholes at the gorge of Bastions numbers 4 and 5 (St Dominic) after 1831. The caponniers, originally planned by de Tignè, were arched over with loopholes provided in each face in order to flank their respective ditches. They were the first fighting caponniers built by the British in Malta. They link the gorges of the ravelins to the land front curtains. A gallery was constructed in the counterscarp of the left face of the left ravelin with loopholes to fire into the dead angle formed by the unfinished part of the glacis. By that time, the countermines were in a ruinous state, partly obstructed, and surely obsolete.[60]

The bastions of Ricasoli needed special attention and maintenance because of the onslaught of the rough sea, as well as due to the needs of the new guns (mostly the RMLs). On 8 February 1821 during a fierce *Gregale* storm, bastion No 2 gave way and slid into the sea with ten cannon. Orsi Tower was the other famous victim of the weather that day.[61] Continuous encroachment by the sea was reported between No. 3 and No.4 bastions in 1934,[62] and the problem still persists. Following reports by Governor Sir William Reid in 1852,[63] and Captain Jervois of the Royal Engineers in 1866,[64] the bastions of the fort had to be rebuilt practically from rock level since granite blocks had to be used for the new casemates which housed the heavy RML guns. The armoured embrasures were attached with iron shields. The construction is massive and strong enough to provide resistance to displacement.

In 1888, the Royal Engineers Lieutenant General Sir Lothian Nicholson and Major General W.H. Goodenough showed concern about the lack of preparedness of the fort, since the parade ground was too high and visible from the sea; there was no covered way between the various buildings inside the fort; and the open sea bastions, with their sharp salient angles, showed too much from the warships, especially during early morning or sunset. They suggested that only the covered way between Nos. 5 and 6 bastions was worth arming heavily, it being the most covered. Therefore after 1890, Ricasoli was rearmed. With the deployment of QF, breech loading guns, *en barbette* emplacements were laid out, with very generous use of concrete. [65] Emplacements for 6 inch guns were laid out on the ravelins in 1890[66] as well as another two emplacements for 11 inch guns on bastion No. 5, in 1898.[67] No major alterations to the fortifications were carried out during the twentieth century, except for improvements in the ventilation system of the galley in 1955,[68] the aforementioned searchlight towers, and the new road into the fort through curtain No. 6 and the retrenchment, which were thus partly demolished in 1976.

---

[60] Spiteri (1996), 91, 110, 182-184. The retrenchment was almost completely demolished in 1976 when a new road was opened for the bonded stores.
[61] Malta, Government Gazette, 14 February 1821.
[62] NAM Plans, Ricasoli 127.
[63] A. Samut Tagliaferro (1989), 75.
[64] J. Q. Hughes, *Britain in the Mediterranean and the Defence of her Naval Station*, (Liverpool 1981), 8.
[65] Spiteri (1996), 103, 122, 185-186.
[66] NAM Plans, Ricasoli 235.
[67] Ibid., 227.
[68] Ibid., 260-262.

Expense magazine and Anti Motor Torpedo Boat Searchlight tower on Bastion Number 4.

The gunpowder magazines

The Knights of St John had built a large gunpowder magazine with a capacity of 650 barrels. In 1807 this magazine was intentionally destroyed during the escape by mutinous soldiers of the Froberg Regiment.[69] This magazine was rebuilt on the earlier model, although enlarged to hold 800 barrels in 1831 according to plans by Colonel Whitmore, at a cost of £1,429.[70] It was rectangular in shape with very thick walls, which were holed to let air in to keep the powder dry. Four larger windows near the ceiling provided light. These were opened or closed by shutters protected by an iron plate. After a report by engineer Adye in 1872, the walls of this magazine were thickened to about 10 metres. Ricasoli is a large fort, and carrying ammunition from the main magazine to the guns took a long time. When QF guns were developed, the need was felt as early as 1854 for small magazines known as expense magazines or expense cartridge stores to be built on the gun floor level close to the guns themselves. These were constructed in 1872, following the design of Lieutenant W.F. Spaight of the Royal Engineers. After the deployment of the breech loading guns in the 1890s, steel and cartridge magazines were

---

[69] See Chapter 10, and Q.P. Badger, *Historical Guide to Malta and Gozo*, (Malta 1869), 269 for Froberg Mutiny.
[70] Hughes (1993), 171.

147

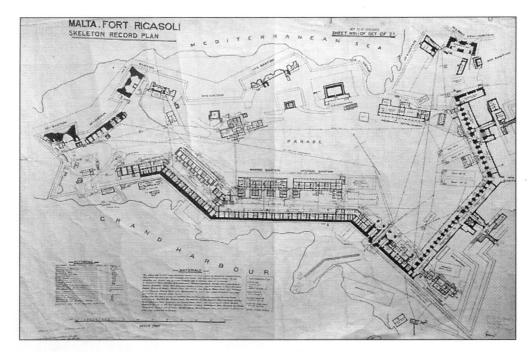

1931 General skeleton record plan of Fort Ricasoli showing details of each room including number of people residing therein. (Courtesy: NAM)

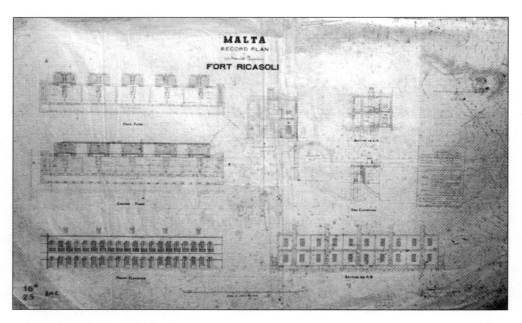

Record plan of Married Quarters. (Courtesy: NAM)

encased in concrete beneath the *en barbette* gun emplacement. The ammunition was conveyed to the gun by means of a lift.[71]

Other buildings inside the fort

Most of the buildings inside Fort Ricasoli, especially those used for soldiers' barracks, were built during the time of the Knights. But the British Military Authorities constructed other buildings which served the armament or the garrison. Table XIII shows a list of buildings, with dates of commencement and completion, as well as estimated and actual cost.[72]

The table proves that the 1890 to 1910 period was the one in which most developments were taking place inside the fort. Not only were barracks, cook houses, messes, and ablutions constructed, but also alterations of purely military nature were made. There was greater awareness to the physical, mental and moral well-being of the garrison as attested by the building of the recreation establishment. Ninety years later in 1956, a new recreational building was built at the north-west end of the soldiers' quarters near Ricasoli Point, which included a Mess, galley, lounge, and terraces.[73] The increased amount of power needed was later satisfied by the building of an engine and generator room by the Main Gate in 1934. It was partly casemated and partly underground.[74] In 1860, the ground floor of the Governor's House was used for soldiers' and officers' guard rooms, while the first storey was used for Field Officers' quarters, Mess room, ante room, kitchen and pantry.[75] By 1931,[76] Fort Ricasoli included most buildings that were needed for its efficient functioning, many of which still stand today, alas in a ruinous state due to abandonment, lack of use and maintenance, and due to vandalism.

The Barracks

The barracks as built by the Knights were more than satisfactory for housing the British troops until 1836, when it was deemed necessary by Governor Bouverie to improve them in order to accommodate a total of 416 men which were being evacuated from Fort Manoel when the latter's barracks were put at the disposal of the Quarantine Department.[77] More Quarters for married soldiers were purposely built in 1867 and 1872 on the South East Front of Ricasoli. These cost a total of £9984 They were built with walls of ashlar masonry of Malta, sandstone selin lime and sand mortar. The damp course was done in puzzolana. The roofs were made of 93 cm. soft stone set on beams of yellow

[71] Spiteri (1996), 79, 91, 95, 114, 123-124, 130, 182, 184, 185.
[72] NAM Plans, Ricasoli 103.
[73] Ibid., 112.
[74] Ibid., 89.
[75] Ibid., 272.
[76] Ibid., 6.
[77] NLM, Despatches 17, (1838), Governor Bouverie to S.o.S. Lord Glenelg, 29 September 1838.

Table XIII		
Buildings inside Fort Ricasoli, 1865-1929		
Building	*Date* *Commenced - Completed*	*Cost* *(£)*
1. Officers' quarters and married quarters adjoining	Apr.1865 - Mar.1867	7999
2. Recreation establishment	Aug. 1866 - May 1869	2129
3. Married quarters N.W. block	16 Sep. 1871 - 19 Jun.1872	1985
4. Steam engine room, right land-port	20 Jun. 1888 - 31 Mar. 1890	367
5. A.A. workshops	7 Aug. 1894 - 21 Feb 1895	171
6. Engine and accumulator rooms, and store by torpedo installation	20 Jan. 1895 - 20 Mar. 1900	46
7. Oil engine room, left land-port	Jun. 1897 - August 1899	730
8. Gun shed in the ditch	25 May 1898 - 15 Feb. 1899	444
9. Latrines near engine rooms (6)	15 Feb. 1900 - 20 Mar.1900	46
10. Directing station	1 Jan. 1900 - 20 Mar. 1900	65
11. Sergeants' Mess	26 Sep. 1901 - 28 Jul. 1902	1719
12. Canteen	6 Dec. 1901 - 1 Aug. 1902	1269
13. Latrines and ablution at right land-port	2 Jul. 1904 - 2 Jan. 1905	115
14. Latrines at left land-port	19 May 1905 - 26 Jan 1906	152
15. Conversion of torpedo installation to engine room	28 Nov. 1905	
16. Ablution	29 Apr. 1907 -29 Nov. 1907	144
17. New cook house	2 February 1929	1051

pine terraced and rendered with diffons (*deffun*). The floors of the rooms were laid of 3 inch thick softstone, but the door steps and verandahs of hard stone. The woodwork was in red pine, but the inside fittings were in white deal. All this for a total floor area of 6522 square feet over two floors.[78]

---

[78] NAM Plans, Ricasoli 223.

The canteen built in 1902.

By the end of the nineteenth century, the need for more accommodation for the garrison was being felt and since it had by then become clear that Ricasoli was part of the inner circle of defence and the land outside the glacis was safer for habitation, land was requisitioned by the military in order to build Married Quarters with laundry; a school; and a church outside the fort. These were built outside St John's (No. 7) bastion, overlooking Rinella valley and Creek, between 1901 and 1905. Their respective cost was £5256, £1073, and £500.[79] It seems that the first construction of the northern Married Quarters, the church and the school by M. Sill of the Royal Engineers[80] was defective. They were reconstructed to a great extent in 1908 by B.M. Pirie.[81] Further alterations to these quarters were effected in 1946.[82] They are now serving as private residences. Land which was close to any military establishment could not be developed by its owner without the consent of the Military Government. In August 1902, the Military demanded the Public Works Department to demolish a cart shed which had just been erected near the new Married Quarters by the owner, B. Borda.[83]

---

[79] Ibid., 103.
[80] Ibid., 255.
[81] Ibid., 305.
[82] Ibid., 119.
[83] NAM, PWD, 142, ff. 15v.-16.

The main soldiers' barracks of Ricasoli, with part of the large place of arms (parade ground).

A barrack room in the main soldiers' barracks.

The casemated barrack rooms at the back of the Grand Harbour tenaille curtain walls. (Hospitaller period). These particular rooms served as civilian barber; carpenter's shop; bathroom; plumber's shop; and tailor and shoemaker's shop in the 1920s.

The Officers' and Married Quarters (1867-1872).

Other development outside the fort

The foreshore of Fort Ricasoli came under the jurisdiction of the Civil Government of Malta. In 1892, the Civil Government granted permission to the Royal Artillery to build a boathouse near the condensing rooms on the rocks outside the walls on condition that the Civil Government could requisition or knock it down at will without compensation; and at an annual lease of 1 shilling. The Royal Artillery needed the boathouse since the boats had until then been left in the open ramps near the slipway, exposed to all kind of weather and sometimes obstructing traffic into the Main Gate. The boathouse was built of masonry with arches and with an iron gate so that the inside might be inaccessible yet visible.[84]

In 1895 more land at Wied Ghammieq was requisitioned by the Admiralty from the Civil Government against a payment of £114, part of which went in compensation to the farmer who had been working the land for three years. The land was turned into a skirmishing ground.[85] In 1899, the naval cemetries at Kalkara were laid out and all buildings to within 200 yards distance were removed.[86]

---

[84] Ibid., Bundle 578 F, 120-126.
[85] Ibid., 138, f. 172.
[86] Ibid., 141, f. 144v.

9

The Garrison

Units

The first British troops to enter Fort Ricasoli on 4 September 1800 were the 35th Foot Regiment, later renamed the Royal Sussex Regiment. Their colours were the first British Regimental Colours to be hoisted in Malta.[1] They were soon replaced on 20 September 1800 by five companies of the 89th Regiment and one company of the *Cacciatori Maltesi* (the Maltese Light Infantry).[2] Except for a short period of time between 1806 and 1807, when the fort hosted the Froberg Regiment which was made up of Slav soldiers recruited from the Balkans, the soldiers that manned Ricasoli during the British rule were mostly British infantry soldiers, British soldiers of the Royal Artillery, and Maltese soldiers of the Royal Malta Fencible Regiment, and later the Royal Malta Artillery.[3] When the coastal batteries were closed down in the 1950s, Ricasoli was occupied by the Admiralty until it was ceded to the Government of Malta on 21 September 1964. After that date, the fort was not used for military purposes any more.

Nationality

The relative proportion of British and Maltese soldiers varied considerably through time. Before 1798, that is during the Knights' rule, the absolute majority of soldiers and their dependants was always Maltese. But the short-lived French rule changed that. Most Maltese were transferred or sent away during the blockade, and by 1801, there were only fourteen Maltese persons living in the fort, of which only six had been there since 1797.[4]

---

[1] *The Times of Malta*, 1 May 1947, 7; *The Sunday Times of Malta*, 4 May 1947; J. Schembri, "The fortifications of Malta - Fort Ricasoli", in the *Malta Land Force Journal,* No. 7, July 1971, 70-74. The flag was preserved in the Armoury, Valletta, but was damaged during an air-raid in April 1942. It was later part of a collection pertaining to the Malta Land Force in Fort St Elmo.

[2] All the Maltese corps mentioned in this chapter were paid troops of the British Army.
[3] Some units are treated separately later in this chapter.
[4] ACCV, LSA, 1765-1805, no pag.

Although a company of a hundred Maltese Light Infantry was stationed at Ricasoli on 20 September 1800, these were transferred by Easter 1801, as evidenced by the *Status Animarum* register of the Vittoriosa parish church, and by Easter 1805 there were only twenty-three Maltese inside the fort.[5] The only death of a Roman Catholic registered at Ricasoli in 1800 was that of Maria Cromeor, the two year old daughter of the Irish soldier Bernard Cromeor and his wife Mary. The girl was buried in St Nicholas chapel.[6] After 1798, there were few periods when Ricasoli was inhabited by a majority of Maltese persons. One such period was between 1815 and 1837, when the four companies (about 400 soldiers) of the Royal Malta Fencibles Regiment (Right Wing) was stationed there.[7] After 1840, with the increased strategic importance of Malta and the rapid build up of the base, more British troops manned the fort, until their rundown after World War I, when Maltese soldiers of the RMA were again in a majority.[8] This fact may add meaning to the events of 1798. Malta had been effectively colonised. The following table shows the (partial) list of units stationed at Ricasoli through the years. It also shows the number of men. It must be noted that some battalions used the barracks at Ricasoli as a temporary station on their way to or from the East. Most of the time, dependants of the soldiers lived in the married quarters of the fort (see table XIV).

Number

In 1800, the British military authorities believed that 320 officers and men were necessary to suitably man the fort, out of a total 4,750 considered necessary for all the harbour defences. Therefore Ricasoli was adequately garrisoned between 1800 and 1840 with about 400, enjoying its fair share of the actual 2,000 total number of troops in the harbours.[9] With the opening of the Suez Canal, there was a build up of the British garrison in Malta, reaching 5,690 that year, and the men at Ricasoli increased to 683, although this was proportionately less than in 1800.[10] Except for the short period of occupation by the Froberg Regiment in 1806 and 1807, the maximum number of people inside the fort was reached in 1901, when Malta was the important naval station at the centre of the routes of the great British Empire. That year there were 652 officers and men inside the fort, and a further 161 dependants for a total 813 people, out of a total garrison of 10,882 (including dependants) for the whole of Malta.[11] It was at this time that the barracks outside the fort overlooking Rinella Valley were constructed to provide more space for the soldiers.

---

[5] Ibid.

[6] ACCV, Liber Mortuorum, V, 1786-1837, 109.

[7] Chesney, 93, 96-97. The six other companies (Left Wing) were quartered in Valletta and the countryside towers

[8] From 1837 to 1863 no death of Roman Catholics at Ricasoli is recorded. After that deaths become more frequent but not of any Maltese soldiers. In 1865 alone ten Roman Catholic persons aged between 11 and 39 died at Ricasoli, of which three were wives of Irish soldiers. ACCV, Liber Mortuorum VI, 1837-1875, 263.

[9] Spiteri, (1996), 53-54.

[10] D. Galton and J. Sutherland, *Report of the Barrack and Hospital Improvement Commissions on the Sanitary Condition and Improvement of the Mediterranean Stations,* (London 1863), 147-150.

[11] Malta, Census, 1901.

[12] In 1911, there were 7,093 total garrison (including dependants) in Malta. Malta, Census, 1911.

[13] Malta, Census, 1931.

	Table XIV	
	Units stationed at Ricasoli, with number of men	
dates	*unit*	*number*
4 - 20 Sep. 1800	35th Foot Regiment	2 battalions
20 Sep. 1800	89th Regiment	5 companies
20 Sep. 1800 - before Easter 1801	Maltese Light Infantry Regiment	1 company (100 men)
1806 - 1807	a. Froberg Regiment (Slavs) b. Royal Artillery (RA) c. Maltese Military Artificers	1000 men (circa) 19 (a few)
1816 - 1861	Royal Malta Fencible Regiment	4 companies (400 men)
1838		416 men added
1840	a. 60th Rifles of 59th Foot Regiment b. 77th Regiment (from Canada)	a. 173 b. 2 officers and 168 men
Nov. 1841	2nd Regt R.A.	4 men
1842	59th Foot Regt and 88th Foot	
1860		412
1864		15 officers and 676 men
1865	68th Light Infantry	
Nov. 1867	No. 7 Battery R.A.	
1869		683 men
1892	Malta Division of Submarine Miners, Royal Engineers (RE)	67
22 Jul. 1897	a. East District R. Garrison A. b. Infantry c. Royal Malta Artillery (RMA)	
1901		652 officers and men (excluding 161 dependants)
1903	Nos 81, 93 and 96 Cos., East District R. Garrison A.	
1911		438 officers and men (excluding 150 dependants)
1913	No. 1 and 102 Co. R. Garrison A.	
1914 to World War II	ditto ; 1 co. R.M.A.	
1921		35 officers and men (British, excluding 26 dependants)
1931		203

[1] Ibid.; Testa, iii (1982), 743; Malta, Censuses, 1901, 1911, 1921, 1931; A. Darmanin, 31-32; A. Samut Tagliaferro, "A History of the Royal Malta Artillery, I, 1794-1802" in *The Malta Land Force Journal*, No 10, 1-32, April 1972 (Malta), 14; *The Malta Times - Broadsheet of the Mediterranean* 20 April, 1840, 15; NLM, Malta Duplicate Despatches, 1838, ff. 444v-445v; Chesney, 93, 96-97; *Malta Army and Navy Directory* 1903.

Henceforth the garrison was in decline,[12] there being only 3,146 total garrison in Malta, of which only 203 in Fort Ricasoli in 1931.[13] The number of men in Ricasoli only soared again to the previous records for about three years during World War II, when the Recruits Training Depot of the RMA was established there.[14]

The composition of the garrison

In 1860, the garrison was made up of the following officers, men and dependants quartered as follows:[15]

338 men in the six large land-front barracks (barrack rooms 1,2,5,6,11, and 12);
44 men in five smaller rooms in the same barracks (rooms 4, 7, 8, 9, 10);
40 other men in eighteen rooms in the South West Grand Harbour Front;
20 Sergeants using 29 rooms in the same area (rooms 17 to 34, 53 and 65);
8 married people in thirteen rooms also in the same area (rooms 35 to 44, 65,66,66a, and 67); 1 man in the guard room;
6 men in 2 prison cells.

For a total 412 regulation number of men and 45 other people.

According to the report about barrack accommodation by D. Galton and J. Sutherland, conditions were unsanitary mainly because of overcrowding. By 1869, the problem was increased, since there were the following number of men as follows:[16]

5 field officers
23 officers
2 staff sergeants
18 sergeants
622 men
13 married soldiers.

The garrison in 1901 and 1911 was made up as shown in table XV.[17]

The rundown of British servicemen after the First World War is evident when one analyses the return for the (British) garrison at Fort Ricasoli in 1921.[18] There were only a total 61 British persons inside the fort of which 45 were males and 16 females. Thirty five were officers and men; 12 were wives; 10 sons, and 4 daughters, and all lived in barracks, not in the houses. At that time, there was an influx of Maltese personnel of the RMA.

---

[14] A. Samut Tagliaferro, (1976), 424.
[15] Galton and Sutherland, 150.
[16] NAM, Maps, Ricasoli, 239
[17] Malta, Censuses 1901 and 1911.
[18] Malta, Census, 1921.

Table XV — Composition of Garrison in 1901 and 1911			
	Malta	**Ricasoli**	**Ricasoli**
	1901	*1901*	*1911*
total persons	10882 (7093 in 1911)	813	633
males	9784	708	531
females	1098	105	102
officers and men	9224	652	483
school mistresses and nurses	11	nil	nil
wives	584	50	51
sons	560	56	48
daughters	503	55	51
houses males	321	13	29
houses females	293	9	23
barracks males	9463	695	502
barracks females	805	96	79

In 1931, there was a total 405 people inside the fort, including 343 men and 20 non-commissioned officers quartered in the Soldiers' Barracks; one field officer and another nine officers in Single Officers' Quarters; one officer in the Governor's House; and two officers and twenty married soldiers in the Married Quarters.[19] After the War, the commanding officer's residence was in the north-west part of the Officers' Mess and Quarters behind the Chaplain's Quarters.[20]

Some special units

The Royal Garrison Artillery and the Infantry

Since Fort Ricasoli was turned into a formidable battery by the British, the Royal Garrison Artillery always stationed troops there. For example in 1867, the No. 7 Battery

[19] NAM, Maps, Ricasoli, 6.
[20] Ibid., 259.

which had just been transferred from Canada, was deployed there. In spite of the impressive array of gunners which stood unchanged until 1914, there always remained that pressing requirement for the infantry to help with maintaining the guns, scrapping shot on site, and a multitude of other tasks with which the gunners alone were still unable to cope.[21]

The Maltese Light Infantry (M.L.I. - Cacciatori Maltesi)

This battalion was raised on British pay by Colonel Thomas Graham, General Officer commanding troops in Malta, in March 1800 in order to accelerate the surrender of the French garrison. It was made up of eight companies of 100 men each and on 3 October 1800, one company was stationed at Fort Ricasoli performing regular garrison duties,[22] but by Easter 1801, the company had already been transferred elsewhere, and the battalion was disbanded in 1802. Their uniform included a grey hat with green cockade and dark grey band, as well as black cross belts, haversacks, shoes, and dagger hilt. The soldiers also wore nankeen trousers and red waist band. In Summer, dress included a nankeen cotton coat with shoulder straps and epaulettes. In winter they wore blue-grey serge coat with red facings and gold lace; red button cuffs, shoulder and collar straps. On enlistment, each soldier received two uniforms to serve for the whole period of two years, as well as a one-time bounty of 5 *scudi* once. He also received a daily ration of 24 ounces of bread when in barracks. Each company, such as the one at Ricasoli, consisted of the following ranks, all except the first three, being Maltese:[22]

Table XVI
Ranks of one company of Malta Light Infantry
1 Captain (British);
1 Lieutenant (British);
1 Ensign (British);
1 Adjutant at 7 *tari* per day, (17 *scudi* 8 *tari* monthly) ;
4 Sergeants at 5 *tari* 10 *grani* per day, (13 *scudi* 9 *tari* monthly);
5 Corporals at 4 *tari* per day, (10 *scudi* monthly);
2 Drummers at 3 *tari* per day, (7 *scudi* 6 *tari* monthly);
100 Privates at 3 *tari* per day, (7 *scudi* 6 *tari* monthly).

---

[21] A. Samut Tagliaferro, (1976), 222-223.
[22] The other companies were stationed at Senglea. A. Samut Tagliaferro, (1972), 14-15, 19.
[23] Ibid.

Comparing the above wages with what the soldiers of Ricasoli used to get sixty years earlier,[24] one can notice that there was an increase in the salary of all ranks. However, one must state that the blockade of the French between 1798 and 1800, as well as the lack of regular trade with the continent, had inflated the prices of most commodities and it is safe to assume that the standard of living of the soldier was roughly the same as had been in the mid-eighteenth century.

The Royal Malta Fencibles Regiment (R.M.F. Regt)

The four companies (about 400 men) of of the Royal Malta Fencibles Regiment's Right Wing were stationed at Fort Ricasoli between 1815 and 1837, mostly to act as Coast Guard against smugglers and breaches of quarantine, although other companies performed the duties of Civil Police. They developed into expert gunners by means of adequate training in the fort. The Lieutenant Colonel at Ricasoli, who was also second in command of the whole Regiment, was Count de Gatto. The regiment was raised by Colonel Count Francesco Rivarola under the direction of the Governor, Sir Thomas Maitland, in lieu of all the previous Maltese corps. Rivarola kept the overall command until 1835, but he was stationed at Valletta, directly commanding the regiment's four Left Wing companies, which also manned St Julians, Qawra, St Paul's Bay and the Mellieha areas. The regiment was later increased from eight to ten companies, but those at Ricasoli were kept at four.[25] The uniform was red with blue facings and gold lace, having in their appointments the royal cypher and the arms of Malta. Each recruit engaging for five years received a bounty of 30 *scudi,* and if for three years only, a bounty of 20 *scudi*. Out of this bounty and the man`s pay, the of necessities shown in table XVII had to be provided and kept up.

The officers received some rations as officers of the line. The non-commissioned officers and men received 2 pounds of wood; one and a half pounds bread; and one half pint wine supply service each day for which a stoppage of 1 *taro* daily was made from their pay. Table XVII is a list of ranks of the Royal Malta Fencible Regiment with the approximate number stationed at Fort Ricasoli and their monthly wage.[26] At first glance it would seem that the pay given to these ranks were miserable when compared to the higher pay which the Malta Light Infantry troops were given fifteen years before, or even that given to the soldiers in the 1750s. One must realise, however, that these wages do not include the 1 *taro* daily stoppage which used to be detracted so that each soldier would be provided with his supply service. This would increase the total monthly wage of a private to 4 *scudi* 10 *tari* 16 *grani*. Neither does it take into account the once-given bounty which if divided, would amount to 6 *tari* a month. The wage earned by the privates of the R.M.F. Regt was less than that of the M.L.I., but not as much as one would think. One must add that employment in the R.M.F. Regt was guaranteed for five years and therefore more in demand.

---

[24] See Chapter 6.

[25] In 1861 the Regiment was converted into an artillery corps styled "Royal Malta Fencible Artillery". Chesney, 116.

[26] Ibid., 177-178.

Table XVII
Necessities of a soldier of the R.M.F.Regt, 1815-1837
1 knapsack (every five years) costing 6 *scudi*;
1 pair of trousers at 3 *scudi* 7 *tari* 4 *grani*;
2 shirts costing 8 *scudi* 4 *tari* 16 *grani*;
1 pair of shoes at 3 *scudi* 7 *tari* 4 *grani*;
1 stock and clasp at 7 *tari* 4 *grani*;
2 pairs of socks costing 10 *tari* 16 *grani*:
1 pair of gaiters at 2 *scudi* 1 *tari* 4 *grani*;
3 brushes costing 1 *scudo* 9 *tari* 12 *grani*;
1 forage cap at 1 *scudo* 6 *tari*;
1 great coat strap at 1*scudo* 2 *tari* 8 *grani*;
comb, sponge and other at 7 *tari* 4 *grani*.

[1] In 1861 the Regiment was converted into an artillery corps styled "Royal Malta Fencible Artillery". Chesney, 116.

The Royal Malta Artillery (R.M.A.)

In 1861 the R.M.F.Regt was turned into a corps specialised in artillery styled Royal Malta Fencible Artillery. On 23 March 1889, the word "fencible" was eliminated from the title of the corps; it was hence designated The Royal Malta Artillery (R.M.A.), whose gunners took such a conspicuous part in Malta`s defence during World War II. The R.M.A. intermittently manned the coastal batteries at Fort Ricasoli as in other coastal batteries, and during the 1930s it also developed some anti-aircraft batteries.[27]

Artillery Drills

The Royal Garrison Artillery and other Maltese corps in Fort Ricasoli had the onerous task of defending the mouth of Grand Harbour and the south-east coast of Malta from any sea-borne attack, as well as defend the fort itself from any hostile occupying troops coming from the Zabbar and Rinella areas. Therefore they had to be expert gunners. They

---

[27] *History of the Royal Malta Artillery,* (Malta 1944), 10. For the part played by the R.M.A. during World War II, see Chapter 15.

Table XVIII

Number, Ranks and monthly wage of the Four Companies of R.M.F. Regt at Fort Ricasoli,1815-1837:

Number	Rank	Monthly Wage (Sc., t., gr.)
1	Lieutenant Colonel	38, 2, 8.
1	Major	33, 9, 12.
5	Captains	22, 7, 4.
10	Lieutenants	15, 7, 4.
4	Ensigns	7, 2, 8.
1	1st Adjutant	20, 4, 16.
1	2nd Adjutant	16, 9, 12.
1	Quartermaster	15, 7, 4.
1	Surgeon	22, 7, 4.
1	Assistant Surgeon	13, 2, 8.
1	paymaster	36, 0, 0.
1	chaplain	14, 4, 6.
1	Sergeant Major	6, 7, 4.
1	Asst Sergeant Major for Coastal Artillery	6, 7, 4.
1	Quartermaster Sergeant	6, 7, 4.
1	Asst Quartermaster Sergeant for Coastal Artillery	6, 0, 0.
1	pay or colour sergeant	5, 4, 16.
15	Sergeants	4, 2, 8.
1	paymaster clerk	4, 2, 8.
1	drum major	4, 2, 8.
1	school master	4, 2, 8.
1	armourer	4, 2, 8.
25	Corporals	3, 0, 0.
11	drummers	2, 9, 0.
350	privates	2, 4, 16.

developed their skill by means of practice which was a regular duty of the artillery and the helping infantrymen. Practice was important in view of the progress in gun range, accuracy and tactics. Already by 27 January 1841, one finds that out of six rounds fired by the R.M.F. Regt at Ricasoli, three hit the target at 800 metres out. The intensified instruction of the infantrymen in guns and gunnery continued on an increasing scale down the years, since there were not enough professional gunners to cope with the armament of the garrison.[28]

In 1848, identification and security night signals were introduced by the Royal Navy for use by the guard boats of the ships. That same year, special posts at Fort Ricasoli, as well as Forts St Elmo and Tignè were established by the army for the same purpose under the commander of the Artillery Lieutenant Colonel Whitty upon a request by Vice Admiral Sir William Parker. The forts made signals by a flash of gunpowder on their observing boats or vessels approaching the harbour, or in the event of such vessels being first noticed by the Navy, to report the signals made by boats. These signals were also made by the detachments of the R.M.F. Regt deployed on coastal duties on the coast of Malta. All occurrences of sights of signals and vessels were reported to the vice admiral.[29]

By the 1880s the coastal searchlights system had been perfected. On 11 May 1889, a military drill was held outside Grand Harbour. Four ships and two torpedo boats manoeuvred there with Forts Tignè, St Elmo, and Ricasoli following their movements by searchlights and engaging each other in an experimental night assault on Malta.[30] Such drills kept being held for most of the time and half a century later served well for Malta's defenders against the Italian E-Boat attack on Grand Harbour during World War II. Whenever the Royal Artillery and the Infantry held gun practice, no sailing was permitted in the area to be covered.[31] Often the practice was held by the gunners of Fort Ricasoli in conjunction and in concert with the other coastal batteries to its south-east and north-west such as Fort St Leonardo or Fort St Rocco.[32] The Royal Malta Artillery engaged themselves in such practice too.[33] As the years passed, the gun practice became more elaborate and even took more time. By the 1920s for example, the Royal Artillery used to practice from Ricasoli, in conjunction with Forts Madliena, Tignè, and St Elmo for a whole week,[34] and that must have been a lean time for the fisherman of that part of the Maltese coast! Such practice continued down into the 1950s when the batteries were definitely dismantled. In 1941 events proved that such practice turned the artillery-men inside the fort into expert gunners.

---

[28] A. Samut Tagliaferro (1976), 187.
[29] Ibid., 142.
[30] *Daily Malta Chronicle*, 14 May 1889, 3.
[31] Ibid., 12 and 14 April 1897, 2.
[32] Ibid., 12 April 1897, 2.
[33] Ibid., 14 April 1897, 2.
[34] Ibid., 23 January 1926, 9.

10

The Froberg Mutiny

The Froberg Regiment

During the Napoleonic Wars, most of the regular experienced troops were stationed close to the different fronts. The Malta garrison was somewhat depleted of its best regiments who had been transferred to Sicily to strengthen the army there. Therefore the garrison had to be supplemented by troops levied from different Balkan countries by speculators who had been commissioned for the job by the British Government on a contractual basis. As a result of such arrangements the regiments raised proved to be at best, untrustworthy.[1]

One such regiment was raised by an unscrupulous French Count, M. de Montjoye de Froberg[2] early in 1806. It was given the English banners with the title of Froberg's Regiment. The regiment, which was stationed at Fort Ricasoli, was composed of about 1,000[3] Greeks, Albanians, Turks, Bulgarians and other Slavs.[4] The officers were mostly German, their commander being Captain Schummelketel.[5] Other officers included two English drill sergeants. About nineteen gunners of the Royal Artillery remained in the fort as usual to superintend the guns[6] under Captain Fead.

The soldiers distinguished themselves during rescue operations at Vittoriosa on 18 July 1806, after that a gunpowder magazine exploded there, killing 160 people and destroying many buildings.[7] However the high esteem they enjoyed among the Maltese population only lasted for a few months. Most of the soldiers were unruly, and since they could

---

[1] Badger, 266.
[2] The noble Gustave Brunone, Count of Froberg was a knight novice of the Langue of Germany in 1785. It is not certain whether he was a relative. AOM 163, ff. 289v-190.
[3] A. Darmanin, "The Mutiny at Fort Ricasoli", in *The Malta Independent*, 12 January 1997, 29 and 19 January 1997, 31-32.
[4] A.V. Laferla, *British Malta*, (Malta 1946), I, 58.
[5] P. Pullicino, "Froberg`s Regiment", in *Heritage*, ii, 481. (Malta 1979).
[6] Badger, ibid.
[7] Pullicino, 482.

not communicate easily, they became unpopular with the rest of the garrison, and the Maltese people in general. Cases of fights with local people were frequent.[8] The lack of confidence between the Maltese and the Froberg men was also the result of false accusations spread by some Maltese people.[9]

The Mutiny

The Froberg soldiers were the rowdy and ruffian type, but the commanding officers did their part to foment trouble when they resorted to frequent corporal punishment, often inflicted by caprice. On 4 April 1807, the soldiers mutinied after that an officer struck a drummer on the face with a cane.[10] The Major of the regiment was attacked while returning to the fort after a hunting trip. He shot at the rebels, who in turn cut him and numerous other officers to pieces, throwing their jarred corpses down a well. Other officers were imprisoned.[11] The British flag was torn off its mast and the Russian flag was hoisted instead. The gunners were ordered to point Ricasoli's guns towards Valletta.

General Villettes, the officer commanding the troops in Malta, second only to Sir Alexander Ball, the Civil Commissioner for the affairs of Malta, was quite apprehensive about the situation, since there were about 1,000 French prisoners in Malta. He ordered a blockade of the fort in order to starve the rebels out. He was also prepared to order the fort bombarded if the Frobergs fired shots at Valletta. Although there was tension in the harbourside towns, the French prisoners of war were kept under lock and key, and the civilian population kept calm.

After four days, the effects of lack of food supplies were being felt inside the fort.[12] The rebels quarrelled against each other, and Ricasoli was again the scene of internal violence and bloodshed. On 8 April the majority of the regiment went out of the fort and surrendered to the besieging British troops, leaving behind a diehard remnant of 150 rebels, mostly Bulgarian and Albanian.[13] These latter mutineers fired shots into Valletta. General Villettes ordered an escalade. Before dawn on 10 April, thirty Maltese non-commissioned officers of the Malta Military Artificers under sergeant-major Collins of the Royal Navy, climbed over the walls at the re-entrant curtain to the right of the Main Gate, into Ricasoli and opened the gates to admit the besiegers. All but six of the rebels were caught.[14]

---

[8] Ibid., 481.

[9] Ibid., 482.

[10] Badger 266-267.

[11] In 1898, a marble tablet inside the fort's gateway was erected to commemorate gunner John Johnson who killed several of the mutineers in a narrow passage leading to the gunpowder magazine before falling victim. A replica of the tablet was presented to the National war Museum by Brigadier Maurice Calleja. The tablet does not mention the heroic death of the two Froberg officers or three sentries who were probably men of the Maltese Military Artificers or even the whole incident itself! Darmanin (1997), 32.

[12] Laferla, I, 58-59.

[13] Badger, 268.

[14] Laferla, I, 59.

The re-entrant curtains of the Grand Harbour tenaille Front to the right of the Main Gate, where Maltese soldiers scaled the wall in order to open the gate for loyal troops to enter and subdue the Froberg mutiny of 1807.

These latter insurgents took possession of the gunpowder magazine and, confident of contracting advantageous terms with the Governor, persisted in their resistance by threatening to blow up the whole place.[15] The Governor, on the other hand, refused them supply of provisions and any conditional surrender. After another six days of tension, the last six rebels issued an ultimatum which was not heeded. In the evening, a great explosion blew up the gunpowder magazine and part of the fortifications. Some garrison soldiers lost their lives or were wounded.

It was generally believed that these last six rebels had blown themselves up with the magazine. However, after some days had elapsed, one of them assailed a priest who was riding home on a donkey from Rinella. The priest managed to escape and informed the police, who soon discovered the last six men in their hide-out. They had escaped through a countermine while blowing up the magazine with a fuse. The rebels had already risked being caught when they tried unsuccessfully to seize a boat in order to escape from the island.[16] They were later executed in public.

---

[15] Badger, 270.
[16] Ibid., 271-272.

167

Harsh retribution

The extent to which insubordination and mutiny were dreaded by the authorities may be attested by the "inhuman and barbarous manner" (according to Badger writing in 1869) in which thirty ringleaders were executed at the parade ground in Floriana after being court-martialled. They were not blind-folded, and their coffins lay within sight. Fifteen were hung and another fifteen were shot. The second five were hung by the first five; and so on; the third group were hung by a fourth group of five. Percy Badger described the scene most eloquently:[17]

> "...after the first volley fired at them, several still clinging to life, rose up and ran about the plain pursued by the soldiers like so many hares. One in particular made great efforts to escape; after stumbling close by a well into which he had attempted to throw himself, he managed to reach the bastions, from which he cast himself headlong the height of one hundred and fifty feet. The soldiers in pursuit followed him to the place of his fall, there finding that he still lived, they soon put an end to his miserable existence."

After the Froberg mutiny, Fort Ricasoli was once again destined for a sizeable troop of loyal Maltese soldiers belonging to the newly amalgamated Maltese Provicial Battalion's two corps. The rest of the battalion was stationed at St Helen's Gate of the Santa Margherita Lines at Cospicua, and Zabbar Gate of the Cottonera Lines.[18] Partly due to the commotion raised by the Froberg mutiny, the punishments for cases of insubordination or rebellion were made harsher. A soldier could be executed, exiled for life or for seven years; he could be given up to two hundred lashes or imprisoned with or without hard labour for taking part in a mutiny, according to personal responsibility in the case.[19] Later on in the century, when a soldier at Fort St Elmo was condemned to death for allegedly firing at his superior, he was executed in the parade ground of Fort Ricasoli, lest the garrison there might emulate their Balkan predecessors.

---

[17] Ibid., 269-270.
[18] A. Samut Tagliaferro, (1976), 46, 63.
[19] Ibid., 47-48.

11

A Place for Penance, Punishment and Prisoners

Lucien Bonaparte's imprisonment

As has already been seen in the part dealing with the earlier Hospitaller history of Rinella and Fort Ricasoli, the situation and the circumstances of the place made it an excellent well-guarded and secluded spot where prisoners could be kept in tight security. This characteristic was shared with the other fort guarding the entrance of Grand Harbour, St Elmo, where many political prisoners and errant knights had been locked up too.[1] In 1775 cleric Guzeppi Dimech, who had taken part in Reverend Dun Gaetano Mannarino's attempted uprising against the knights was imprisoned at Fort Ricasoli.[2] In 1797, a conspicuous prisoner at Ricasoli had been Mikiel Anton Vassalli.[3] Right down to 1972, there were still suggestions being made for turning Ricasoli into Malta's main prisons.[4] On 23 August 1810, a famous prisoner, together with members of his retinue, got the shock of their lives when they were locked up in the fort.[5]

This was non other than Lucien Bonaparte, younger brother of Napoleon, Emperor of the French.[6] Lucien had been instrumental in Napoleon's rise to power by his support in the coup d'etat of 1799, when he was president of the Council of 500 during the Directory of France. He was later Ambassador in Spain, but when Napoleon became Emperor in 1804, jealousy crept in and Lucien retired to live at Canino near Rome. He

---

[1] Don Gaetano Mannarino and some of his rebel friends of 1775, as well as insubordinate knights were detained inside Fort St Elmo. A.P.Vella, *Storja ta' Malta*, ii, (Malta 1979), 183. See also Chapter 7 for Fra Emanuel Cotoner's imprisonment there in 1798.

[2] Vella, ii, 183.

[3] See Chapter 6.

[4] see the final chapter.

[5] Lucien Bonaparte's retinue included his wife and six children, a nephew, a physician, a tutor-chaplain, a secretary, and about twelve servants.

[6] Laferla, I, 76.

never reconciled with his brother, not even when the Emperor offered him the throne of Spain. Lucien knew the Spanish rebellious character better than his brother. When Napoleon annexed the Papal States, Lucien no longer felt safe enough there and left on board the United States ship Hercules for Austria, but inclement weather forced the ship to harbour at Cagliari. When she left harbour, British ships intercepted the *Hercules* and escorted her to Malta.[7]

As soon as Lucien entered Fort Ricasoli, he protested with General Hildebrand Oakes, the British Civil Commissioner at Malta, for such a treatment. Evidently, Lucien and his family were not used to a Spartan living as being 'host' at Ricasoli entailed. After taking instructions from the British under- Secretary of State for War, Oakes transferred Lucien Bonaparte and his family to San Anton Palace.[8] On 18 October King George III ordered the immediate transfer of Lucien and his suite to England on the British warship *President* of Captain Warren. He was given asylum under parole there, not being allowed to proceed to the United States of America. Since Bonaparte did not wish to travel in winter, Oakes decided he should proceed immediately.[9] By December, Lucien and his retinue had already settled in England.[10]

The hanging men's place - *"Ta' l-Imgħallqin"*

Another episode which made Fort Ricasoli a veritable place for punishment had a similar ending to that of the Kara Saim Rais case of 1531. Once again in 1820 as in 1531, Ricasoli was chosen for the site of macabre warning to sailors lest they challenge authority. Once again the name of the locality was changed because of such signal.

Captain Delanis piracy case

In August 1819, a certain Captain Charles Christopher Delanis of the brig *William of Liverpool* and ten of his crew forcibly carried away all the merchandise from, and tried to scuttle another British brig, the *Helen* off Cape Gatta in Spain.[11] They probably did this because Captain Delanis was heavily in debt.[12] The crew of the latter ship, however, made a lucky escape from inside the sinking hull, sailed on a Greek vessel which rescued them to Alicante, and hence to Malta to report the case. Governor Sir Thomas Maitland immediately sent an armed ship to Izmir in Turkey, where the *William of Liverpool* had meanwhile put anchor after calling at Malta where the Delanis men had attracted suspicions upon selling their stolen goods at incredibly low prices. Nine of the pirate crew were retrieved. Two gave King`s evidence and another, being a minor, was

---

[7] J. Murray (ed.), *The Court and Camp of Buonaparte*, (London 1831), 47-48.

[8] Laferla, I, 76.

[9] S(ecretary) o(f) S(tate) Lord Liverpool to Governor Oakes, 18 October 1810.

[10] After the war, between 1816 and 1840, Lucien returned to Italy as Prince of Canino. Murray, 1, fold-out.

[11] Laferla, I, 123.

[12] R. Attard, "The Maltese pirate trial", in *The Malta Independent on Sunday*, 9, 16, 23 August 1998, 29.

pardoned. The six others, being Captain Delanis; pilot Thomas Thompson; Chef John Lewis; able seaman John Smith; second pilot Benjamin Wilcock; and John Webb were condemned to death by a newly established Piracy Court at Valletta.

On 4 February 1820 they were hanged from the yards of the *William of Liverpool* which was berthed in Grand Harbour near Fort St Angelo. The corpses of the first four were later wrapped in tarred sacks and put in iron cages on gibbets on the seaward coast of Fort Ricasoli to serve as warning to other prospective sailor-mutineers. They were never pulled down and dangled in the air for years before the rough *Gregale* gales laid them to rest at sea.[13] The spot was henceforth called "*ta` l-Imghallqin*" (the hanging men`s place) by the local people.[14]

Edward's execution

On 20 December 1861, the parade ground of Fort Ricasoli hosted the execution by firing squad of gunner John Edwards of the Royal Artillery, witnessed by a substantial representation of all the garrison troops stationed at Malta. Insubordination within the ranks was a very serious matter punishable by death, as already seen in the case of the Froberg mutiny. The British military authorities wanted to show each and every member that no subversive element would be tolerated, even when the motive was personal.

Edwards was stationed at Fort St Elmo with the 3rd Brigade Royal Artillery. On 3 December he shot at Captain Keate from about ninety metres away, but hit a spot four metres above his human target. He was caught reloading.[15] Both during interrogation and court martial held at the Palace, Valletta, Edwards chose not to defend himself. He only answered in a confused manner, claiming that he had been mistreated by Keate. Most probably what prompted Edwards to shoot was a mixture of home- and army discipline-sickness. He was condemned to death.[16]

On 20 December, hours before daybreak, no less than three brigades,[17] under the overall command of Major-General Blucher-Ward C.B., marched or were ferried from Cottonera, Valletta, Floriana, and even Pembroke Camp to Ricasoli. They arrived there three quarters of an hour before sunrise, and paraded in a large rectangle leaving only the north-east (seaward) side of the ground clear. The forced night march on empty stomachs, and the

---

[13] Wilcock and Webb were buried outside Ricasoli.

[14] Faurè, iv, 186-190.

[15] *The Malta Times and United Services Gazette*, 19 December 1861, 3.

[16] *Mediterraneo*, 21 December 1861, 8. The weekly newspaper *l'Ordine*, which was critical of the British in Malta, claimed that Edward's case fell under the civil courts' jurisdiction, since it was a case of common delinquency. In such a case the accused would not have risked more than twelve years' imprisonment with hard labour. In claiming so, *l'Ordine* ironically referred to an 1828 Government proclamation as binding for all British subjects, and not only priests! *L'Ordine*, 13 December 1861, 3.

[17] Including troops of the 2nd Battalion; 22nd Regiment; 4th Battalion Rifle Brigade from Cottonera; and from other barracks.

grim prospect of assisting to a comrade's execution, were the causes for several of the soldiers fainting while they waited for Edwards.

The prisoner, accompanied by the Church of England chaplain of the forces, Reverend W. Hare and the provost-marshal, was led out of his cell at 8.00 a.m. The mournful procession consisted of the band of the 15th Regiment playing funeral marches, an armed escort, the coffin borne by fellow gunners of the Royal Artillery, the prisoner accompanied by the chaplain, and another escort bringing up the rear. It passed in slow time from right to left in front of each regiment and proceeded to the centre of the parade ground; the chaplain reading the psalms and the band still playing. Here it halted, the band and escorts retiring, leaving the prisoner with the chaplain and the provost-marshal, the coffin being placed at a short distance behind the prisoner.

The sentence of the court martial was then read to Edwards by Colonel Hallawell, army assistant adjutant-general, and the chaplain, having prayed with the wretched man for the last time, rose from his knees, shook hands with him and retired. The prisoner's eyes were then bandaged by the provost-marshal, who also shook hands with him. At this time the firing party consisting of twelve artillerymen, whose carbines had been previously loaded, six with shot and six with blank cartridge, advanced to within ten paces of Edwards who was resting on his right knee with his face towards them. At preconcerted signals they raised their carbines and discharged them at the poor gunner. Although death seemed instantaneous, according to custom, the provost-marshal discharged a pistol at the body, that no doubt should exist. The shot, however, did not take effect and he had to fire a second.

Each regiment then passed in fours, slow time, past the corpse, the bands playing the funeral dirge. This closed the sombre ceremony and the troops were marched off the ground.[18]

It is believed that the execution of John Edwards was celebrated in such grave pomp and circumstance in front of such a large body of troops to serve as a severe example and to deter other similarly disposed men from imitating the poor gunner's act. Shortly before 1861, such violent insubordination had become frequent in the army. Indeed many people thought that Edward's intent had only been that of committing an act which would relieve him from the monotony of the service or procure him with a transfer. Probably he mistimed his calculations.

---

[18] *The Malta Times and United Services Gazette*, 26 December 1861, 2.

12

Ricasoli the Hospital

The cholera epidemic of 1837

From 15 to 28 June 1837, Fort Ricasoli passed through its darkest hour. No less than 336 persons died there of cholera. The scene was horrific. Panic and misery reigned supreme.[1] This particular Asiatic cholera epidemic had a very remote origin. It was really a pandemic that had originated in Bihar in North East India in 1826. Unlike the first cholera pandemic of 1817-1823, it spread to Europe too. Moscow was invaded from the Urals in 1830 and Russian soldiers carried it to Poland in 1831. By the end of that year all of northern and central Europe was infected. In December 1834 Marseilles was infected. Over the next two years southern France and Italy were attacked. Malta and Sicily in fact were the last places to be infected in Europe, notwithstanding the fact that both London and Tunis had suffered in 1831.[2]

Cholera first appeared in Malta on Friday 9 June 1837 at the *Ospizio* at Floriana. The *Ospizio* was a hospital for the aged and the poor. Two old male inmates died there after a few hours' illness, and others were successively attacked by the disease.[3] By noon of 13 June, seventeen more persons died and twenty-seven others were infected.[4] By now the epidemic had been identified by the doctors and Governor Bouverie ordered the removal of 645 out of 750 inmates and mental patients from the *Ospizio* to Fort Ricasoli in the hope of arresting the progress of the malady in the isolated and well aerated position occupied by the fort.[5] The troops were evacuated. All these persons were transferred on boats on the 13 and 14 June and placed in the barracks under the overall

---

[1] T. Chetcuti, *Notizie Storiche e Patologiche Climatiche sul Cholera che divampò in Malta e Gozo nel estate del 1837*, (Malta 1838), 7.
[2] G.C. Kohn, *Encyclopaedia of Plague and Pestilence*, (New York 1989), 8-9. After this second pandemic, cholera visited Europe five other times, the last being in 1961 to 1973.
[3] NAM, Governor Bouverie to S.o.S. Glenelg, Despatch 16, 2 July 1837.
[4] *The Malta Government Gazette*, 14 June 1837, 209.
[5] Bouverie to Glenelg, ibid.

direction of Charles Satariano; the medical care of the Maltese young doctors Giuseppe Desalvo of the *Ospizio* and Antonio Grech; nurses and servants.[6]

Far from ceasing the epidemic continued to spread with unabated vigour both among the inmates who had been removed to Ricasoli and among those who had been left at the *Ospizio*.[7] The daily/weekly returns for the situation at Ricasoli are illustrated in table XIX.[8]

As can be seen from the table, the total deaths at Ricasoli amounted to 390, of whom 336 between 15 and 28 June. The mortality could have been higher had the healthy patients not been allowed to leave the fort on 25 June to recover in their families' homes.[9] What happened inside the fort during that fortnight is subject to speculation, however, it is certain that the situation ran out of control of the director. The barracks had not been readily converted into a proper hospital arrangement. This was only done after that a new director, Dr Antonio Speranza, took over the hospital-fort on the 21 June since Satariano was infected and left for Valletta. The perpendicular rays of the June sun; the number, the age, and the agony of the ailing old people, completely demoralised the two young Maltese doctors, the nurses, and the servants. The former two contracted the disease, and together with the panic stricken junior staff, abandoned the fort. The chaplains too were infected and could do little to console the sick.[10] Earlier on, some British doctors of the navy, including Doctors Clarke, Liddell and Sankey went to the fort to help their Maltese colleagues. Other Maltese doctors, including Gavino and Michele Portelli, Luigi Pisani, and Gaetano Micallef did the same. But all these doctors could do little since the most efficient cure had not as yet been identified. Governor Bouverie visited the fort twice on 16 and 25 June. Neither were these doctors helped by their nurses or juniors. The corpses were left abandoned and unburied, sometimes lying in filth.[11]

For this purpose on 18 June, eighteen convicts were released from prison and promised asylum on condition that they bury the dead. But since there was no proper armed surveillance, these prisoners abused the sick. It is said that they robbed the patients of their belongings, and in some cases they buried people who were still giving signs of life in a mass grave at Wied Ghammieq outside the walls of the fort.[12] The day after, these convicts were re-admitted to prison.[13] On 20 June another nine convicts were released for the same purpose, but with the same results.[14] By 21 June all three remaining

---

[6] Chetcuti, 10.

[7] Cassar, 193.

[8] Chetcuti, 7; and *The Malta Government Gazette*, 12, 19, 26 July 1837.

[9] Chetcuti, 13.

[10] Ibid., 10-11.

[11] *Harlequin*, 20 September 1838, 83-84.

[12] Fauré, iv, 217. The convicts were later exiled from Malta. The farmers at Wied Ghammieq used to unearth human remains in this field until 1881, when it was decided that a proper cemetery be laid out for them. A chapel was also erected. The cemetery is a place of religious devotion, popular with pilgrims. Guillaumier, 173-174.

[13] Cassar, 193.

[14] Chetcuti, 11.

Day	remained from last report	new cases	total cases	died	healed	remained
June						
13	-	2	2	2	-	-
14	-	7	7	7	-	-
15	-	30	30	13	-	17
16	17	52	69	20	-	49
17	49	42	91	36	-	55
18	55	50	105	39	6	60
19	60	60	120	38	-	82
20	82	40	122	34	-	88
21, 22	88	80	160	68	1	99
23	99	17	116	25	-	91
24	91	12	103	14	7	82
25	82	8	90	14	-	76
26	76	10	86	10	-	76
27	76	6	82	15	39	28
28	28	8	36	10	-	26
29	26	16	42	5	6	31
30	31	5	36	7	4	25
Jul. 1	25	13	38	7	-	31
2	31	9	40	6	-	34
3	34	1	35	8	1	26
4	26	2	28	1	4	23
5	23	3	26	3	-	23
6	23	3	26	3	3	20
7	20	-	20	-	20	-
8-11	-			3		
12-18				2		

Table XIX

Daily/weekly cases of Cholera at Fort Ricasoli; 13 June to 25 July 1837

19-25: remaining patients transferred back to Floriana

Maltese doctors, as well as the director Satariano showed symptoms of acute diarrhoea and had to leave the fort too. On that day Dr Sankey moved in to help, and in the evening Antonio Speranza, the newly appointed director, arrived at Ricasoli and took over the fort. He found it in utter confusion. The only medicine available were doses of calomel, to be dissolved in water.[15]

The following morning, 22 June, Speranza engaged Mr Lanfranco for financial advisor. He promised generous remuneration to newly recruited convicts who obliged by burying forty-five corpses.[16] Speranza also organised better accommodation in a proper barrack hospital. More Maltese doctors were transferred there and did excellent service, same as the two newly arrived Capuchin monks who administered the Sacraments to the patients, so that when Governor Bouverie made his second visit on 25 June, he was satisfied with the general progress.[17] It was at this stage that permission was granted for all the healthy inmates to leave the fort. One hundred and fifty-one left within four days. The emergency at Ricasoli was over.[18]

But not in the rest of the country though! By 17 June the epidemic had infected the rest of Floriana; by the 18 Pietà; a day later Fort St Elmo was attacked; and by the 20, it was the turn of Valletta, Senglea, Fort Manoel, and a ship which had to quarantine in St Paul's Bay.[19] Although the figures above suggest otherwise, many of the 'healthy' inmates who left Ricasoli after 25 June may have been infected with the disease, since it was after that date that cholera spread most quickly to most villages in Malta. From 5 to 11 July, only nine died at Ricasoli, but 558 died throughout the island.[20] From 12 to 18 July, 802 died in all, only two being at Ricasoli.[21] During the rest of summer 1837, a further 2,076 persons died[22] for a total of 4,253.[23] The last seventeen patients were transferred back from Fort Ricasoli to Floriana shortly before 25 July.[24]

The events at Fort Ricasoli produced a trail of bitter controversy within the local population. The Anglophile media reported that the majority of Maltese medics, with only a few exceptions, had abdicated their duties generally, and that the patients prayed that they might be treated by British doctors, whose splendid services avoided rebellion as had happened in Sicily.[25] The opposition papers on the other hand defended the work of the Maltese doctors. It was the latter who had diagnosed the disease properly and

---

[15] Ibid., 11-12.

[16] Due to the high mortality rate that year, the archpriest of Vittoriosa to which Ricasoli was then attached, could not register all those who died , and none at Ricasoli. ACCV, Liber Mortuorum, vi, 1837-1875, introductory note before page 1.

[17] Cassar, 194.

[18] Chetcuti, 13.

[19] *Malta Government Gazette*, 21 June 1837, 220.

[20] Ibid., 12 July 1837, 248.

[21] Ibid., 19 July 1837, 260.

[22] Ibid., July-September 1837, passim.

[23] Laferla, I, 164.

[24] *Malta Government Gazette*, 26 July 1837, 268.

[25] *Harlequin*, 9 August 1838, 38; 15 September 1838, 75; 20 September 1838, 78-80, 83-84.

Wied Ghammieq Cemetery where the 1827 cholera victims where buried *en masse*.

recognised its true nature, while the British doctors continued to find alternative names to it even after it was evident that it was cholera. Never had cholera patients been more promptly helped by doctors as at Malta. The Government showed its confidence by putting all the hospitals under Maltese doctors' direction.[26]

Cholera spread because its real causes, let alone cures, were not yet known. It was thought that miasma, or noxious putrid matter or particles emitted from corpses entered and infected human organism, but also that a predisposition existed in fearful individuals and others oblivious of basic sanitary norms.[27] The only medicine prescribed was various doses of calomel dissolved in water. Dr Giuseppe Maria Stilon of the Royal Navy was a firm believer in its efficacy. Others, however, openly criticised him and did not administer it.[28] In order to prove the efficacy of calomel, Stilon published a treatise about cholera in 1839.[29] The fact is that this medicine was only effective if administered with a great amount of water. It was the latter which really helped the successful cure.

[26] *Mediterraneo*, 30 August 1838.
[27] L. Gravagna, *Ragguaglio Sul Cholera Morbus*, (Malta 1837), 3-4.
[28] G.M. Stilon, *Sul Cholera Morbus*, (Malta 1839), vii.
[29] Ibid.

Cholera also spread because sanitary and sewerage facilities in Malta were only satisfactorily developed in parts of Valletta at the time. Therefore it was quite feasible for water or food to be contaminated by the vibrio. It was only after other cholera and plague epidemics struck Malta that the sewerage system was planned for most towns and villages in the 1880s.[30]

Early hospitals at Fort Ricasoli

When the British forces occupied the fortified towns of Malta in 1800, they could not man all the fortifications built by the knights. Fort Ricasoli's function as a hospital originated much earlier than the cholera epidemic of 1837.[31] The first Royal Navy hospitals in Malta were at the Armoury in Vittoriosa (Birgu) and at the former slaves prison at Valletta,[32] while the army used the General Hospital at Valletta also.[33] But besides this, part of Fort Ricasoli was converted into a military hospital to replace another one that had been housed in the Inquisitor's Palace at Vittoriosa. A number of high bomb proof arcades that run along the inner face of the land front of the fort were cut off by wooden walls from the rest of the arcades occupied by the healthy troops. A wooden floor was thrown across an end of the upper part of these arcades so that two storeys were formed. The upper one was partitioned off into two wards and a surgery; in its wooden floor, gratings were cut to promote the ventilation of the ground floor which was reserved for the convalescent soldiers and other patients requiring segregation. This hospital had a complement of 54 beds which could be increased to 100 in an emergency. In 1822 it sheltered the invalids and discharged men belonging to regiments stationed in the Ionian Islands, as also the ophthalmic patients of the 85th Regiment who were moved from Valletta in 1822. Eye diseases were common in the lower ranks in the early nineteenth century.[34]

The hospital at Ricasoli was also used by wounded Russian sailors from November 1827 through 1828. These sailors had arrived at Malta on the Russian fleet which had participated in the Battle of Navarrino together with the British and French Royal Navies against the Turko-Egyptian fleet. Other wounded Russian sailors were hospitalised in the Armoury hospital at Vittoriosa.[35] Many more Russian sailors stayed on at Ricasoli for almost two years,[36] since in February 1830, a British sailing ship brought with it

---

[30] Laferla, ii, 70-73.

[31] Cassar, 98.

[32] W.A., Griffiths, *A Brief Outline of the Foundation and Development of H.M. Naval Establishments at Malta*, (Malta 1917), 23.

[33] Cassar, 95.

[34] A. Samut Tagliaferro, (1976), iii. Six new urine tubs were issued to the fort to be used as washing tubs by the patients!

[35] D. Fenech, 'Birgu during the British period', in L. Bugeja, M. Buhagiar, and S. Fiorini (ed.), *Birgu: A Maltese Maritime City*, (Malta 1993), 139.

[36] Griffiths, 16. The cost of victualling the sick and wounded Russians at Fort Ricasoli between 1 January and 31 March 1828 was £879. 16s. 10d. as follows:
  3461 full diets @ 3s. 6d. each;
  2052 half diets @ 2s. 4d. each;
  592 low diets @ 1s. 2d. each.

the smallpox contagion to Malta which affected the Russian troops, whose sick were again quartered at Ricasoli. But by that time the defects of the fort as a hospital were already evident. This occasioned the building of a proper naval hospital at Bighi in 1830.[37]

By the 1850s the fort hospital was no longer in use.[38] It had been found wanting in the cholera epidemic of 1837 and even the normal barrack accommodation and sanitary facilities of the fort had been condemned by the Barrack and Hospital Commission of 1860.[39] Between the 1860s and 1922, British soldiers were treated at Forrest Hospital established at Villa Spinola at St Julian's,[40] and also at Cottonera Hospital built near Zabbar Gate of the Cottonera Lines in 1873, capable of 128 patients.[41] It was only due to exceptional emergencies during World War I that Fort Ricasoli again functioned as a hospital for one last time.

Bighi Naval Hospital

Salvatore or Bighi promontory, the one which lies next to Fort Ricasoli towards the south-west across Rinella Bay, witnessed very important developments after 1822. Bighi palace had been almost totally destroyed during the blockade of the French.[42] When a division of property between the various Government departments was agreed upon in 1822, Bighi Palace and grounds were ceded to the Royal Navy. On 23 March 1830 the first stone was laid of a naval hospital at Bighi. The architect was Salvatore Xerri, later replaced by his own brother Gaetano. It was completed in 1832. Later on, especially in 1871, 1877, 1879, and 1886, baths were built by the sea below Bighi.[43] Major structural additions were undertaken in 1901 to accommodate better the zymotic and surgical wards.[44] Since 1832, the unmistakable columns of the neo-classical Bighi hospital have been a distinguished landmark of Grand Harbour opposite Rinella Creek. Bighi was evacuated by the Royal Navy in 1964. In 1972 it was turned into a trade school, and partly an Institute for Scientific Research in 1994.

Ricasoli: a hospital during World War I

On 28 July 1914 Austria-Hungary declared war against Serbia and within a few days most of Europe's countries were engulfed. In October Turkey joined the central powers. This made the Eastern Mediterranean a most important theatre of operations in which

---

[37] Faurè, iv, 203.
[38] Cassar, 98.
[39] See further down the chapter about the sanitary facilities at Ricasoli.
[40] Ibid., 99.
[41] Ibid., 100. It ceased to be a hospital in 1920 when it became a grammar school for boys.
[42] Griffiths, 24.
[43] Ibid., 23.
[44] Cassar, 98.

Malta played her part. By February 1915, the Turks invaded Egypt to the Suez Canal line, and on the 25 April 1915 allied troops landed at Gallipoli peninsula in the Dardanelles, intent on knocking Turkey out of the war. But within the first month of fighting there, the British alone had suffered more than 30,000 casualties. The war in the East enhanced Malta's position on the lines of communication and made her 'the nurse of the Mediterranean'. Starting on 4 May 1915 with 600 men, wounded soldiers were brought over to Malta for convalescence in twenty-seven newly established or re-equipped hospitals around the islands which could house 25,000 beds.[45] By the end of May over 4,000 cases were being treated in eight hospitals; by September 10,000. The number of beds had by then risen to thirteen and again to twenty thousand by March 1916.[46]

During September 1915 there was an alarming increase of casualties from Gallipoli. An expansion of the existing hospitals now included Fort Ricasoli, where the barrack rooms and parade ground could be made available. The same reasons considered when the cholera cases of 1837 were transferred there, were again the cause for Ricasoli being chosen: a healthy site; closeness to the sea; a harbourside location; convenient disembarkation; and its isolation. The larger eight barrack rooms were arranged for the accommodation of 224 patients, while tents were pitched in the parade ground for a further 576 wounded soldiers. The hospital was prepared and equipped in October 1915; received its first patients on 6 November, and by 30 November there were 503 sick men. During December 1915 and January 1916, 942 patients were admitted, but after 27 January no further cases were referred to there. The evacuation of Gallipoli had by this time markedly reduced the number of sick. Neither had the wounded from the Salonika expedition started to use Malta as yet. At the end of March 1916, Fort Ricasoli hospital was closed, same as Spinola.[47]

It was during March 1916, with the prospects of more cases from the newly opened Salonika front that part of Fort Ricasoli was again turned into a hospital, together with Forts Manoel, Chambrey, and Spinola Palace, but by June 1916 they were again closed because of comparative inactivity in the campaign.[48] Ricasoli had served its wartime purpose well, contributing its fair share towards Malta's job as 'nurse of the Mediterranean'.

Sanitary conditions and improvements in the nineteenth century

As has already been noted earlier, the sanitary facilities obtaining both at Fort Ricasoli and in Malta as a whole were much the same in the 1850s as in the eighteenth century for various reasons, not least because the British military authorities only started to

---

[45] Laferla, ii, 201.
[46] Ibid., 202.
[47] G.R. Bruce, *Military Hospitals in Malta during the War*, (Malta), 35.
[48] Bruce, 32.

appreciate Malta's strategic value after the Crimean War of 1853-1856, and more especially after the opening of the Suez Canal in 1869. Another reason was that before 1921 Malta lacked a fully responsible and autonomous self-government, and the local population doubly loathed any form of taxation for whatever purpose.

The water supply

Therefore the water supply situation in 1843 was still that described by Romano Carapecchia a century and a half earlier. Fort Ricasoli was still being served by ten cisterns capable of holding 10,278 *botti* (443,877 litres) of water.[49] By 1860 three cisterns had lost their water, and water for drinking and cooking had to be supplied by the commissariat, and was stored in open barrels in the barrack ground, exposed to dust and the heat of the sun. One tank yielded brackish water after stormy weather. Much water was wasted to flush latrines which could otherwise use the near sea water.[50]

After 1883 the water supply problem in Malta was tackled with fervour by engineer Osbert Chadwick. Water under pressure was laid in towns. By 1900 at the latest, Fort Ricasoli had running water with new cisterns for storage.[51] A few years later water pipes for the new Married Quarters were laid.[52] By 1902 a water meter owned by the Public Works Department (PWD) was operative near Ricasoli coal yard,[53] and in 1904 the lighthouse keeper's quarters were supplied with running tap water by the PWD on the military authorities' expense.[54] During drought years water cuts had to be made. During 1904 and 1905, most public taps were throttled, while the military establishments including Ricasoli, had their flow curtailed by night.[55] By the outbreak of the First World War, the fort no longer suffered from any lack of running water, and could thus successfully serve as military hospital.

Drainage and sewerage facilities

Concern over the sanitary condition of Malta involved not only the adequate supply of running water, but also the drainage and sewerage network; the need for which was being felt throughout the nineteenth century with the rapidly expanding population and the rather frequent occurrence of both cholera and typhoid.[56] The civil government of

---

[49] V. Azzopardi, *Raccolta di Varie Cose Antiche e Moderne Utili ed interessanti riguardanti Malta e Gozo*, (Malta 1843), 144. At Fort St Angelo there were two reservoirs and two cisterns with a total capacity of 6,230 *botti* (113,582.07 litres).

[50] D. Galton and J. Sutherland, 149.

[51] NAM, PWD 142, ff. 294v-295.

[52] Ibid., 143, ff. 59v-60.

[53] Ibid., 144, f.1.

[54] Ibid., 145, ff. 87v-88.

[55] Ibid., 145, ff. 44v-45; Ibid., 146, ff.24v-25.

[56] Apart from 1837, cholera visited Malta in 1850, in 1865 (1,873 deaths); in 1887 (435 deaths); and 1911 (85 deaths).

Malta already contemplated the construction of the water carrier system in 1858. Until then the sewerage of the harbour towns poured into Grand Harbour. Even at Fort Ricasoli, the soil from the latrines was flushed through a main drain 75 centimetres wide and 150 centimetres high with an outlet cut out to the north of the fort, and opening on the surface of the rock above sea level. At times this outlet formed a pool of foul water from which the most offensive effluvia proceeded. A cutting in the rock was made in the 1850s to remedy this but with little success. During summer sixty men were employed daily in carrying water to flush the drains.[57] After 1865, sewers started to be ventilated with clay.

In 1885 the government remodelled the drainage system in Malta after a long drawn out battle in the Council of Government against the elected members who were not at all convinced of the worth of such a project. They also thought that the military government should foot the bill since the barracks soiled Maltese waters as much as private residences did. House drainage was remodelled in towns and the sewerage removed by steam power to an outfill in the sea at some distance south-east of Fort Ricasoli at Wied Ghammieq, nearer to St Rocco. The 1887 cholera epidemic served to show the urgency of the project.[58]

Following the 1860 report on barrack and hospital improvement by D. Galton and J. Sutherland, glazed pipe drains of 22 centimetre diameter were laid for drainage for latrines, the cook house and ablution rooms of Fort Ricasoli. This was discharged into the sea by iron pipes below sea level.[59] In 1882, the drainage pipes of the church still drained onto the rocks outside the fort. That year it was connected to the main sewer.[60] These same drains were again found defective and needed repairs in 1900.[61] Meanwhile the main sewer of the fort was connected to the general (Malta) sewer draining at Wied Ghammieq. In 1901 the drainage system of the whole fort was remodelled by the PWD at a cost of £45, being charged on the Superintendent of Public Works.[62]

Sanitary condition of the barracks, 1860

The barrack and hospital improvement commission of 1856, which visited Malta in 1860, had been commissioned following the exposure by Florence Nightingale and others of the terrible conditions under which the troops lived and died in the Crimean War. Its report authored by D. Galton and J. Sutherland is a long one,[63] and contained many important recommendations on most aspects of health. The report is invaluable since it

---

[57] Galton and Sutherland, 148.
[58] Cassar, 323. It was only after 1899 that the larger suburban villages were connected to this sewerage system. Until then houses there had only been connected to unsanitary cesspits.
[59] Galton and Sutherland, 148, 150.
[60] NAM, Public Works bundle 578, ff. 169-172.
[61] Ibid., PWD 142, ff.66v-67.
[62] Ibid., ff. 223v-224, 267v-268.
[63] See also Chapter 9 for details of barrack accommodation.

provides a detailed picture of the state of Ricasoli and the other forts in 1860, and since very little improvement had occurred since the British occupation, the description may be said to apply for Hospitaller Ricasoli too.

The main conclusion of the commissioners was that the barrack rooms were overcrowded and ill-ventilated, not only at Fort Ricasoli, but in all forts and barracks. At Ricasoli there were only 7.476 cubic metres per person. At Fort San Salvatore there were 8.876 cubic metres. The minimum space acceptable then was 16.8 cubic metres.[64] Most men at Ricasoli only disposed of 4 square metres of floor space.[65] Following upon this recommendation,[66] half the men in barracks were placed under canvas tents, being pitched on barrack squares and roofs. This also happened at Ricasoli. The good effect of this measure was vouched for in later reports which showed the men in the tents being fifty per cent healthier than those remaining in barracks.[67] The lack of ventilation and light at Ricasoli barracks was due to the fact that the main barrack rooms are situated in the casemate in the South East land front bastions and curtains, and only one wall which faces the parade ground could have windows. The other old (knights') barrack rooms in the south-west wall fronting Rinella Creek are also casemated. Moreover they have a wall in front of them to screen them from the Officers' Quarters which run parallel to them to the north-east, effectively blocking the fresh air and the more feeble light that could enter the north-facing windows. Only during high winds was the air not stagnant.[68] In 1860 there were no fireplaces and lighting was still done by oil lamps, not by gas.[69] Galton and Sutherland strongly recommended that all windows in the barrack rooms be raised and widened; that there was space for no more than 300 persons rather than for the 412 living there in 1860, and that the Married Quarters in the smaller rooms be removed from there.[70]

Ablution rooms and latrines

The latrines were situated in an underground casemate in the north-east, open sea wall, about 45 metres from the nearest barrack room. They were flushed, but the ones for men were close to the ones for women. The main drainage outlet was beyond the walls on the rocks. There was only one ablution room with no baths in the south-east land front. It was seldom used since it was inconvenient. The commissioners recommended that suitable ablution rooms be provided with baths and water laid on, and that latrines and urinals be reconstructed on Macfarlane's and Jennings principle - properly drained and supplied with water.[71]

---

[64] A. Samut Tagliaferro, (1976), 218-219.
[65] Galton and Sutherland, 147-148.
[66] Ibid., 150.
[67] A. Samut Tagliaferro, (1976), 219.
[68] Galton and Sutherland, 147.
[69] Ibid., 148.
[70] Ibid., 147-148, 150.
[71] Ibid., 148-150.

The cook-house, guardroom, cells, library and schoolroom

The cook-house was situated between the Main Gate area and Bastion No. 7, in a casemate. The ventilation was abundant and the kitchen was cool. It was provided with old boilers but no oven. It did not even have running water supply. There was another smaller cook-house near the latrines used by the married people. The barrack and hospital commission recommended that the cook-houses be supplied with new steel boilers and ovens. The canteen, consisting of two rooms and a yard, was dark and uninviting. It required considerable improvement.[72]

The guardroom and cells were near the Main Gate. They were badly ventilated and needed total reconstruction. There was also a schoolroom on the other side of the Main Gate. It was well ventilated and lighted. The library consisted of three contiguous and joined rooms in the south-east (Rinella) front, well lighted and ventilated, and had a shed outside so that men could sit there to relax, read and smoke. There were no workshops (the barracks were used), no ball courts or skittle alley.[73] These were constructed later.

A thrust towards general improvement

Following these recommendations, the military authorities embarked on a massive barrack building campaign throughout Malta especially in the period between 1870 and 1910. Until 1860 the conditions obtaining at Fort Ricasoli were much the same as in 1798. The frequent epidemics; overcrowding; the 1860 commissioners' report; and the obvious discernment that Malta was becoming more important for the Empire, especially after that the Suez Canal was opened in 1869; led to the improvement of the sanitary situation of the whole islands, and Fort Ricasoli benefited from these developments.

---

[72] Ibid., 148, 149, 150.
[73] Ibid., 149.

13

Life inside the Fort

Development of infrastructure (1800-1945)

Although Fort Ricasoli was primarily a military establishment, it still maintained the characteristic of being also a small town with its own married quarters, church, school and sports facilities, since there was always a sizeable number of wives and children. People were born, lived, worked, played, and died inside the fort, same as during the Knights' rule. For example Charles Thomas van Straubenzee (later Sir), was born at Ricasoli on 17 February 1812, a second son of Major Thomas van Straubenzee, a gunner. Charles Thomas became Governor of Malta on 3 June 1872, holding the highest office in the island until June 1878.[1]

Therefore Fort Ricasoli always needed to be well equipped with the latest infrastructure not only to perform its military role efficiently but also to serve its dependant civilian population. It therefore housed public places such as a church, school, barber's shop, clinic, shoemaker, carpenter and other workshops.[2]

Town Gas lighting

Town gas was firstly introduced to light 400 lamps in Valletta and another 240 lamps around Marsamxett Harbour on 8 August 1856. By 1858 it had been connected to the Cottonera area.[3] In 1861 The Malta Gass Company erected a branch gas works of two acres at Rinella, and Fort Ricasoli had gas connections installed.[4] In 1907 gas mains were also laid at 2 shillings (s.) 6 pence (d.) per main encroachment fee, by the gas

---

[1] Laferla, ii, 1.
[2] NAM, Plans, Ricasoli, 6.
[3] Faurè, iv, 254-255.
[4] A. Samut Tagliaferro (1976), 219.

company after permission had been granted by Military Government.[5] From Rinella a 10 centimetre underground gas entered the Main Gate after passing outside the flank of No 7 bastion. Inside the fort, four smaller pipes, each of 4 centimetres diameter, spread out of the main one to serve the Married Quarters, the Breakwater Lights, the batteries on curtain 1, and the soldiers' (land front) quarters.[6]

Electrification

The first power station in Malta started functioning at Floriana in 1895. Valletta, and later the harbour-side towns were soon served with this important commodity which gradually took the place of gas in lighting most places. By 12 February 1898, Fort Ricasoli was also connected to the power station by means of rubber insulated cables which entered the fort from behind the left ravelin on to the flank of Bastion No 5, and from this north-east side on to the rest of the fort, including the Point, to serve the lighthouse too.[7] But it had to wait until 1902 so that there could be electric current and light, also because of conflicting competencies between the Military and the Civil Government of Malta in the project of electrification. The Civil Government had not as yet decided the rates per unit to charge the Military Government. Private owners were charged 7d. per unit. The Civil Government suggested that 6d. should be charged since the Military were large consumers; 5d. per unit would be charged if the latter assumed maintenance costs. Eventually 650 electric bulbs were installed at Fort Ricasoli, Rinella and Fort St Rocco, out of a total of 4,950 for seven sets of barracks. The wiring and filling would still be the Civil Government's property.[8] By 1908, Ricasoli's 400 electricity points were consuming 18,000 out of the total 396,000 units per annum being consumed by all seven major barracks in the island. Because of this large consumption, the British Military Authorities were already considering building their own power station.[9] This was done much later though.

Telecommunications

The telegraph system was set up in 1867, but was replaced by the telephone around 1900.[10] When wireless telegraphy was invented, the Admiralty took over part of the already existing gunpowder stores buildings and other areas at Rinella Valley to construct a station. In 1909, a wall was built by the road leading to Ricasoli Ranges to avoid access by the public, and the Wireless Telegraphy Station was completed with its masts by 11 January 1911.[11]

---

[5] NAM, PWD, 146, ff. 252v.-153.
[6] Ibid., Maps, Ricasoli, 6.
[7] Ibid., 220.
[8] The total cost for the 4950 points and connections amounted to £26,000. NAM, PWD, 143, ff. 158v-159, 216v-217, 261v-262, 272v-273.
[9] Ibid., 146, f.400v.
[10] N. Samut Tagliaferro, 59-60.
[11] NAM, PWD, 147, 52v-53, 109v-110, 141v-142, 152v-153.

Telephone lines were introduced at Fort Ricasoli in 1898. In 1908 the line was extended to the breakwater. A direct line connected it to the Dockyard. By 1917, cables connected the fort to St Elmo too.[12] In 1935, cable radio was introduced in Malta, and all quarters of Fort Ricasoli were soon connected to the network.[13]

Transport

Ever since 1670, the normal way to and from Valletta and other places was by boat. This remained so until the introduction of the first automobiles in Malta by the 24th Company of the Royal Engineers in 1903. In 1881 the boat fare from Valletta Marina to Ricasoli or vice-versa was 3d. by day but 4 and a half pence by night.[14] By 1903, the day fare had increased to 4d. This was also the fare for a boat ride to any of the three cities.[15] This was not the only way to and from the fort. A road connected it with the Rinella area and on to Vittoriosa or Zabbar, and to the country. In the late nineteenth century, all connecting roads were tarmaced. In 1903 a cab ride from Valletta to Ricasoli (about 11 kilometres) cost 2s. 4d. if drawn by one horse; 6s. 6d. if drawn by two. A cab ride from Marsa (about 5.5 kilometres) only 4d. By 1913 the fare of the one-horse ride had increased to 2s. 6d., and remained so until 1925 at least.[16]

Water supply

Ever since Romano Carapecchia's visit, the water was derived from rainfall collected in underground tanks. By 1860 two out of three large underground tanks had lost their water and had to be repaired later.[17] By 1869 the water tanks contained 1,759,937 gallons of water derived from rain. There was an aqueduct leading from two cisterns of 2500 gallons capacity each which supplied the wash-house and the Officers' Mess.[18] During World War I new reservoirs, boreholes, and distribution networks were prepared. Work on new drainage systems was taken in hand by the Royal Engineers in the 1870s and the 1880s.[19] The four largest cisterns are situated under the parade ground near the cookhouse of the land front barracks. Each one is 30 metres long and 6 metres wide and can be reached by portholes and stairs.[20]

---

[12] Ibid., 146, ff.339v-340, and Ibid., 148, f.70v.
[13] Ibid., Plans, Ricasoli, 283.
[14] *Guida Generale di Malta,* 1881, 109-111.
[15] *Malta Army and Navy Directory* 1903, 85-86. By 1913, the fare was unchanged. Ibid., 1913, 96.
[16] Ibid., 1903, 84-85; Ibid., 1913, 94; and Ibid., 1925, no pag.
[17] Galton and Sutherland, 149.
[18] NAM, Plans, Ricasoli, 239.
[19] N. Samut Tagliaferro, 59-60.
[20] NAM, Maps, Ricasoli, 6.

Religious observation

Roman Catholic

Little information is available about the functions held inside St Nicholas Chapel between 1800 and 1881. One may presume that in certain periods when the garrison was predominantly Anglican, few services were held, if at all. The Roman Catholic Chapel is not mentioned in Azzopardi's 1843 detailed description and guide of the Maltese Islands, although the one at Fort St Angelo is.[21] By 1881, however, Reverend Raffaele Patiniott took care of the spiritual needs of the Roman Catholic population of Ricasoli, although he resided at Vittoriosa, and was also chaplain for all Catholic troops of the Cottonera.[22] He was still chaplain in 1906.[23] He was helped in his work by Rev. M. Lorenzo Camilleri.[24] The chaplain usually said Mass every Sunday morning at 7.30, and sometimes Parade Service was held at 8.00.[25] The chaplain could live in a house, which was held as a benefice, just behind St Nicholas Chapel. He was held responsible for all maintenance work and repairs to be done.[26] There was some controversy regarding the tenure of the chapel and priest's quarters between the Civil and Military Authorities in Malta. Repairs were made at the expense of the Public Works Department, as in February 1919, when repairs amounting to £13 were completed.[27] One such example of blurred jurisdiction is the case of the picture of Grand Master Cotoner which originally hung in the sacristy of the chapel.

Grand Master Cotoner's portrait incident

In 1901, the Officers of the Royal Artillery Eastern District stationed at Ricasoli, discovered the series of coat of arms of the various knight Governors of the fort in the ante-room of the officers' Mess in the former Governor's House. They took interest in collecting memorabilia of the fort, and shortly before July 1907 they acquired a portrait of Fra Giovanni Francesco Ricasoli and hung it in the Mess. They also requested the Civil Government to borrow a picture of Grand Master Nicholas Cotoner in half bust from the sacristy of St Nicholas Chapel.[28] The request was made by the commander of the Artillery Brigade, Colonel H.T. White on 16 July 1907 to the Brigadier General in charge Administration, who later made the request to the Lieutenant Governor, on condition that no objection would be forthcoming from the Civil Government or the

---

[21] V. Azzopardi, *Raccolta di Varie Cose Antiche e Moderne utili ed interessanti Riguardanti Malta e Gozo,* (Malta 1843).

[22] *Guida Generale di Malta,* 1881, (Malta 1881), 56, 58.

[23] NAM, PWD, 146, f.160v.

[24] Ibid., 1882, (Malta 1882), 66, 62. Other chaplains included Rev. J. Darmanin of Zejtun in 1903 (for all the Eastern District also), and Rev. Mgr Canon Cavendish in 1913 (Ricasoli only). *Malta Army and Navy Directory,* 1903, 25; and Ibid., 1913, 22.

[25] *Daily Malta Chronicle,* 7 December 1907, 7.

[26] NAM, PWD, 146, f.160v.

[27] Ibid., 148, f.244v.

[28] This was a copy in half of an original in the State Dining Room of the Grand Masters' Palace in Valletta.

Ecclesiastical Authorities. But since the church was Government property, the latter's consent was not even sought, and the Civil Government had no objection so long as it would be returned to the sacristy if it was no longer needed. Other conditions were that a marble plaque commemorating the picture had to be put in its place in the sacristy; that under the picture a plate should be attached stating that it was on loan from the sacristy; and that the move had to be recorded in the inventory of Government pictures.[29] The picture was thus moved in 1907. But barely thirteen years had elapsed when the picture was going to be lost for Ricasoli in a most impudent way. On 12 July 1920, the Colonel in Charge Admiralty, Ricasoli, requested to transfer the oil painting of Grand Master Cotoner from the Officers' Mess at Ricasoli to Fort Tignè. Ten days later, the Director of Public Works, L. Gatt advised the Governor that if the picture was no longer needed at the Mess, it should return to the sacristy.[30] When the fort was given over to the Malta Government in 1964, all the pictures and works of art were transferred to the National Museum collection.

Church of England

Little documentation is available regarding the Services held for the Anglican troops at Fort Ricasoli in the nineteenth century. Part of the barracks must have been used as a chapel. In 1903 the chaplain in charge was Reverend H. Marshall. He celebrated the Services according to the following schedule:[31]

Sundays	- Holy Communion		7.30 a.m.
	also 1st Sunday		9.30 a.m.
	3rd Sunday		10.15 a.m.
	Parade Service		9.30 a.m.
	Evensong		6.30 p.m.
	Sunday School	1st Sunday in month	3.00 p.m.
	other Sundays		2.30 p.m.
Wednesdays	- Children's Guild		5.00 p.m.
	C.E.M.S.		8.00 p.m.
Saturdays	- Intercessions		6.30 p.m.

Matins and Sermons were also celebrated on occasions.[32] Other similar Services used to be held in the other major barracks of the British garrison in Malta.

On 24 November 1904, authority was given for the construction of an Anglican Church in the new barracks outside the fort at Rinella. The church was started on 17 January

---

29 NAM, PWD 146, ff.262v-263, 266v-268, 281v-182.
30 Ibid., 149, f.3v.
31 *Malta Army and Navy Directory* 1903, 83.
32 *Daily Malta Chronicle*, 7 December 1907, 7.

1905 and was completed the following 22 September, at a cost of £500, £100 less than had been estimated.[33] The Church was dedicated to St Matthew.[34] Henceforth, the same services could be held in better comfort there.

The school

An infants' school was functioning at Fort Ricasoli by 1869 at the latest. Both the school rooms and the Mistress' quarters were situated in the South-West (Grand Harbour) Front just behind the Officers' and Married quarters.[35] The classrooms were found to be wanting for the pedagogical needs of a greater child population of the turn of the twentieth century. Therefore a larger school consisting of three classrooms; teachers' room; library; a play-shed; and a corridor[36] was built between 11 September 1905 and 17 April 1906, for a total cost of £1,078, £68 more than the estimated cost.[37] The new school was situated outside the fort near the new Married Quarters above Rinella Valley. It catered for a maximum of 36 primary, and 48 infants schoolchildren.[38] In 1903, the Army school master and mistress were a married couple, Mr T.H. and Mrs M.J. West.[39] Ten years later Mr A.L. Hill, a married teacher, was schoolmaster in the new school, while Miss M. Watt acted as schoolmistress.[40] When the new school was completed in 1906, the old classroom in the casemate was turned into a school for adults.[41]

Leisure activities

Swimming and fishing

Fort Ricasoli is surrounded by the attractive Mediterranean for the most part, and ever since swimming became more popular during the eighteenth century, the soldiers at Ricasoli have bathed in the sea for their own leisure and distraction from the monotonous life inside the fort.

The sea there is often rough, and there are instances of death by drowning. For example on 27 July 1854, three soldiers of the 68th Light Infantry Regiment drowned while swimming. One of them found himself in difficulties while bathing beneath the fort. The other two dived to save him when he was no longer visible, and they were drowned too.[42]

---

[33] Ibid., Maps, Ricasoli 103.

[34] *Malta Army and Navy Directory*, 1913, 83.

[35] NAM, Plans, Ricasoli, 228.

[36] Ibid., 106.

[37] Ibid., 103

[38] Ibid., 106.

[39] *Malta Army and Navy Directory*, 1903, 26.

[40] Ibid., 1913, 27

[41] NAM, Plans, Ricasoli, 6.

[42] *Il Portafoglio Maltese*, 29 July 1854, 3. *The Malta Mail and United Services Gazette*, 1 August 1854, 3, rebutted the former newspaper's claim that the three soldiers were found "in a deplorable state".

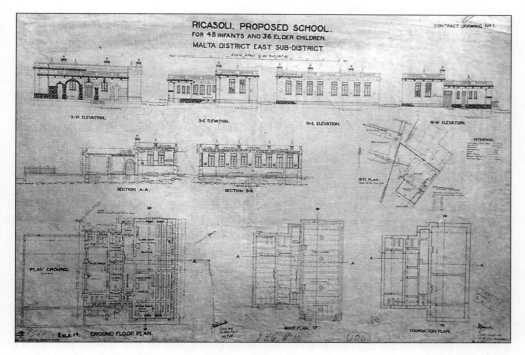

RICASOLI. PROPOSED SCHOOL.
FOR 48 INFANTS AND 36 ELDER CHILDREN.
MALTA DISTRICT EAST SUB-DISTRICT.

1908 plan of the school outside Ricasoli.   (Courtesy: NAM)

Exactly eleven years later to the day, John Graney, a Roman Catholic English soldier of 39 years, met the same fate while bathing.[43]

Fishing too was a normal activity around the fort same as it still is today. In May 1870, a report was submitted to the Governor of Malta by the Lieutenant Colonel of Fort Ricasoli against fishermen who used to break rocks by the side of the road in order to seek shell fish, thus rendering the road hazardous for (cab) traffic.[44] Fishermen on boats were always restricted from entering the zone of the arc of fire of Ricasoli's guns when artillery drills took place.

Sports Day

An annual sports day used to be held too. For example on 17 April 1889, the Royal Artillery East Division held a Sports Day at Fort Ricasoli in the afternoon. The band of the Berkshire Regiment played marches. There were numerous lady and gentlemen spectators among whom Major General King, the Aide de Champ of the Governor. The

---

[43] ACCV, Liber Mortuorum VI, (1837-1875), 289.
[44] A. Samut Tagliaferro (1976), 229.

191

most interesting event was the gun-mounting competition. It was won by the 3/1 North Irish Division. There was also a tug- of-war won by the 4/1 Western.[45]

Recreation Establishment and other sport

As for indoor leisure activities Fort Ricasoli was endowed with a very inclusive Recreation Establishment which was built between August 1866 and May 1869, at a cost of £2,129 on the northern side of the Parade Ground, just inside the retrenchment at the neck of Bastions 4 and 5. It was 55 metres long and 8 metres wide on the inside, with an arched veranda overlooking the ground, 3 metres wide. The Establishment was a place where the soldiers could meet in a relaxed atmosphere. It included a reading room (12.5 x 8 metres) and an adjoined stage (7 x 8 metres)); a small library and a librarian's office (3 x 3 metres each); a coffee bar (4 x 8 metres); a grocery shop (8 x 4 metres) and a grocery store (3 x 3 metres). Two extensions to the building housed a kitchen and a writing room.[46] Occasionally some soldiers would abuse in drink. Therefore a temperance bar was located at the farthest north-east corner of the fort, barely eighty metres away from the establishment at the neck of No 4 bastion, to take care of drunken or rowdy men.[47]

Other sports and pastimes practised by the troops inside the fort included skittles, raquet, tennis, and football. By 1927 there were two tennis courts, one beside St Nicholas Chapel for the officers, and one on Bastion No 7 for the Sergeants. The skittle alley and the raquet court were both near the Recreation Establishment. Association football was played in the parade ground, at least since 1902.

Association football

The first ever recorded Association football match in Malta was played at the Marsa between the Royal Engineers and the Garrison teams on 4 March 1882.[48] Since Fort Ricasoli hosted units of both regiments and boasts the largest parade ground in any fort in Malta, it may be presumed that football was already being played there in the 1880s. The first ever recorded football match at Ricasoli was played between St George's of Cospicua and the 88 Company of the Royal Garrison Artillery on 22 February 1902, ending in a 0 - 0 draw after a fairly quiet first half, and an even but contested struggle with attacking football in the second half.[49] That day the heroes of Ricasoli were attacker Evans, as well as Brazier, Scott and assistant bombardier Chew - though for once they had only their feet for guns![50]

---

[45] *Daily Malta Chronicle*, 19 April 1889, 4.
[46] NAM, Plans, Ricasoli, 6 and 246.
[47] Ibid., 6.
[48] C. Baldacchino, *Goals, Cups and Tears: A History of Maltese Football*, vol. I, (1886-1919), (Malta 1989), 7.
[49] Ibid., 75.
[50] *Daily Malta Chronicle*, 26 February 1902, 5-6.

The recreation establishment built in 1869.

By 1908, Ricasoli was home ground to the Royal Garrison Artillery Trumpeters football team, who took part in the Junior League. They played just one match at home, beating the Lyceum team 3-0 on 11 January 1908.[51] They were also due to play against Melita at Ricasoli in the same tournament, however, Melita conceded a walk over since they wanted the match to be played in a neutral venue.[52] In 1909 the Ricasoli Garrison School football team was founded, but they amalgamated with the school teams of St Andrew's and Mtarfa before playing in the Malta Garrison Schools Football League which was played in 1909 and 1910 on a home and away basis. Some of the matches involving this united team were also played at Ricasoli.[53] The Malta Football Association was founded in 1900. Ricasoli Parade Ground may indeed be considered as one of the cradles of Maltese football.

---

[51] Baldacchino, I, 141.
[52] Ibid.,
[53] Ibid., 183, 411.

Some other major events

Shipwrecks

Fort Ricasoli is a coastal fort situated in a very busy sea lane at the mouth of Grand Harbour. It therefore follows that it witnessed a number of shipwrecks through its history, also since the sea there may be very rough during fresh gales. At times it was the garrison of the fort which brought help to the unfortunate travellers first, such as on 7 April 1806, when Ricasoli's men saved all the crew of the Turkish schooner *Sibilla* that had shipwrecked at Ricasoli Point.[54] The same thing happened in August 1854 when the transport ship *Urgent* struck Ricasoli Point and lay on the rocks until she was released by workers from the fort.[55] They could do nothing though on 27 October 1851, when during an exceptionally violent *Gregale* storm, a Swedish ship was shipwrecked at il-Kalanka tal-Patrijiet just beyond Wied Ghammieq. All twenty-four crew as well as the Captain's family were drowned. That day the waves were so high that some of the water found its way into Rinella Bay from Wied Ghammieq.[56]

On 9 April 1897, five British soldiers who were in a boat outside Fort Ricasoli capsized and were saved by Maltese fishermen who let the soldiers cling to their small boat until four were rescued by the Marine Police. Meanwhile a boat sailed from Fort St Elmo for help. This boat capsized too and its crew were only saved with difficulty. There was only one casualty, Gunner J. Brady, aged 26.[57] On 19 April 1907, the *Ariel* torpedo destroyer shipwrecked just beneath Ricasoli's bastions while participating in naval night manoeuvres. The pilot was probably blinded by the searchlights of Ricasoli. Some men went out of the fort and saved all of the crew except for one.[58]

The worst sea disaster to which the garrison of Fort Ricasoli reluctantly assisted was that of the ship *Sardinia*, which left Malta bound for Alexandria on 25 November 1908, with 191 passengers, 39 crew, and general cargo on board. When the ship was six kilometres outside harbour, she caught fire at the boilers first, and then on to the deck. Although the Captain veered the ship back towards Grand Harbour, they were not allowed in for safety reasons, and the *Sardinia* shipwrecked on the St Rocco coast. That day 121 perished, including the Captain, and the men who went out of Fort Ricasoli, navy launches, and the Gozo ferry boat *Gleneagles*, could only save 72 persons. The people watching the tragic event from Ricasoli's ramparts could do nothing but despair at such a pitiful sight.[59]

---

[54] Faurè, iv, 138.
[55] Ibid., 248.
[56] Ibid., 1047-1048.
[57] Ibid., 410.
[58] Ibid., 672.
[59] Ibid., 696-701; *Daily Malta Chronicle*, 26 November 1908, 2-3.

Other events

The garrison in Fort Ricasoli was in a festive mood whenever a royal celebration or visit was taking place. As has already been seen in the section about armament, the saluting battery fired gun salutes on such occasions. At 12.00 noon on 22 June 1897, the fort's batteries joined others around Grand Harbour to celebrate the Diamond Jubilee of Queen Victoria.[60] The same happened when King Edward VII's royal yacht *Victoria and Albert* entered and left harbour on 16 and 21 April 1903.[61] Whenever the royal visitor was a direct superior of the armed forces serving in Malta he would tour the barracks. The Duke and Duchess of Connaught were in Malta on an inspection tour from 10 to 15 March 1905. The Duke was Inspector General of the Forces. He arrived in port at 10.00 a.m. and as if to underscore the importance of Fort Ricasoli, he had already inspected the garrison there by the afternoon.[62]

Personal and working relationships inside the fort were not always harmonious. In 1842 ill-feeling and a final altercation resulted in Captain John Levick of the 59th Foot Regiment fighting a pistol duel against Lieutenant Septimius Adams of the 88th Foot outside the walls at Wied Ghammieq. Their first shot went astray. Adams insisted on a repeat and was mortally wounded by Levick.[63]

The Andrews Case and Riots

By 1889 the British presence in fortress Malta were being increasingly felt by the local population. Since the opening of the Suez Canal in 1869, and the subsequent build up of the garrison, the naval dockyard, and the modern fortifications, the Maltese had found employment with the Military. However, the mixing of the two communities was not always harmonious, and sometimes there was ill-feeling between the Maltese and the British troops. The progressive requisition of the foreshore in the Grand Harbour area; the discernment of a new, culturally akin and powerful rival and neighbour such as Italy had become; and the mere physical presence of so many troops, sometimes led to friction between the British and the Maltese. The garrison viewed the Maltese as local natives meriting little or no respect to their rights. The promulgation of the 1887 Constitution, which gave the elected representatives of the people a majority in the Council of Government was not enough to quell the inhabitants' aspirations for self government, and by 1889, it was evident that the Constitution was not working well, especially since the Governor often resorted to his right to Order in Council to legislate to Imperial advantage. Moreover the late 1880s were a period of relative economic slump in Malta, and the political situation then can be described as uneasy - a dormant volcano.

---

[60] Faurè, iv, 407.
[61] Ibid., 556, 562.
[62] *Daily Malta Chronicle*, 10 March 1905, 2.
[63] A. Samut Tagliaferro, (1976), 454.

This is the background and part explanation to the riots that took in Malta, more especially in the Cottonera area, between the 22 March and 8 May 1889. It is relevant for the history of Fort Ricasoli, since the spark that lit the fuse of the powder-keg took place at the foot of Ricasoli steps in front of the fort's Main Gate. Also, because of the incident, the Berkshire Regiment stationed at Ricasoli and the local Maltese population found themselves pitted in a war of nerves, scuffles, stone throwing, and sometimes gunshots, claiming some casualties and causing grave injury. Had the ill feeling in the capital city of Valletta been comparable to that in the Cottonera area, then the riots of 7 June 1919 would have been greatly anticipated.

The Case

On 22 March 1889 at 11.00 p.m., privates James Casey and John Andrews, and trumpeter William Sutton of the Berkshire Regiment, Royal Garrison Artillery, hired a boat from Valletta Marina to ferry them to Fort Ricasoli.[64] The boatmen were Silvestro Bartolo, 26, and Salvatore Attard, 19, both of Cospicua.[65] When they arrived near the foot of the steps leading to the Main Gate of the fort, the three soldiers offered two shillings to the boatmen, but the latter insisted that they be paid three shillings when Casey and Sutton had already set foot ashore.[66] The three soldiers took offence and started a fist fight. The boat rocked and Andrews fell overboard. He could not swim and instead of helping him out of the water, Attard hit Andrews several times on the head with an oar, causing his death.[67] While the other two soldiers immediately went inside the fort to report the case, the boatmen gagged Andrews' corpse and landed it at Senglea Point. His body was only found on 30 March in Kalkara Creek near Fort St Angelo.[68]

Attard and Bartolo were arrested on 23 March by police Inspector Bonaventura Consiglio of Senglea. On 11 April, after interrogating witnesses, he formally accused them of the wilful homicide of Andrews and of putting the life of the other two soldiers in danger.[69] The trial by jury was held between 15 and 18 May 1889 presided by Judge Sir Adrian Dingli. The jury found Attard guilty by 7 to 2, and he was sentenced to life imprisonment with hard labour. Bartolo was unanimously found not guilty and was released.[70]

The riots

As soon as news spread of the murder at Ricasoli steps, the garrison troops and the Berkshire Regiment stationed at Ricasoli in particular, began to show their anger by

[64] Faurè, iv, 334.
[65] NAM (Mdina), Atti d'Istruzione, April-May 1889, KK, (last item).
[66] *Daily Malta Chronicle*, 26 March 1889, 3.
[67] Faurè, iv, 334-335.
[68] *Daily Malta Chronicle*, 2 April 1889, 3.
[69] NAM (Mdina), Atti d'Istruzione, April-May 1889, KK, (last item).
[70] Ibid., Procedimenti Criminali, 1888-1889, 136-142.

attacking Maltese people wherever they met, since they were certain that the Maltese boatmen and other dealers had been overcharging them for quite some time. The local people, especially the people of Birgu, Senglea, Cospicua and Zabbar did not hold back in answering to the provocation of the British troops and they attacked the Shropshire Regiment troops also, thinking they were men of the Berkshire Regiment. The situation was rendered grave since both the Military and the Civil Police were often ineffective in dealing with the rioters[71], and there were instances when the police sided with them. The *Daily Malta Chronicle* contended that the civil courts were giving lenient sentences to Maltese rioters.[72]

From 23 March to 18 April, incidents occurred daily both by day and by night.[73] In the majority of cases, they were provoked by the British troops. Some grave incidents involved soldiers from Ricasoli. On 8 April, a troop of soldiers from Ricasoli attacked a boatman from Zabbar who was on his way to work. He was hospitalised with serious injury at the backbone.[74] Another soldier attacked a priest at Zabbar.[75] On 16 April, a private of the Berkshire Regiment was killed and others of the Shropshire Regiment were stabbed in scuffles.[76] That day some soldiers of the Berkshire Regiment stationed at Zabbar Gate, Cottonera, stoned two persons who were on their way to work. One of them fled, while the other one was unjustly held by the same soldiers at their barracks. Four Maltese policemen from Zabbar went to fetch the man. They fired some shots in the direction of the British troops and released the man. The Berkshires counterattacked and entered Zabbar armed with their rifles and bayonets. In the fight which ensued, four Maltese policemen were wounded, including the same Inspector Cassar. Three British soldiers were wounded and another one died.[77] Two days later, an unknown person fired shots at a picket of British troops which went out of Fort Ricasoli.[78]

After that the two boatmen had been formally charged, the situation was coming back to normal, but the *Malta Times and United Services Gazette* of 19 April reproduced an article which had been published in the *Admiralty and Horse Gazette* of London. The article instigated the British Garrison in Malta to take the law into their own hands, by saying:

> "...It is satisfactory to know that the supposed murderers are in custody; but this case is only another instance of the conduct of some of these Maltese gentry, and we fancy that a little application of lynch law administered by the comrades of some of these victims of extortion would seem to be much to blame for allowing the admittedly disgraceful state of affairs to continue..."

---

[71] Malta, 17 April 1889, 2.
[72] *Daily Malta Chronicle*, 7 May 1889, 7.
[73] NAM, Despatches, Governor Torrens to S.o.S. Knutsford, 18 April 1889.
[74] *Malta, Corriere Mercantile Maltese*, 9 April 1889, 1.
[75] Ibid.
[76] *Daily Malta Chronicle*, 19 April 1889, 4.
[77] *Malta*, 18 April 1889, 2.
[78] Ibid.

The report was ill-timed, if not absolutely uncalled for at that moment. The newspaper *Malta* criticised the report as being impertinent and seditious, and many clubs and outlets in Malta boycotted the *Malta Times* for some time.[79] To make matters worse, the order of confinement of troops in barracks was derogated on 22 April[80] when the annual Garrison Sports Day was going to be held at the Marsa grounds, and many of the soldier-spectators who had read the article were intent on trouble and revenge. The shop-owners at Sliema were ordered by the police to shut down early, and pickets positioned along the roads leading to Marsa. When the competitions were over, British troops returning to their barracks at St Francis in Cottonera and Fort Ricasoli started, and engaged in fighting and rioting against the local people. Three Shropshire Regiment soldiers bayoneted a helpless donkey at Marsa and were later attacked and given their due by its owner and some of his friends in a fistfight.[81] Later on that day, 25 soldiers of the same regiment assaulted an old man and his son at Ghajn Dwieli Gate only to be attacked in turn by a mob from Cospicua, who forced them to retreat into St Francis Barracks.[82]

The Cottonera Gates were again closed and the troops were again confined to barracks. On 26 April, in order to separate the two communities, all the area to the north-east of the Paola to Delimara road, and including Paola and Tarxien, Zabbar and Zejtun, was declared out of bounds for British troops until further notice.[83] On 1 May, the troops were ordered to wear their helmets at all times by day.[84] The situation might have flared up again on 9 May when an inconsiderate Irish gunner stationed at Delimara sexually assaulted a ten year old Maltese farmer girl of Zejtun in a field at Tas-Silg, Marsaxlokk.[85] But since it was known that the trial of the two boatmen was imminent, and that there would soon be a thorough redeployment of troops in the eastern (Cottonera and Ricasoli) district, the crises was over, and the soldiers in the fort could hope for better relations with their Maltese neighbours.

---

[79] Ibid., 22 April 1889, 2.
[80] Ibid., 19 April, 1889, 2
[81] Ibid., 23 April 1889, 2.
[82] Ibid., 24 April 1889, 2.
[83] *Daily Malta Chronicle*, 26 April 1889, 5.
[84] Ibid., 3 May 1889, 5.
[85] NAM (Mdina), Police, Atti d'Istruzione, LL, May-July 1889.

14

The Building of the Breakwater

Early projects

Before the breakwater was built between 1903 and 1909, the Grand Harbour's main channel and Bighi Bay, that is the large basin between Ricasoli and St Angelo, lay at the mercy of the *Gregale* (north-east) wind which, with a fetch of 400 kilometres across the Ionian Sea to the nearest land in Greece, produces waves as high as six metres when it blows for more days. Moreover, the refraction of waves hitting St Lazarus shore below the Knights' Infirmary (now the Mediterranean Conference Centre), would also produce turbulent waters in Rinella and Kalkara Creek. The problem was further complicated by the fact that the waves broke at the mouth of Grand Harbour because of Monarch Shoal, protruding in an easterly direction from St Elmo Point for about 350 metres. The existence of Monarch Shoal was firstly documented by Captain W.H. Smyth in the map of the Grand Harbour which he published in 1822, after carrying out the first hydrographic survey of the area between 1814 and 1816 on behalf of the Royal Navy.

It was realised by the Admiralty that the capacity of the Grand Harbour could be increased from 11 to 25 battleships or cruisers if calm water was secured in the Main Channel and Bighi Bay by building a breakwater at its mouth. Eventually, Monarch Shoal itself was used by the Admiralty in order to build there the longer (St Elmo) arm of the breakwater, with a shorter arm at Ricasoli Point.[1] That the breakwater was not built before 1903 was for strategic, technical, and political reasons.

Reasons for the building of the breakwater

As long as France was still Britain's rival in the Mediterranean, Malta's position as the base of the Royal Navy was considered as untenable and therefore the need for great

---

[1] W. Soler, "The Breakwater in Grand Harbour" in *The Sunday Times*, 26 June 1994, 38-41; 3July 1994, 40-42; 10 July 1994, 44-47., passim.

defence expenditure was not felt, since the fleet would leave for Gibraltar in time of crises. However, with France as partner in the newly forming Entente Cordialle, Malta was better appreciated as a naval base, and worth the risk defending. The development of the self propelling bomb, or the torpedo in 1866, also precipitated the decision for the building of the breakwater.[2]

Although the first investigation into the practicability of building such a breakwater carried out by engineer Hamilton Fulton was commissioned by the Royal Navy in 1817, it was only very late in the nineteenth century that the development of the steam engine and the advance of the use of cement in concrete made the whole project economically feasible. Other reasons for the building of the breakwater were to facilitate the protection of the harbour entrance by a floating boom in time of war; and to give increased protection for merchant vessels moored stern to shore at Valletta.[3]

The Maltese political situation at the turn of the twentieth century was rather disturbed, and the Admiralty had to tackle any opposition that might come from the Maltese politicians. The fleet was being accused by them as causing pollution in the harbour and that therefore the Imperial Government should pay for any sewerage works. There was serious preoccupation about the scheme since it could produce stagnant waters in the Grand Harbour, further polluting it. This problem was solved by forming a 69 metre long opening in the St Elmo arm, bridged by an iron viaduct, in order to promote circulation of sea currents, but which was also to serve as a passageway for lighters entering the harbour. This viaduct was destroyed by the Italian E-boats in 1941, as shall be seen in Chapter 15. Civil, mercantile and commercial shipping had been excluded from the foreshore of both Dockyard and French Creek, they being exclusively reserved for the Navy. Now it was being proposed that the foreshore of Ricasoli too should be requisitioned by the Admiralty so that the works on the breakwater may proceed without hindrance. In exchange the Admiralty granted the right of promenade to civilians on the new breakwater. The foreshore and ditches of Ricasoli and St Elmo Points were, however, returned by the Admiralty to the Civil Government on 7 September 1911.[4] Furthermore, the Secretary to Government at the time (comparable to today's Prime Minister), Lord Gerald Strickland, who was anglophile, insisted that since the Navy was a source of income for the local population, the Civil Government of Malta should contribute to any expenditure incurred for the development of the harbours. But to this Francesco Azzopardi, President of the *Associazione Patriottica Maltese* reiterated that Italian and Spanish workers should not have been imported for the project since it would have guaranteed employment for the Maltese workers for many more years to come.[5] All these problems were solved by the British Government in 1901. The whole project, estimated at £677,000, but which eventually cost close to £1 million, was financed by the Admiralty.

---

[2] Laferla, ii, 164.
[3] Soler, ibid.,
[4] NAM, PWD 147, ff.186v.-187.
[5] Faure, iv, 632.

Description of the breakwater

The first proposals for the building of a breakwater in Grand Harbour do not feature any sort of mole from Ricasoli Point. Architect William Scamp of the Admiralty produced two alternative schemes in 1859 for the building of a breakwater on Monarch Shoal and the construction of a smaller mole either at l-Imgerbeb Point beneath the Lower Barracca in Valletta, or at St Angelo foreshore.[6]

The breakwater as built between 1903 and 1909, however, has two arms, the 378-metre St Elmo arm, and the Ricasoli arm of 122 metres. The latter arm is 12.5 metres wide at the sea-bed, narrowing to 12 metres at the parapet. The depth below mean sea level increases gradually from the shore to 14 metres at the head. A spur pier planned for l-Imgerbeb Point was never built. Both arms of the breakwater end with a bull nose on which a lighthouse and a machine gun emplacement were built. The breakwater arms are made of great concrete slabs, each one of which was pre-cast at a purposely built concrete factory at Mistra Bay in St Paul's Bay, which were later transported by barge to the Grand Harbour. The aggregate for this concrete was Upper Coralline Limestone (a type of hardstone), quarried and crushed at Hondoq ir-Rummien and Ghar Dorf in Qala, Gozo, which was then transported by barge to Mistra. Therefore the great white hardstone slabs of the breakwater that are so pleasing to the eye, form only the upper and covering part of the whole structure. These slabs were quarried by hand in Gozo too. The foundations of the two arms were excavated, levelled, and filled with concrete by divers lowered in a bell. The Ricasoli arm has a concrete wave-breaker on the seaward side.[7] This was laid in pell-mell fashion in order to dissipate the wave energy and avoid recoil on to the inner face of the St Elmo arm.

Ricasoli Point Lighthouses of 1858 and 1907

While the St Elmo arm has got a subway to allow all-weather access to the head for the servicing of electric cables supplying power to the new lighthouse[8] the Ricasoli arm had no such subway. Since 1858, Fort Ricasoli hosted a huge round lighthouse, with two red lights: one at 18, and another at 26 metres height, which was visible at seven kilometres distance. This lighthouse complemented the more famous Fort St Elmo light. Both feature prominently in early photographs and prints of Malta or Valletta.[9] There had been suggestions that gas should be used for the new lighthouses, however, since gas was obtained from a private company, electricity should be used as a standby.[10] Long lasting improved lamps were also installed at the lighthouse.[11]

---

[6] Soler, ibid.
[7] NAM, PWD 146, f. 248v.
[8] Soler, ibid.
[9] Guillaumier, 171; and Badger, 237.
[10] NAM, PWD 146, f.249.
[11] Ibid., ff. 260v.-261v.

The breakwater lights were administered by the military until 3 February 1911, when the lighthouse, the keeper's quarters, and some stores were declared to be in a good state and safe, and therefore the complex was handed over to the Civil Government.[12] In fact a commission sent by the Lieutenant Governor to the Ricasoli arm of the breakwater in March 1908 had suggested that the Civil Government should request the Admiralty to render passage to the lighthouse safe by placing a chain hand-rail and later on providing a covered passageway for the keeper, so that he would not get wet or washed over. During the visit, the wind was fresh north-east breeze, and heavy water broke and fell on to the lower parapet in sufficient volume to injure a person.[13] In case of heavy seas during a *Gregale*, the lighthouse keeper could always go to the lighthouse on a boat. But if in rough weather he found it difficult to land at Ricasoli Point the Public Works Department asked for, and obtained permission by the Military Authorities that the keeper should be allowed entry into Ricasoli and lower himself to the breakwater by means of a ladder. The above-mentioned old lighthouse in Fort Ricasoli was transferred by the Civil Government to the Military Authorities on 1 January 1910 for an encroachment fee of one shilling per annum,[14] and was demolished soon afterwards. The new breakwater lighthouse had taken over its job.

The building of the breakwater

In February 1900, the Admiralty commissioned the harbour engineers' firm Coode, Son and Matthews to report on the construction of the breakwater.[15] The project was approved by the Cabinet in November 1900, and shortly after by the House of Commons. In April 1901, the Earl of Selbourne, First Lord of the Admiralty, visited Malta and finally decided the line on which the breakwater should be built.[16] Although the invitations to tender by the Admiralty surveyors were only issued on 8 October 1902, preparatory works for the breakwater were already on hand by 11 February 1902, when the Admiral Superintendent requested permission to the Civil Government to construct a small building by the side of the Ricasoli (old) light(house) in order to fix wind-vanes on top of it. The construction was required to serve as a small observatory containing the instruments registering the force and direction of the wind at Ricasoli Point in connection with the new breakwater. The small observatory, however, was not to be. The Admiralty transferred the project to the roof of the Palace (in Valletta), when the Civil Government replied that permission was only forthcoming on condition that a £20 lightning conductor be also installed.[17] On shore staging works started later on in October that year, to the design of Colonel Edward Raban, Director of Works, Admiralty. The Admiralty accepted the tender submitted by contractors Messrs S. Pearson and Son Limited of London. The contract was signed on 18 April 1903, the day appointed for the laying of the foundation stone.[18]

---

[12] Ibid., 147, f. 20v.; ff. 167v.-168.
[13] Ibid., 146, ff. 335v-338.
[14] Ibid., 147, ff. 80v.-81.
[15] Soler, ibid.
[16] Laferla, ii, 164.
[17] NAM, PWD 146, ff. 67v.-68, 91v.-92, 107v.-108, 142v.-143.
[18] Soler, ibid.

General view of Malta's Harbours looking from outside Grand Harbour's mouth towards the south-west. Fort Ricasoli is in the foreground left. Valletta is on the right, with Fort St Elmo at its nearest point. Further to the right is Marsamxett Harbour. Beyond Ricasoli lie Rinella Creek; Bighi (or Salvatore Hill); Kalkara Creek; Fort St Angelo; Galley (or Dockyard Creek); Senglea; French Creek; and Corradino Hill. The Main Channel of Grand Harbour, protected by the breakwater arms, is in the centre of the photograph.

(Courtesy: DOI)

King Edward VII at Ricasoli Point

Although the longer arm of the breakwater is the St Elmo one, Ricasoli was privileged since its arm was the one to be started first. Therefore the ceremony of the laying of the foundation stone by the visiting King Edward VII was held at Ricasoli Point on 20 April 1903, two days after the appointed day, because of inclement weather. The King arrived at Ricasoli Point by boat at 4.00 p.m., after that all the officers had taken their position. The foundation stone is a large granite boulder with an inscription on it commemorating the event.[19] It is situated at the shore end of the Ricasoli arm and a hollow beneath it contains a brass casket lined in satinwood overlaid with ornamented burnished brass, the work of Malta Dockyard artificers Galea, Ginnies and Saliba. In it the King deposited a set of current coins; a record of the ceremony; plans of the breakwater drawn on parchment; copies of two current dailies; and a set of photographs of the harbours.[20] The

[19] Faurè, iv, 558.
[20] Soler, ibid.

gold key that locked the casket and the silver case which held the silver trowel, were manufactured by the well-known Maltese jewellers and silversmiths Messrs Meli and Company of "Strada Reale and Fountain Square", Valletta, while the mortar board and mallet, made of ebony and inlaid silver, and the mason`s glittering silver level, were made by Amabile Mifsud, of 144 Strada Santa Lucia, Valletta. The foundation stone of the St Elmo arm was laid by Lady Lacon, wife of Rear Admiral Sir Thomas Hammet, Commander in Chief, Mediterranean Fleet, on 8 June 1903.[21]

The Ricasoli arm was completed by 1907,[22] while the last block of the St Elmo arm was laid on 20 October 1908. No ceremonies were held on that day.[23] The project took long to complete since most material had to be carried and deposited by barge and the weather did not permit most manoeuvres during winter time. The staging and some completed work suffered during storms. From 19 to 21 February 1904, the place experienced three days of *Gregale* thunderstorms which damaged ships in harbour, and overturned the machines, cranes and blocks of the breakwater which had already been put into place. It caused the contractors £30,000 worth of damages. Two Maltese port wardens were saved from drowning by English artillery men of Ricasoli.[24] The *Gregale* again damaged the works in October that same year.[25] The works also took long because the pre-cast concrete factory at Mistra was only operational months after the laying of the foundation stone.

Concluding Comments

The breakwater has withstood the test of time and war. It needs maintenance work, however, otherwise the sea will win its final battle against this silent gargantuan sentinel. One may conclude by quoting William Soler's observations on the breakwater:[26]

> "...the passage of time and pioneering pre-cast concrete techniques in Malta, combined with extraordinary human endeavour and skill in shaping the individual indigenous parts into an aesthetically pleasing curvilinear whole, have made this structure an integral part of our rich historical building heritage...They (the two arms) are the only two super megaliths not forming part of our prehistoric namesake temple culture, and it is precisely for this reason that we should strive to preserve them for posterity."

---

[21] Faurè, iv, 600-601.
[22] Griffiths, 52.
[23] Faurè, iv, 694.
[24] Ibid., 1062.
[25] Soler, ibid.
[26] Ibid.

15

The Second World War

Preparation for war

After the Nazi invasion of Poland, the United Kingdom declared war on Germany on 3 September 1939. The dark clouds that hung over Europe since the Fascist dictators Hitler and Mussolini embarked on their disconcerted, yet effective policy of aggression, finally produced the reaction of the Allied powers. Malta was not located on the front yet. The war may have been 'phony' on the Western Front, but in Malta the war was 'phonier' still and calm reigned until Italy declared war on Britain and France on 10 June 1940. The quiet dawn of the following day gave way at 6.55 a.m. to the heart rending sound of the siren announcing the first of a series of 3,340 air raids by Italian and German fighters and bombers in four years of war. The war had come to Fort Ricasoli's doorstep. During the first air raid over Malta, six soldiers of the Royal Malta Artillery were killed at their post on Fort St Elmo's Cavalier, just 500 metres away from Ricasoli Point. The Maltese people in general, and the people inside the Fort in particular, were facing the grim reality of a perilous situation, rendered even more dangerous by the general lack of preparedness owing to the fact that the small island had never experienced such a new type of warfare. Although there had been ample time to prepare the defence, the much needed aeroplane-fighters, weapons, ammunition, and other stores were never enough for an island which had always depended on foreign lands for most supplies. For this reason, that is in order to secure the berth of supply convoys coming from Britain via Gibraltar or Egypt, Ricasoli still had an important role to play, against possible attacks by sea or by plane, since the fighters intent on attacking the harbours flew over the fort. With supplies secured, Malta could strike back at the enemy convoys, especially those crossing over from Italy to North Africa, or even at enemy military stations almost as far north as Naples.

In view of the possible assault, shelters for watch on duty were constructed at Ricasoli starting in April 1938.[1] The married quarters had bathrooms built later on that same

---

[1] NAM Plans, Ricasoli 133.

year.[2] New gun emplacements with relative shafts and magazines were started that same year.[3] Anti Motor Torpedo Boat equipment together with fire control towers and ammunition hoists were planned in May. The towers' overall height above surface (emplacement level) was of nine metres. They included three floors with stairs. The control towers were placed behind the gun emplacements.[4] In 1939, the wash-up house in the land front Married Quarters was turned into a boiler house[5] and the cook house was improved too.[6] The lights on top of the wireless masts at Rinella were put off shortly before the war started so that they would not present an easy target to the axis raiders. Still one of the masts fell when it was hit during an air raid in March 1942.[7] In January 1941, Bofors gun emplacements were also projected for Ricasoli by Major Tanner of the Royal Engineers.[8] With the increase in the number of new recruits during the war period, the need was felt for finding more barrack space. In 1944, there was a proposal for thirty-six, 5 x 11 metre Nissen Huts to be built in the north-west section of the parade ground to house 504 men (fourteen in each). The only open space left would have been just inside the Main Gate.[9] Apparently these huts were never constructed, and the ground was left intact for over thirty years. The first raids carried out by aeroplanes in the Italo-Turkish War in 1911, altered defence strategies world-wide, even in the design of existing forts. The concrete casemate was reintroduced as a necessary component of defensive works in order to provide for overhead protection. Partial overhead protection against aerial bombing was provided for some of the twin 6-pounder quick firing guns in turreted mountings protecting the Grand Harbour entrance at Ricasoli, as also in Fort St Elmo.[10]

The State of Defence

The Garrison

The garrison of Fort Ricasoli was composed of the 1st Battalion of the Cheshire Regiment (Infantry of the Line), who were stationed at Ricasoli during the war.[11] The Fort was also manned by one officer and 67 men of the 3rd Heavy (Coastal) Battery of the Royal Malta Artillery under Major Alfred Samut Tagliaferro, who trained their three twin 6-pounder and two 12-pounder guns on the incoming enemy.[12] Moreover, the RMA established a Recruits Training Depot (RTD) at Ricasoli early during the war, increasing the total complement inside the fort to a very considerable number. The RTD occupied the old barracks in the land front of the Fort, as well as the parade ground adjacent to

---

[2] Ibid., 129.
[3] Ibid., 146.
[4] Ibid., 142.
[5] Ibid., 137.
[6] Ibid., 128.
[7] C.J. Boffa, *It-Tlett Ibliet Matul l-Aħħar Gwerra, 1940-1944*, (Malta 1976), 12, 48.
[8] NAM Plans, Ricasoli 121.
[9] Ibid., 266.
[10] Spiteri (1996), 49.
[11] P. Velia, *Blitzed but not Beaten*, (Malta 1985), 44, 214.
[12] Spiteri (1996), 88.

them. Territorially the rest of the Fort, and operationally the whole fort was under the direct command of the "Battery Commander, Fort Ricasoli" who at the time was Major George Fleetwood.[13]

The Coast Defence

As already pointed above, Ricasoli had a dual role during the war. It was a coastal fort defending the harbours and the south-east coast of Malta, but it was also in the path of attacking aeroplanes, and therefore hosted anti-aircraft batteries too. Between August 1938, and 1940, the military authorities erected no less than eighty pill-boxes around the coasts. The small rectangular pill-box on the rocky foreshore of Ricasoli was the first one of a line of thirteen defending the south-east coast of the East District. It is made up of concrete with vision and gun slits.[14] The main feature of pill-boxes was the rapid machine gun.[15]

Fort Ricasoli did not stand alone in the defence of the harbours. There were two rings of fortified batteries around and protecting the harbours area. The Royal Artillery's 4th Heavy Regiment, based on Fort Tignè was entrusted with the Outer Fire Command, consisting of Forts San Leonardo, Benghajsa, Bingemma, and Madliena. The Royal Malta Artillery under Lieutenant Colonel A.J. Gatt, based at Fort St Elmo included the :

> *1st Heavy Battery*, Headquarters Lascaris, manning Fort Delimara, Fort St Rocco, and Fort Ricasoli;[16]
> *2nd Heavy Battery*, Headquarters St Elmo, manning Forts Tignè and Campbell;
> *3rd Heavy Battery*, Headquarters St Elmo, manning St Elmo.

In 1939 the coastal defences were re-deployed in such a way that Ricasoli obtained the two 12-pounder quick firing guns[17] in addition to the three 6-pounders already in position by 1938.[18] The Defence Electric Lights were manned by the 24th Fortress Company, Royal Engineers.[19] The naval defences of the Grand Harbour were completed with a net closing the steel viaduct or bridge-span at the shore of Fort St Elmo arm of the breakwater, as well as a boom defence closing off the entrance of the harbour,[20] spanning from the centre of St Elmo breakwater to the tip of Ricasoli breakwater and on to the shore of Valletta at Taħt iż-Żiemel, below St Lazarus Curtain (wall).[21]

---

[13] A. Samut Tagliaferro (1976), 424.
[14] Ibid., 534-535.
[15] Ibid., 499.
[16] A. Samut Tagliaferro (1976), 406-407.
[17] Spiteri (1996), 51.
[18] A. Samut Tagliaferro (1976), 419.
[19] Spiteri (1996), 87.
[20] Ibid., 178.
[21] W.G. Ramsey (ed.), *After the Battle*, no. 10, *Malta During World War II*, (London 1975), 34.

Casemated machine gun emplacement, as well as Anti Motor Torpedo Boat stores and shelters on Bastion Number 2, facing the open sea.

The air defence

Apart from the obvious air cover provided by the Royal Air Force fighters, in order to defend the ports against air attack, the military authorities built a network of heavy anti aircraft gun batteries, deployed in concentric rings around the harbours and airfields.[22] These anti-aircraft batteries were started after 1933. They were aided by anti-aircraft searchlight companies. The first such British company was formed on 1 September 1934, although searchlight companies to provide vital sea frontage illumination for artillery engagements by night had for many years been integrated into every coast defence fire scheme.[23] The San Pietro Heavy Anti-Aircraft battery, erected in May 1939 adjacent to St Rocco Battery, was the closest one to Ricasoli, only 750 metres to the south-east.[24] It had four 4.5 inch guns in emplacements, manned by the 23rd Battery 11th Heavy Anti-Aircraft Regiment of the RMA (Territorial) under the command of Major Gerald Amato-Gauci, Troop Commander. It was strategically sited, often being the first to sight and engage the increasing raiders on their sorties over Grand Harbour and Luqa airfield. The

---

[22] Spiteri (1996), 52.
[23] A. Samut Tagliaferro (1976), 406-407.
[24] Spiteri (1996), 547-549.

208

Germans tried to wipe out this battery, it being singled out for two attacks every day: one at dawn, in the blinding easterly sun, and another at dusk. During an attack by five Junker Ju 88 (Stuka dive bombers) on 9 May 1942, a stick of bombs fell on the battery, one exploding in front of No 4 gun, killing four men (Seraphim Cauchi, Joseph Falzon, Peter Portelli, and Michael Sammut), and wounding five.[25]

Recruits Training Depot (RTD)

In May 1938, the regiment of the Royal Malta Artillery (RMA) was to be expanded from one to two coast regiments, one of which was to be a Heavy Anti-Aircraft regiment, thus increasing the establishment to 63 officers and 1442 other ranks. To cope with the sudden influx of recruits, a Training Cadre was formed at Fort Ricasoli under Major S.J. Borg with a staff of RMA instructors. The War Office authorised the formation of the RTD on 27 October 1938.[26] RMA officers and NCOs were promoted to Squad, Education, Physical Training and other disciplines' Instructors and posted there. Others were posted as clerks, cooks and in other administrative jobs. The establishment numbered 4 officers and forty-eight other ranks (both Maltese and British). The commanding officer and Regimental Sergeant Major were seconded from British units. Although Borg organised the cadre, Major S. Auld, who had had much experience in the running of similar Depots in the U.K., was specially posted to Malta on 20 April 1939.[27]

The main aim of the RTD was to absorb recruits after their enlistment and to train them in basic military subjects. Originally, each course was planned to cover twelve weeks, though in order to achieve a higher number of recruits the training period was later reduced to ten weeks.[28] On the whole the RMA staff at Ricasoli RTD did miracles in turning a motley crowd of clerks and farmers, shop assistants and masons, intellectuals and illiterates, into soldiers.[29] These ex-civilians, who had formerly led a more comfortable life, found it rather difficult at first to adapt to military duty, having to wake up early at 6.00 a.m., duck quickly straight into the cold shower-room, to be in time for the morning drill in the open parade ground just thirty minutes later. However difficult life was, especially when it came to the forced 15-mile marches around the Maltese coast, the recruits found some measure of satisfaction and relief (if not glory) when the passing out inspection parade came at the conclusion of their period of training at Ricasoli, in front of the General Officer Commanding the Troops or the Commander, Royal Artillery.

The first recruits to leave the Depot helped to form a Heavy Anti-Aircraft battery , the 5th HAA Battery, RMA. This was followed by the 6th HAA Battery and the 7th HAA Battery RMA, which were formed into the 2nd HAA Regiment, RMA on 2 December

---

[25] P. Vella, 104, 108, 296-297.
[26] A. Samut Tagliaferro (1976), 12, 434.
[27] Ibid., 414.
[28] Ibid., 415.
[29] P. Vella, 34.

1939 under Lieutenant Colonel S.J. Borg himself.[30] Some recruits also joined the King's Own Malta Regiment (KOMR) after qualifying from the Ricasoli RTD.[31]

Main Events

The first day of war spelled disaster for the coast defence at Ricasoli, but even more so to three launches of *HMS St Angelo* which, at 3.00 p.m. of 11 June 1940 had been sent outside Zonqor Point to beach a sinking Italian merchant ship. It seems that the Jetty Quarter Master failed to report the movements of the launches to the Military Authorities. Consequently, when the launches were on their return to harbour at 7.00 p.m., the coastal batteries at Fort Ricasoli and Fort St Elmo struck at the craft and were certain of achieving glory when they destroyed two of them. Little did they realise that their first wartime victims were six Maltese naval personnel. The whole incident was hushed up. It would surely have demoralised the coast defence. As a result of this unfortunate action, the Navy had to move most of its commanding staff to Lascaris too for better liaison with the other military chiefs.[32] Barely half an hour later, the second air-raid by the Regia Aeronautica materialised. Some bombs fell on Ricasoli, as well as on Cottonera, Tarxien, Sliema and Gzira.[33]

It is difficult to recount all the action or events which took place during the war, since there was a strict censorship of the media at the time and the authorities feared that a vivid detailed description of all the material losses would demoralise the population, if not the soldiers. The main newspaper *The Times of Malta* regularly published the statements by the Department of Information which only gave the number of aircraft destroyed or damaged (both allied and axis), and the number of civilian dead or wounded. The reports were stark and did not give much detail about localities raided.

One episode which surely put the harbour defence to test was the German onslaught on the aircraft carrier *Illustrious*, which had anchored at Parlatorio Wharf, at the mouth of French Creek on 16 January 1941. Immediately, and for three days running, the Luftwaffe sent in wave after wave of dive bombers intent on sinking the aircraft carrier at her berth. The position of the ship put Fort Ricasoli straight in the path of most dives. A curtain of steel rose from the anti-aircraft batteries around the harbours. The gunners of Fort Ricasoli, same as those of St Elmo, San Pietro, San Leonardo, the Dockyard, Crucifix Hill, Kordin, Barrakka Gardens, Tignè, Tal-Qroqq, ta' Cejlu, Hompesch, and Tal-Borg fired as quickly as their guns allowed them at the bold Germans, helping the RAF fighters in their task of interception. Despite their fierce dive bombing the German Stukas were not accurate enough and only hit the *Illustrious* once, but they hit almost everything else in the neighbourhood.[34] Ricasoli suffered no casualties during those three action filled days.

---

[30] A. Samut Tagliaferro (1976), 13.

[31] Wismayer, 209.

[32] P. Vella, 10-11.

[33] Boffa, 8.

[34] Ibid., 34-35.

Another unfortunate incident happened on 30 April 1941, involving recruits of the RTD. Some soldiers who were on a boat on their way back from the RTD at Ricasoli to Kalkara and Valletta were raided by three axis bombers in mid-harbour. Two bombs fell within short range of the boats which broke to pieces. Joseph Vella and Joseph Calleja, both gunners of the RTD, were drowned. All others were saved.[35] Two days later, the same members of the RTD, together with other RMA soldiers, dived into the mine-infested seas off the coast of Ricasoli to save personnel from *HMS Jersey*, when the destroyer sank after striking a mine at the harbour entrance.[36] The moment of greatest glory for war-torn Ricasoli came early in the morning of 26 July 1941, when its coast defence helped in no small way in repulsing the Italian E Boat attack on the harbours.

The Italian E-Boat Attack on the harbours, 25-26 July 1941

On the 24 July 1941 a convoy reached Malta harbours bringing in supplies needed for the defence of Malta and for arming the aeroplanes based here and which, in their turn, were harassing Italian convoys on their way to the front in Africa. The Italians therefore decided to launch a sea-borne attack on the Malta harbours in order to destroy shipping berthed there and any supplies not yet unloaded. Such daring action, using the motor torpedo boats, or the human torpedo boats, had been perfected by the Italian Navy since the First World War, although the idea of surprise attacks on harbours with small craft was very old indeed. It was Fra Giovanni Francesco Ricasoli himself who had led such an attack on Tripoli three centuries earlier. After some initial failures at Alexandria and at Gibraltar, the Italians successfully crippled the British cruiser *HMS York* at Suda Bay in Crete on 25 March 1941.[37]

The attacking force and the Plan

Table XX shows the units which took part in the action and the mission of each.

The following is an outline of the plan of attack. The flotilla would leave Augusta at 6.15 p.m. of 25 July to rendezvous at point C, 34 kilometres bearing 40 degrees (roughly north-east) from St Elmo Point, with the sloop *Diana* (she had been built in 1940 as Mussolini's private yacht)[38] carrying the nine MTMs and also towing the MTL carrying the two SLCs in turn. The two MAS sailed in formation with MAS 452 towing the MTSM. This part of the plan was faithfully accomplished by 11.00 p.m. as stipulated.

At point C the *Diana* would launch the nine MTMs which would proceed to Point B, 8 kilometres bearing 40 degrees of St Elmo. The MTMs would be led by the MTSM, the

[35] Ibid., 22.
[36] P. Vella, 34.
[37] Ibid., 41.
[38] Ramsay, 37.

					Table XX		
				The X - MAS (Tenth Light Flotilla)			
No.	*Type*	*Name*	*Crew*	*Captain*	*Description*	*Main Task*	
1	E-Boat Carrier despatch boat	Diana	n.a.	Capt. Mario di Muro	1568 ton sloop	to carry the MTMs and to tug the MTL to point C	
1	MAS (*Motoscafo Anti Sommergibile*)	451	8	Sub-Lieutenant Giorgio Sciolette	18 metre motor torpedo boat	for escort and rescue. To tug MTL from point C to point B	
1	ditto	452	8	Lieutenant Gio. Battista Parodi	ditto	for escort and rescue. To tug the MTSM to point B	
1	SLC (*Siluro a Lenta Corsa*)		2	Major Teseo Tesei	7 - metre human torpedo sumbarine/ boat. Also called "maiali" (pigs) baby submarines	to blast the net under the bridge of the Ft St Elmo Breakwater	
12	ditto		2	Capt. Franco Costa	ditto	to attack sumbarines in Marsamxett harbour	
1	MTL (*Motoscafo Turismo Lento*)		6	Steersman Tindaro Paratore	baby sumbarine carrier	to carry SLCs to Point A and to rescue Tesei's SLC	
1	MTS (*Motoscafo Turismo Silurante*)		2	Capt. Giorgio Giobbe	flotilla leader	to lead MTMs from point C to point A and to pick up Costa's SLC	
1	MTM (*Motoscafo Turismo Modificato*)	1	1	Sub-Lieut. Carlo Bosio	Motor torpedo boats. Also called E-Boats or barchini. 5 metres flat bottomed outboard engine at 50 k.p.h. with a 300 kg charge at bow	To lead the other E-boats through the blown net	
1	ditto	2	1	Sub-Lieut. Roberto Frassetto	ditto	to blast the net if Tesei missed	
1	ditto	3	1	Sub-Lieut. Artistide Carabelli	ditto	reserve of MTM 2	
1	ditto	4	1	Signalman Vittorio Marchisio	ditto	to destroy shipping in the harbour creeks	
1	ditto	5	1	2nd Chief Vincenzo Montanari	ditto	ditto	
1	ditto	6	1	2nd Chief Alessandro Foglieri	ditto	ditto	
1	ditto	7	1	2nd Chief Enrico Pedrini	ditto	ditto	
1	ditto	8	1	boatswain Pietro Zaniboni	ditto	ditto	
1	ditto	9	1	Chief 3rd Class Fiorenzo Caprioti	ditto	to attack any interfering boats	
16			37[1]				

[1] excluding the "Diana".

latter in turn being tugged by MAS 452. The *Diana* would lie in waiting at Point C. The MTL, still carrying the two SLCs would be tugged by MAS 451 during this second part of the transit. This operation too was successfully accomplished by the stipulated time, 1.34 a.m. of 26 July. These operations were thus planned in order to avoid detection and not to forfeit the important element of surprise.

At Point B, MAS 451 would release the MTL, which would carry further the two SLCs to Point A, 1 kilometre bearing 40 degrees of St Elmo Point, while MAS 452 released the MTSM which would lead the nine MTMs to Point A. The two MAS would wait at Point A for rescue operations. Point A was reached one hour behind schedule at 3.00 a.m.

At Point A all the smaller craft capable of carrying the charges and exploding, that is the two SLCs and the nine MTMs would be launched or released by the MTL and the MTSM, which would wait for rescue and support at Point A: Tesei's SLC to blast and force open the the net at the bridge of St Elmo breakwater; Costa's SLC to attack the submarines in Marsamxett Harbour; and the nine MTMs each with its own separate task as explained in the last column of the table above. The first explosion at the St Elmo mole was scheduled for 4.30 a.m., when a diversionary attack on Mqabba airport (as Luqa airport was called by the Italians) was also planned. After the attack, all the thirteen floating men would be picked up by either the MTL or the MTSM. The men riding Costa's SLC and those steering MTMs 4 to 8 realised that their rescue was highly improbable since their mission was to penetrate deep into the harbours.

The attack

The mission was ill-fated from the start since the flotilla, unlike earlier single craft reconnaissance missions would be, and in fact was detected by radar at 10.30 p.m., shortly before reaching Point C. Therefore all the gunners at the defences had been on action stations for a long time when the illuminated area was lit as soon as the first explosion was heard at 4.45 a.m. Also, most of these small craft, although being sophisticated and ingenious inventions, were highly susceptible to break down during actual missions. Although the invention of the radar was only suspected by the Italian seamen, this does not detract from their obvious valour. The diversionary attack on Luqa airfield came at 4.14 a.m., a little too early for distracting the attention of the coast defence.[39] Costa's SLC developed a fault and had to turn back. Both Tesei's SLC and MTM 2 failed to explode. When their reserve MTM 3 hit the net at 4.45 a.m., it detonated the MTM 2 charge also, producing a great explosion which brought down the left hand span of the steel bridge. This effectively sealed the harbour further. Within six minutes of the start of the battle, most of the other smaller units of the expedition were destroyed or crippled by the Royal Malta Artillery gunners from Forts St Elmo, Ricasoli or St Rocco, while they were courageously trying to force the main entrance to Grand Harbour after the

---

[39] Ibid., 35.

mishap at the bridge. The Royal Air Force Hurricane IICs aircrafts of Nos. 126, 185 and 251 Squadrons finished off the two MASs. Only eleven men of MAS 452 escaped back to the *Diana* and home, after successfully boarding and directing the MTSM to the mother sloop. Except for the survivors of MAS 452, no other Italian returned from Malta; fifteen men died, including Captain Moccagatta and the valorous Tesei; eighteen were made prisoner.

Ricasoli's Part in the Battle

Since the attack materialised mainly from a North-Easterly direction, Fort St Elmo bore the brunt of the fighting. Even logistically St Elmo stood out as the centre of the defence since its Cavalier hosted the Harbour Fire Command of the Coast Defence batteries which guarded the entrances to the harbours. Orders were received at Ricasoli by standing orders from St Elmo, although the overall command of the Islands' coast defence was situated at Coastal Defence operations room, part of the War Headquarters, deep inside Lascaris bastion near Castille in Valletta. Therefore although Ricasoli RMA and the 1st Battalion, Cheshire RA regiment took a conspicuous part in the action, it was still peripheral to the part played by the gunners at St Elmo who claim most success. Ricasoli guns in action were the 6 pounders A, B, and C, and the Bofors anti-aircraft. There were another four 6-pounders at St Elmo, together with other Bofors at St Elmo and Tigne.

Since the breeze came from North-West, the MTMs were drifting dangerously towards Ricasoli when they shut off their engines. Frassetto had to start his engine to get clear.[40] The Ricasoli guns could only engage the leading MTM since they were advancing directly towards them in line formation. Moreover, the smoke of discharge blew over the gun telescopes and blinded the layers at Ricasoli and the No 1s who could not correct their fire. Since the St Elmo guns fired at right angle to the MTM`s direction, they were in a better position to aim than those at Ricasoli.[41] The 1st Battalion, Cheshire Regiment's medium machine gun on the Ricasoli foreshore claimed its victim at the beginning of the action as soon as the illuminated area was exposed. It engaged and sunk a small craft (probably one of the MTMs) east of Ricasoli Point at close range.[42] At 4.50 a.m., Fort St Rocco's 6-inch guns under Major G. Micallef-Eynaud hit the MTL when it was under cover of the three-mile (five kilometre) buoy. When two abandoned MTMs were boarded again by their men due east of St Elmo, all the coastal guns, including those at Ricasoli engaged them. The fire and the multi-coloured lights of the tracers gave a spectacular, though deadly display of light which the local population watched in awe even at this early hour of the morning, not only from the nearest places of the harbour area, but even from the higher though distant vantage points at Rabat and Mdina.

---

[40] H.A.R. Ferro, "The Battle of Valletta - 26 July 1941", in *The Malta Land Force Journal*, July 1971, No. 7, (Malta), 59.
[41] Ibid., 52.
[42] Ibid., 63.

In conclusion one may note that the battle was a triumph for the 6-pounder 10 hundredweight twin equipment with its high rate of fire, speed of applying corrections and deadly accuracy.[43] The entire credit for maintaining the security of the harbours must go to the Harbour Coastal Defences, decisively helped by the new invention of radar. They had saved the harbour and the shipping therein from the SLCs and the MTMs. When the SLC was developed in the mid-1930s, Tesei already had Malta in mind.

The later course of the War

Although the attack on the harbours was intrepid and dangerous for the defenders, Ricasoli, together with the whole Island passed through its worst ordeal in the spring of 1942, when Hitler and Mussolini had decided to try to subdue Malta by an invasion, preceded by intense bombing of the airfields and all other military establishments. In April 1942 alone, over 6700 tons of bombs were dropped on Malta. The blitz continued until mid-May, when the axis powers realised that Malta would not submit by air-raids alone. Fortunately for Malta, the 80,000 men needed for the invasion of Malta were requested by Field Marshall Rommel in summer that year. He desperately needed them for his final drive towards Alexandria. Malta was the most densely bombed place on Earth, considering its small area of 250 square kilometres. On 26 April, no less than 55 German aircraft attacked Grand Harbour and several other localities. The anti-aircraft artillery were continuously in action. The fiercest aerial combats on Ricasoli took place on 9 and 10 May 1942. On the 9th, two raids hit Grand Harbour. During one of these raids, San Pietro Battery was hit, as already seen earlier on. Fort Ricasoli received a direct hit and four men of the Cheshire Regiment died. That evening the sky above the harbour looked like the outside of some fantastic wasps' nest, with aircraft milling about in a breathless hectic rough-house.[44] Sunday 10 May was no less grim for the defence. There were two raids in the morning, one concentrated on the Dockyard, and another two raids after 5.00 p.m. During those forty-eight hours alone, the enemy lost 22 aircraft, six of which were downed by the anti-aircraft artillery.

The monotonous military life of the fortress was only occasionally broken by the odd screening of a movie or the visit of the *Whizz Bangs Concert Party*, a dance company made up of six British girls who not only worked at the operations rooms at Headquarters, Lascaris, but who also toured barracks, gun-sites, searchlight batteries and aerodromes in Malta giving shows to servicemen. In fact they visited Ricasoli regularly upon request by Major and Mrs George Fleetwood who were staunch supporters of the concert party, and who presided over dinner in honour of the *Whizz Bangs*. The major also assisted backstage during the show![45]

The ordeal lingered on through the rough summer of 1942. When the Governor of Malta had decided to surrender, a substantial part of the convoy *Pedestal* got through in August,

---

[43] Ibid., 65.
[44] *The Times of Malta*, 11 May 1942, 1, 4.
[45] C. Ratcliff, "Carve Malta on My Heart", serialised in *Malta News*, pt 10, 12 July 1974.

bringing enough supplies for Malta to withstand for some time longer. By November 1942, Rommel's Afrika Korp, had been expelled from Egyptian soil after the decisive battle of El Alamein. Soon the second great siege of Malta was lifted. Fort Ricasoli and its men had successfully withstood the onslaught of the enemy. The modifications done at the Fort both in its structure and in its armament had been effective and had obtained the desired results. The Fort had suffered though, especially between December 1941 and December 1942. All of the twenty-one casualties of the Cheshire Regiment during the war died during those thirteen months. The Maltese men of the RMA and the RTD also paid their share for the final victory. The Fort itself lost Blondel's Governor's House, and Valperga's Main Gate. Only the latter was subsequently reconstructed after 1958.

16

Ricasoli after the War

Ricasoli's history after the Second World War follows the same pattern as that of Malta. Same as for Malta, the fort went through reconstruction; redeployment, rundown and evacuation of military forces; industrialisation; commercialisation; and finally, tourist development. During the post war period, missiles were developed and perfected. These new weapons rendered the coastal batteries, such as at Fort Ricasoli, as well as anti-aircraft batteries obsolete. By 1960 most forts and batteries in Malta including Ricasoli, were closed down and disarmed by the army. By 1956, the fort had been taken over by the Admiralty and turned into a Royal Navy Barracks, temporarily hosting, as it had done all too often between 1840 and 1918, a huge number of different crews in barracks. From 1800 to 1813, Ricasoli had been occupied by the British Military Forces in the name of the King of Naples under the title of 'perpetual user'. When Maitland became first British Governor of Malta, all forts became 'crown property'. On 21 July 1964, two months before Malta became independent, a defence agreement of ten years was signed between the Governments of the United Kingdom and Malta. By Article 3 of the annex, the rights and facilities to be used by the British forces were defined. Although many forts and barracks were still held by the British, Ricasoli was evacuated on 21 September 1964. It had become property of the Government of Malta.[1]

Reconstruction

During World War II, Fort Ricasoli had suffered two devastating direct hits: one of them completely destroyed Blondel's Governors House together with the upper part of Valperga's Main Gate; another hit blasted and shattered the porte-cochere.[2] The Main Gate was rebuilt after August 1958 by drydocks craftsmen under the direction of the civil engineers in the Chief's Department, Admiralty.[3] The four spiralling columns flanking

---

[1] Keasing's Almanac, 1964; L. Zahra, "Fort Verdala and Fort Ricasoli", in *Malta News*, 4 February 1976, 3.
[2] H. Braun, 7.
[3] NAM, Plans, Ricasoli, 251 and 279.

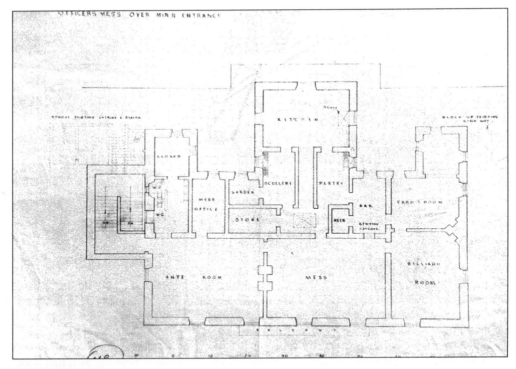

1958 archival plan of the proposed reconstruction of the Governor's House (Officers' Mess), over the Main Gate. The house was never rebuilt.
(Courtesy: NAM)

the gate were reconstructed with five instead of six twists.[4] The other two buildings were never re-erected, and the curtain flanking the Main Gate to its right (West) still bears the scars of war.

The Malta Drydocks tank cleaning installation

During the late 1950s and the early 1960s, the Malta Drydocks was in a state of transition from a naval to a commercial dockyard. Since it started servicing and repairing an increasing amount of tankers, it needed an installation for tank cleaning. Fort Ricasoli's position near the entrance to harbour, and the space available for large tankers in Bighi Bay, made the fort an ideal location for such a facility. Work by Drydocks employees started shortly before 24 June 1964.[5] It was completed at a cost of £600,000 and was fully operational by 4 October 1965.[6] It was opened by Sir Anthony Mamo,

---

[4] J.M. Wismayer, "Fort Ricasoli", in *The Sunday Times of Malta*, 19 July 1998, 47.
[5] *The Malta Review*, 24 June 1964, 8.
[6] *The Malta Year Book*, 1966, 23.

The Malta Drydocks Tank Cleaning Facilities boom equipment, (1965) at Ricasoli Steps.

the Acting Governor-General on 1 December 1965.[7] During the ceremony, the then General manager of Malta Drydocks, N.S. Thompson, claimed that the installation was the most modern such facility in Europe. Indeed it still serves the same purpose most efficiently.

The installation is made up of two parts: jetty and approach (in front of the steps which lead to the Main Gate) - 100 metres long and capable of receiving tankers of 85,000 deadweight tons; and the reception and treatment area (in the ditch starting from Rinella Creek right up to the salient angle of Bastion No 6) - where tank washing is carried out at a rate of 2000 tons per hour, simultaneously with the disposal of oil ballast at a maximum rate of 2000 tons per hour.[8] The jetty is complete with boom equipment, pump room on the foreshore, and gate. The pipes lead into the ditch, that is where there is the reception and treatment area. This latter area comprises four large 3000 ton tanks, office block, boiler house, water wash tank, transfer pumps, sludge incinerator, condensate tank, observation tank, and effluent discharge pipe that lead to the open sea at Wied Ghammieq.

---

[7] Ibid., 1967, 11, 22.
[8] Ibid., 22.

219

The installation does not only clean tankers for drydocking, but repairs and surveys tankers for repair. Work goes on round the clock, and security is also guaranteed. The three main tasks performed are: washing with hot water at 60 degrees at a pressure of 14 kilogrammes per square centimetre; gas-freeing and trunking, with five compressors and eight ventilators; and steam supply at the jetty. The installation also makes distilled water for sale to ships. The whole area is strictly regulated for safety according to the Institute of petroleum Codes for Installations storing Class A Petroleum.[9] For any lover of Malta's architectural heritage, the installation is an eyesore. Great steel tanks and pipes, together with modern offices and constructions for pumps and boilers, are out of tune with the fine weathered limestone fortifications of the baroque era.

1964 - 1977: Into oblivion

Fort Ricasoli was handed over to the Government of Malta in 1964 by the Admiralty in impeccable shape, newly whitewashed and all installations functioning. It is a pity that the government had no plans about the future use of most of the services establishments which it inherited, and since Fort Ricasoli fell into disuse, it fell prey to vandalism, and became derelict in a short time.[10] The well-known commentator of a Sunday newspaper, Roamer, first suggested that some of these establishments should be turned into a tourist resort, since they command positions that are the prospector's dream. Although the Department of Information denied such allegation,[11] by 1970 surely the fort was in an abandoned and ruinous state.[12] Fortunately, most of the relics and paintings inside the chapel were transferred to the National Museum, and were thus saved from pillage.[13]

In March 1972, a new seven-year Military Facilities agreement was signed by the Governments of Malta and the United Kingdom, and many other military establishments were also handed over to the Maltese government. Public suggestions for the future use of all the existing vacant establishments were sought. One interesting suggestion was that of transferring the prisons from Paola to Ricasoli, thus releasing a vast area at Paola for future residential development. However, a special commission set up for the same purpose suggested that the fort should be given over to industrial or tourist development.[14]

Ever since the mid-1950s, Malta was fast industrialising in order to be able to transform its economy from one based on defence spending by Great Britain, into one that was more self-supporting. Many industrial estates were built, and the programme was completed in the 1970s with the building of such estates at Hal Far, Kordin and St Rocco. The industrial estate between St Rocco and Xghajra lies about one and a half kilometres

---

[9] *Malta Drydocks: At Your Service in the Centre of the Mediterranean* (booklet), 14-15.
[10] "Roamer", in *The Sunday Times of Malta*, 11 April 1965, 7.
[11] Malta, Department of Information, *Malta Review*, 28 April 1965, 6.
[12] L. Zahra, "The History of Fort Ricasoli", in *The Sunday Times of Malta*, 6 December 1970, 30.
[13] Ibid., (1976), 3.
[14] N. Samut Tagliaferro, (1976), 118-119.

The main soldiers' barracks of Ricasoli, (Hospitaller period), one time also used for hospital and later for bonded stores.

away from the nearest bastion of the fort, however, it was named Ricasoli Industrial Estate after the historic fort.[15]

The Bonded Stores

In 1977 the parade ground and the great land front barrack rooms were transformed into Bonded Stores for those merchants who did not have enough and immediate warehouse space for all their imported goods. In order to transform the fort into such a station, alterations were necessary. The north-west (Ricasoli Point) half of the fort, which includes the Church, the Officers' Quarters and Married Quarters was separated from the rest of the fort by a twelve course high wall, and thus continued in its state of abandonment. Unfortunately, since the trailers with their cargo of containers could not possibly enter the fort by way of the old Main Gate, a new road into the fort was built. It starts at Wied Ghammieq, flanks the northern ravelin, and enters the fort through the No 5 curtain and the retrenchment that had to be both breached. The deep ditch there was also infilled.

---

[15] It is a pity that many Maltese are oblivious of the historic fortress, and are only aware of the industrial \ estate when they hear the name Ricasoli.

Other structural changes in the fort included the building of ten course high partitions in the long barrack rooms in order to separate the goods according to the importer. At the new gate (or rather breach), a large heavy metal mash gate was installed, and immediately inside the fort, a raised stone booth was constructed for the Revenue Security Officers who controlled entry and exit of vehicles.

By 1982, it was clear enough that some importers were unhappy with the facilities being afforded by the Ricasoli Bonded Stores for various reasons, including lack of security from the outside, since entry into the fort could be gained from the abandoned part. There was also lack of security against theft, fire, vandalism or damage inside the stores themselves, since the walls separating the cubicles did not reach the ceiling but were only ten courses high, and were built on the existing ground, not on solid foundations. The Chamber of Commerce complained about lack of sanitary facilities and the existence of manholes that led to the old countermines outside the fort.[16] It also contended that there was not enough space for all the goods in the stores, and therefore much cargo was being deposited in the open in the parade ground. Although the government of the day tried to rebut all this criticism, and assured the Chamber of Commerce that necessary action was already being taken,[17] the Ricasoli Bonded Stores were never popular with Maltese importers, and by 1988, they had stopped operating, and Fort Ricasoli was again left in an abandoned state until the present.

Ricasoli today and plans for a heritage park

As soon as the bonded stores closed their gates indefinitely, plans for the future development and use of Fort Ricasoli were drafted by the newly established Planning Authority as well as by the Secretariat for Tourism. In 1994 plans were in hand to develop the fort into a heritage and cultural park based on the island's history and village life, incorporating entertainment, enactments and leisure and catering facilities.[18] But although a British firm had already shown great interest in investing several million pounds in developing the fort, the project did not materialise. The idea was not dropped, however. In April 1997, the government had short-listed three companies after submitting similar plans to the Planning Authority. That year, the Authority published a development brief about Ricasoli, confirming the intention to turn it into a historical cultural theme park to include various recreational facilities and limited tourist accommodation together with the restoration of the fort. A major constraint was the oil tank cleaning facilities in the ditch and foreshore.[19] It further stated that the development should be carried out by one single consortium; the definite plans were to be submitted by September 1997; and

---

[16] Chamber of Commerce sub-committee, "Ricasoli Bonded Stores" in *Commercial Courier*, 6 September 1982, 620-621.

[17] "Il-Verita` dwar il-Bonded Stores tar-Rikazli", in *it-Torca*, 10 October 1982, 15, 22.

[18] J.A. Mizzi, "Fort Ricasoli to be turned into a heritage park," in *The Sunday Times of Malta*, 8 May 1994, 1.

the consortium chosen would be bound to spend at least £m1.5 million to restore the walls and the historic buildings inside the fort.[20]

The Ricasoli theme park or tourist complex plan seemed good on paper. However, until March 1998, it seems not to have attracted enough serious private investors, since most often, the latter only venture where there is little risk.[21] On 2 April 1998, a press release issued by the Vintage Cars Association suggested that Fort Ricasoli might be turned into a vintage cars or automobile museum, but there was no official reaction to it by the Planning Authority or the government.

From March to May 1999, the fort hosted a purposely built colosseum for the shooting of Steven Spielberg's film *The Gladiators*. For weeks on end the parade ground was turned into a Roman Forum, and amongst Ricasoli's latest inhabitants were famous actors, hundreds of extras, and also exotic animals such as elephants and tigers who gave birth to cubs there. The wall that was built across the fort in 1977 when it had been turned into Bonded Stores was pulled down for the shooting of the film and thus Ricasoli was no longer physically divided. This was not the first time that the fort was used as a set for shooting films, since it lies very near to the Mediterranean Film Studios in the Wied Ghammieq to St Rocco area, but surely the 1999 shots were the most spectacular.

Something needs be done for Fort Ricasoli. It must be developed in such a way as to put it to use without in any way detracting from its historical, architectural and military character. The fort is evidence and part of Malta's heritage. It witnessed more than three centuries of Malta's history, and not only military. Fort Ricasoli is part of world heritage. It should not suffer further abandon. But while the Maltese people go about their daily chores, quite oblivious of their glorious past, the fort still lies in a derelict state. Most buildings have been left to rot. The limestone of the bastions is slowly sliding into the Mediterranean, resting where it had formed twenty million years ago.

---

[19] G. Cassar, The proactive role of the Planning Authority, " in *The Times*, 11 February 1998, 23.
[20] Television Malta, News Broadcast, April 1997.
[21] "Editorial", *The Malta Independent*, 16 March 1998.

Glossary

Bailiff - a senior knight.

Banchette - A passage situated just behind the *parapet,* whence the defenders could fire on the enemy.

Bastion -A part of the fortress jutting out of the main line of the wall intended to cover all ground just outside the fort. The bastion developed in modern fortification from the ancient tower.

Battlements - a *parapet* with *embrasures.*

Caponnier -an *outwork* consisting of a covered passage in the *ditch* joining the main walls to the *ravelin.* The defenders could station themselves in the *caponnier* to fire on troops inside the *ditch.*

Casemate - the wall could be hollow in order to afford space for guns or for rooms.

Cavalier - an *outwork* made up of a small fortification in front of a *bastion.*

Commandery - a (smaller) estate in Europe that was administered by a knight.

Common Treasury - the central financial institution of the Order of St John. It was made up of nine procurators or director-knights under the presidency of the Grand Commander or head of the Langue of Provence. It was responsible for every material aspect of the running of the Order and its Government.

Convent - the Order and the country where it was established, such as Rhodes between 1310 and 1523, or Malta between 1530 and 1798.

Cordon - a course of rounded stone protruding from the face of the walls just below the P*arapet*. Apart from its aesthetic value, it could make scaling more difficult.

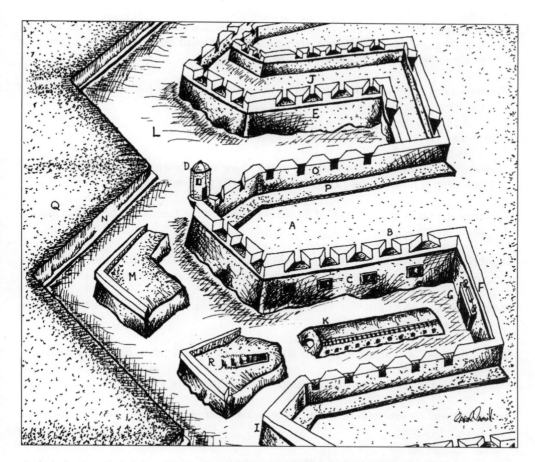

Artist's impression of the main parts of baroque fortification, including:

A.	bastion	G.	main gate	M.	counterguard
B.	embrasure	H.	scarp	N.	counterscarp
C.	casemated gun emplacement	I.	salient angle	O.	parapet
D.	vedette or sentry box	J.	fausse-braye	P.	banchette
E.	flank	K.	caponier of communication	Q.	glacis
F.	curtain	L.	ditch	R.	ravelin

Council - together with the *Grand Master,* the Council of the Order decided all matters of importance in the running of the Order and Malta. The Ordinary Council was made up of the Grand Master and the head knight of each Langue. The Complete Council was made up of the same dignitaries with two other senior knights from each Langue. The latter decided matters of greater importance.

Counterfort - the thick masonry behind the walls.

Counterguard - a diamond-shaped outwork in front of a *bastion.*

Countermine - mines and underground passageways that lead from the bastion to under the ditch and glacis. At the extreme end there would be a room with gunpowder ready to be fired if the enemy is heard digging.

Counter-scarp - the wall of a *ravelin* or *counterguard* which faces the main walls of the fortress. It is the outer wall of the *ditch*.

Covert-way - a passage on top of the *counterscarp*.

Crown-work - a small fort or *outwork* in the shape of a crown, that is it is made up of one central *bastion* and two lateral demi (half)-bastions.

Curtain - the main straight wall of a fortress, between the bastions. The gate is usually in its centre.

Dead Ground - land outside the walls which cannot be seen, therefore shot at, from the *flanks* of the *bastions* where there was usually greatest concentration of ordnance.

Demi-bastion - a half *bastion*, having only one *flank*. Its *salient angle* is flanked by a *curtain* and only one face.

Ditch - the land just outside the walls was dug up to great depth to harass the attackers.

Embrasure - the indentures on the parapets where the guns were placed.

Entrenchment - a low wall of fortification usually defending a long, but less important stretch of coast.

Face - the *scarp* or outer part of the wall or *bastion*.

Fausse-braye - a wall running parallel to and lower than the main walls of the fortress situated in front of the *ditch*.

Flank - the side wall of a *bastion*. It usually hosted the guns since the flank guarded and dominated the *curtain* wall, the main gates and the next bastion.

Fra - the title given to any member of the Order, literally meaning brother, since these members made the vows of obedience, poverty and chastity.

Glacis - the land outside the walls and outworks of a fortress was levelled in a gentle gradient so that the defenders on the parapets could see and fire at the attacking forces.

Grand Marshall - the head knight of the Langue of Auvergne was also head of the Order's military forces, including infantry, cavalry and navy.

Grand Master - the head of the Order of St John and also feudal prince of Malta.

Keep - the innermost, strongest and usually the highest place of a fort, usually having walls which could be defended independently of the main parts of the fort. It was meant to host the troops making the last stand.

Outworks - parts of a fortress lying outside the main walls, affording a first line of defence. These included the *ravelin; cavalier; ditch; fausse-braye; caponnier; glacis;* and *countermines.*

Palissade - pointed logs driven into the ground and used as a first line of defence or as an advanced gate in front of the drawbridge and main gate.

Parapet - the uppermost three or four courses of a wall behind which the defenders could position themselves.

Place of arms - the main ground of the fort where drills and calls for arms were effected.

Porte-cochere - the inside of the main gate of a fortress.

Priory - a (large) estate of the Order of St John in Europe.

Ravelin - a kite-shaped outwork in front of a curtain wall.

Retrenchement - a wall built inside a fortress in order to afford a second line of defence in case of an occupation by the attacking troops of any weaker main bastion. A retrenchment would effectively divide a fort into two parts, with the stronger part becoming a keep.

Salient angle - the outermost point or tip of a bastion.

Tenaille - a series of successive curtain walls in zig-zag plan, each one defending the other, and with no bastions in between.

Terreplain - the earth between the masonry which formed the outer cover of the walls.

Traverses - parapets and low walls, built at right angle to, and on the walls or covert ways in order to defend lateral parts of the same walls from flanking fire, especially if parts of the same walls would have been scaled.

Conversion Tables

Linear Measurement:

1 canna = 8 palmi = 6 feet 10½ inches = 2.095 metres
1 foot   = 0.3048 metres

Weight:

1 cantara / quintale / qantar (hundredweight / cwt) = 20 wizna = 100 rotolos = 79.378 kg.
1 wizna = 5 rotolos   = 3.968 kg.
1 rotolo = 30 uqija / oncie / ounces = 0.793 kg.
1 ounce   = 0.026 kg.

Volume:

1 modd (salma) = 16 tomna (tummoli) = 2.909 hectolitre (h.l.)
1 tomna   = 6 mondelli   = 0.1818 h.l.
1 mondello   = 10 misure   = 0.0303 h.l.
1 misura   = 0.0030 h.l. (*circa*)

Currency:

1 scudo = 12 tari = 240 grani = 1440 piccioli = 1 shilling 8 pence = 20 pence =
8 (Maltese) cents
1 taro = 20 grani   = 120 piccioli
1 grano = 6 piccioli
£1 = 20 shillings = 240 pence
£m1 = 100 cents

note: when the Maltese currency was changed to the British one in the 1830s, the *scudo* was equivalent to 1 shilling 8 pence. One must appreciate that since the seventeenth and eighteenth centuries, there has been continuous inflation, devaluation of the currencies, and changing cost of living.

Appendices

APPENDIX I

Approval of Bailiff Alessandro Orsi's proposal for the construction of San Petronio (Orsi) Tower[1], 29 January 1629.

Fabbrica d'una Torre con casamatta proposta dal Signor Commendatore ORSI a sue proprie spese nella bocca del Porto.

Die eadem. Havendo il Serenissimo signor Gran Maestro esposto al Venerando Consiglio il desiderio del signor Commendatore Fra Alessandro Orsi di voler a spese proprie far edificare una Torre con Casamatta (conforme al disegno dimostrato) nella bocca del Porto, e punta della Renella gia detta sottile, con che si difficultarebbe assai la fuga alli schiavi, Sua Altezza Serenissima et il Venerando Consiglio approvando e gradendo l'affetto e lodevole pensiero di esso commendatore verso il servitio della Religione hanno dato il loro consenso à quest' opera, come molto necessaria, e già altrevolte ordinata per il suddetto fine, et alla medesima altezza rimasero il dar tutti gl'ordini opportuni, e convenienti alla totale, et intiera assegutione di essa.

APPENDIX II

Genealogy of the Ricasoli Family[2]

Fra Giovanni Francesco Ricasoli, born (b.) 1602 - died (d.) 1673, 5th son (s.) of
Paolo, (b.) 1561 - d. 1620. married (m.) 1589 to Contessina Serristori. 6th issue and 4th
    s. of
Filippo, b. 1511 - d. 1600. m. to Maddalena di Ubertino di Rucellai. 4th issue and 3rd s.
    of

---

[1] AOM 109, f. 164v.
[2] Passerini, opposite p. 95, and opposite p. 57.

Gaspero, b. 1472 - d. 1521. m. to a) 1502 Piera Arrighi, and b) 1520 Dianora Galli. 2nd
    s. of

Gaspero di Andrea, b. 1425 - d. 1472. M. in 1470 to Annalena Canigiani. 6th issue and
    4th s. of

Andrea, d. 1457. M. 1412 to Lapa Tosinghi. 3rd s. of

Rinaldo, b. 1357 - d. 1392. m. to a) Andrea Salimbeni di Siena and b) Ghita di Cione
    del Frate. 3rd issue and 2nd s. of

Ranieri, b. 1322 (?). 2nd s. of

Rinaldo, d. 1318. m. to Lapa. 2nd s. of

Ranieri di Alberto, b. 1247 - d. 1268. M. to Margherita di Angiolieri. 2nd s. of

Alberto, b. 1213 - d. 1253. m. in 1229 to Frisia Pannocchieschi di Travale. 2nd s. of

Ranieri, d. 1203. m. to Adelisia. 1st s. of

Berengarius, b. 1136. S. of

Guido, b. 1095 - d. 1120. 3rd issue and 2nd s. of

Albert, m. to Adelasia Ranieri. 2nd s. of

Hugh, b. 1059. 2nd s. of

Rudolf, s. of

Geremias, s. of

Hildebrand.

APPENDIX III

*Inscription on Giovanni Francesco Ricasoli's tombstone in the Conventual Church of
St John in Valletta*[3]

Deo exercituum
FR. JOANNES FRANCISCUS DE RICASOLIS
Praeceptor Commandar S. Magni de Gradulo S. Jo. De Bettona
Et s. Sepulchri de Florentia
Hoc tumulum vivens posuit A.D MDCLXIIII

APPENDIX IV

*Foundation of Fort Ricasoli by Fra Giovanni Francesco Ricasoli. Entry in the register
of State matters of the Council of the Order (Liber Conciliorum Status)*[4]

Si rendono grazie al Commendatore Ricasoli per il suo generoso donativo, il quale
si applichi nella fortificatione della punta della bocca del porto, e si chiamerà
RICASOLI.

---

[3] H.P. Scicluna, *The Church of St John in Valletta*, (Rome 1955), 315.
[4] AOM 261, f. 166.

Die XV Mensis Junii 1670. Havendo il Commendatore Fra Giovanni Francesco Ricasoli fatto donativo alla religione di 20 mila scudi, per supplire in qualche parte alle grandissime spese, che gli conviene di fare nella fabrica di tante fortificationi, l'Eminentissimo e Serenissimo Signore Gran Maestro conformemente al parer di tutti I venerandi Consiglieri, chiamato in pieno Consiglio il detto Commendatore gli rese molte gratie à nome suo, e di tutta la Religione per un'attione così pia, così esemplare e così generosa; et insieme fù determinato unanimi voto dal venerando Consiglio che detto danaro si applichi nella fortificatione che dovrà dimandarsi Ricasoli, et in essa debbano porsi le armi di detto Commendatore e collocarsi nel luogo più cospicuo della medesima con iscritione a nome della Religione in gloria e memoria di un Religioso così zelante, et in esempio, e stimolo di tutti gli altri.

APPENDIX V

(Partial) list of Commissioners of Cotoner Foundation

There were three knight commissioners at any one time. According to a decree of 13 August 1693, one had to be Aragonese, and the other two of different nationality, serving for a term of two years. They were nominated by the Grand Master and elected by the Council of the Order.

Commissioner	*date of election*	*reference*
Arnaldo Moix	13 August 1693	AOM 131, f. 40.
Carlo Felix Doraison	13 August 1693	Ibid.
Cristoforo Balbiani	13 August 1693	Ibid.
Carlo de Thezan Venasque	24 April 1694	Ibid., f. 97
Diego de Serralta	12 September 1696	AOM 6430, f. 126.
Anselomo Cays	25 February 1696	AOM 132, f. 145v.
Giorgio de Puigdorfila	25 February 1696	Ibid.
Ramon Despuig	10 April 1698	AOM 133, f. 3v.
Traiano Gironda	5 March 1699	Ibid., f. 66v.
Mario Bichi	27 October 1699	Ibid., f. 131.
Amadeo de Cays	14 February 1707	AOM 136, f. 61v.
Traiano Gironda	17 August 1711	AOM 137, ff. 184v.
Ramon Despuig	14 September 1711	Ibid. f. 190v.
Guglielmo Sanazzaro	9 May 1712	AOM 138 f. 10v.
Ottavio Gallean	3 October 1715	AOM 139, f. 73v.
Silvio Sortino	12 July 1716	Ibid., f.184v.
Giovanni Battista de Mons Savasse	9 June 1720	AOM 140, f. 189v.
Giovanni Bichi	15 July 1721	Ibid., f. 363v.
Francoise de Mouche	21 February 1724	AOM 141, f. 214v.
Vittorio de Ferà de Rouccuille	10 March 1729	AOM 143, f. 87.
Ramon Despuig	(as on) 12 April 1730	Ibid., f. 229v.
Nicola Puigdorfila	17 December 1736	AOM 145, f. 275v.
Giorgio Montaner	14 May 1738	AOM 6430, f. 126.

Ignazio Lembo	1 September 1740	Ibid.
Joseph d St Jay		Ibid.
Anne de St Mauris (as on)	23 May 1746	AOM 149, f. 31.
Sebastian de Sarassa (as on)	23 May 1746	Ibid.
Pietro Gerolamo Net	9 March 1758	AOM 152, f. 319v.
Giovanni Battista Amalfitano	9 March 1758	Ibid.
Giovanni Battista Amalfitano	(as on) 14 December 1773	AOM 158, f. 125.
Paulin de Guast (as on)	14 December 1773	Ibid.
Pietro Gerolamo Net (as on)	14 December 1773	Ibid.
Giovanni Battista Amalfitano (as on)	16 January 1786	AOM 163, f. 301v.
Douray de St Pois (as on)	16 January 1786	Ibid.
Fra de Compredon (as on)	16 January 1786	Ibid.

APPENDIX VI

Partial list of Governors of Fort Ricasoli[5]

Governor	date of election
Ramon Despuig	13 May 1698
Giorgio Puigdorfila	
Ramon Despuig	14 September 1711
Giorgio Montaner	17 December 1736[6]
Michele Bordils	20 January 1741[7]
Francisco Ximenes de Texada	
Antonio Ribas	1 March 1777[8]
Charles de Clugny[9]	
Charles Louis Odouarde de Tillet	9 June 1798[10]

APPENDIX VII

Partial list of Lieutenant-Governors of Fort Ricasoli[11]

Lieutenant-Governor	elected
Lelio Savini	13 May 1698
Geronimo Ribas	
Antonio Puigdorfila	

---

[5] Derived from AOM 264, f. 166v; AOM 6430, ff. 218, 223; NLM 142d, f. 459, or as otherwise noted.
[6] AOM 145, f. 275v.
[7] AOM 147, f. 94v.
[8] AOM 159, f. 137.
[9] Terrinoni, 16.
[10] Ibid.
[11] Derived from NLM 142d, ff. 459-459v., AOM 6430, f. 127, or as otherwise noted.

Giacomo Togores
Vincenzo Ortin
Matteo Duretta
Giorgio Montaner
Matteo Duretta
Matteo Duretta
Nicola Puigdorfila
Agostino Erasso
Nicola Descallar
Martino de los Rios
Nicola Descallar
Fra Carvajal
Martino de la Plata
Giovanni Espeleta

25 June 1712[12]
1 April 1713
(as on) 27 January 1720[13]

20 January 1741[14]

(as on) 4 February 1775

APPENDIX VIII

Papal Brief dated 29 September 1693, establishing St Nicholas Chapel in Fort Ricasoli as a Conventual Parish Church:[15]

Die 29 Septembris 1693 Sacra Congregatione Eminentorum Sacris Ordinis Religionis Cardinalium Acciaioli, Mariscotti, Casanate, et Bichi a sanctissimo Domino Nostro particulariter deputata, attentis peculiaribus circumstantiis, et signantur ab fundationem unius Ecclesia erigenda in Fortalitio Ricasoli nuncupato muniendo ad immediatam Conventus defensam, ob qualitatem situationis eiusdem, ob periculosum mari, et longum, asperrime Terra accessum, ac a Parochia distantiam, censuit si sanitati sua placuerit, petitam facultatem fundandi ecclesiam, seu Cappellam praedictam sub infrascriptis conditionibus quod ea sit regularis, membrum, et pars, ac de partenentiis Ecclesia Prioralis Conventualis principalis Conventus, et Hospitalis Sancti Ioannis ab ea dependens, erigetur pleno Iure subiecta, et quod Cappellanus qui sit de ordine fratrum cappellanorum eiusdem Religionis professus, si fieri potest, sin minius novitius, vel in eorum defectum, etiam Presbyter secularis ad nutum Eminentissimi Magni Magistri in eadem preficiendus, omnibus, et singulis in eodem Propugnaculo degentibus sacramenta etiam sanctissimi Viatici, et Extremae Unctionis nomine Prioris eiusdem Ecclesia Conventualis administrat per litteras Apostolicas in forma Brevis concedi posse, reservata tamen Episcopo quoad Personas sibi subiectas approbatione Cappellani etiam Regularis ad nutum dicti Eminentissimi Magni Magistri amovibilis nec non salvis Parocho Emolumentis, et Juribus Parochialibus quoad Baptismata, Matrimonia, Praeceptum Paschale, Funeralia, tumulationem cadaverum, quatenus commode alio deferri, et asportari contigerit: Ita tamen, ut praesens Indultum

---

[12] AOM 138, f. 19v.
[13] AOM 140, ff. 140-140v.
[14] AOM 147, f. 94v.
[15] AOM 264, f. 21v.

non transeat in exemplum: facta ergo de praemissis per infrascriptum sancti Congregationis Concilii Secretarium relatione sanctissimo: Sanctitas sua praedictae particularis Congregationis sentiam in omnibus approbavit sub die Octobris - 1693. E Cardinalis Mariscottus Praefectus. R. Pallavicinus Secretarius.

APPENDIX IX

Partial lists of chaplains and vice-chaplains of St Nicholas Chapel in Fort Ricasoli[16]

a. *Chaplains*	*notes*
Matteo lo Castro	before 1692 (probably not resident).
Domenico Gambigallo	born (b.) in Senglea. Died (d.) on 16 February 1730. As on 5 January 1692 and on a later term.
Giacinto Signorino	as on 25 April 1694.
Giovanni Battista Bosa	b. in Senglea. d. 23 August 1753.
Gaetano Reboul	b. in Valletta c 1707, d. 14 April 1759. As on 24 December 1743 and 14 June 1755.
Andrea Fenech	d. 6 November 1796.
Adriano Leonardo	as in 1797

b. *Vice-Chaplains*	*notes*
Geronimo Signorino	as on 19 September 1693.
Gasparo Azzopardi	d. 3 May 1698.
Giovanni Battista Bosa	
Carlo Refalo	b. in Senglea. As from 1717 (ad interim); Appointed 18 February 1730; d. in office on 12 May 1735.
Gaetano Reboul	Appointed 7 May 1735.
Claudio Ricca	b. in Valletta; d. 17 January 1771.
Gaetano Galea	as in 1797.

APPENDIX X

List of all the 121 inhabitants of Fort Ricasoli in Eastertide 1702 (not including knights and chaplains)[17] *, and including Number of room or hearth; name; state; and age. N.B. w.= wife; d. = daughter; s.= son*

1. Musan Giovanni 61
   Musan Paulica w. 56
   Gratia (maid) 30
2. Cuschieri Lorenzo 65

Cuschieri Aloysetta w. 53
Cuschieri Maria d. 9
Cuschieri Diana d. 18
Cuschieri Giorgio s. 12

---

[16] Derived from NLM 142d, ff. 459v.-460; NLM 1029, no pag.; AOM 152, ff. 37v.-38; AOM 495, f.105v.; AOM 497, ff. 133v., 81v.; AOM 498, f. 109; AOM 523, f. 130v.; AOM 533, ff. 184v. - 185; AOM 539, f. 126; AAF, LSA Vittoriosa, 1797, f. 39.

[17] AAF, LSA, Vittoriosa 1702, ff. 38v. - 40.

3. Cugnet Giovanni Maria 50
   Cugnet Euphemia w. 30

4. Gambigallo Speranza 45

5. Seichell Antonio 40
   Seichell Giovannella w. 40
   Seichell Catarina d. 9
   Seichell Rosa d. 4 months

6. Busuttil Giovanni Maria 45
   Busuttil Antonia w. 45
   Busuttil Giacomo s. 3
   Busuttil Francesco s. 5

7. Buttigieg Domenico 46
   Buttigieg Domenica w. 41
   Buttigieg Giovanni s. 22

8. Curmi Salvatore 65
   Curmi Gratia w. 50
   Curmi Catarina d. 17
   Curmi Giovanni Maria s. 19
   Curmi Giuseppe s. 15
   Curmi Bartholomeo s. 12
   Curmi Vincenzo s. 8

9. Schembri Bartholomeo 70
   Schembri Lorenza w. 70

10. Gioia Paolo 56
    Gioia Maddalena w. 51
    Gioia Clementia d. 16

11. Russo Stephano[18] 20
    Russo Florenza w. 32
    Russo Theodora d. 9
    Russo Francesca d. 5
    Russo Maria (mother) 70

12. Grech Alfonso 45
    Grech Clementia w. 51
    Grech Gratia d. 19
    Grech Matteo s. 17

13. Zarb Tommaso 50
    Zarb Domenica w. 51

14. Cugneri Paulo 63

15. Galea Giovanni Maria 55
    Galea Giacobina w. 41
    Galea Rosa d. 19

16. Vella Clementio 60
    Vella Giacobina w. 30

17. Portelli Horatio 70
    Portelli Lucretia w. 40
    Portelli Maria[19] d. 15
    Portelli Maria d. 8
    Portelli Sapientia[20] d. 11
    Portelli Sapientia d. 4

18. Callus Andrea 45
    Callus Vittoria w. 41
    Callus Maddalena d. 13
    Callus Giuseppe s. 10
    Callus Antonio s. 5
    Callus Michel Angelo s. 3

19. Galea Giovanni Luca 60
    Galea Catarina w. 41
    Galea Ursola d. 16
    Galea Alberto s. 9
    Galea Rosa d. 8
    Galea Anna Maria d. 4

20. Di Natale Natale 51
    di Natale Margarita w. 40
    di Natale Maria d. 13

21. Gauci Domenico 45
    Gauci Laurica w. 41

22. Farrugia Alessandro 70
    Farrugia Catarina w. 65

23. Casha Maruzzo 50
    Casha Maddalena w. 55

24. Piccinino Serafino 32
    Piccinino Agata w. 63

25. Rizzo Nicola 70
    Rizzo Margarita w. 65

---

[18] "Under-Sergeant".
[19] from first wife.
[20] from first wife.

26. Azzopardo Flaminio 60
    Azzopardo Margarita w. 51

27. di Bono Giovanni Battista 45
    di Bono Angiolina w. 40
    di Bono Maria d. 13
    di Bono Gratiulla d. 11
    di Bono Tomaso s. 8
    di Bono Margarita d. 4
    di Bono Teresa d. 7

28. Borgan Francesco 45
    Borgan Catarina w. 40
    Borgan Giovanni Maria s. 11
    Borgan Stefano s. 8
    Borgan Anna Maria d. 8 months

29. Xuerep Andrea 66
    Xuerep Catarina w. 45

30. Xeberras Tomaso 45
    Xeberras Margarita w. 41
    Xeberras Maria d. 9
    Xeberras Alonza d. 6

Xeberras Michele s. 11

31. Buttigieg Clementio 60
    Buttigieg Evangelista w. 62

32. Farrugia Cosimo 60
    Farrugia Catarina w. 41
    Farrugia Cleria d. 18
    Farrugia Gabriele s. 14
    Farrugia Vincenzo s. 10

33. Psaila Pietro[21] 55
    Psaila Clara w. 50

34. Muscat Salvatore 60
    Muscat Domenica w. 45
    Conti Margarita d. 11
    Conti Lucretia d. 11

35. Vella Flaminia 87
    Vella Giuseppe s. 37
    Vella Pietro s. 44
    Vella Maria d. 22
    Vella Rosa d. 19

APPENDIX XI

List of all the 109 inhabitants of Fort Ricasoli in Eastertide 1754 (not including knights and chaplains) and including number of room, name, state and age[22].
N.B. w = wife; s. = son; d. = daughter; m. = mother

1. Costa Francesco 62
   Falzon Anna 20

2. Fenech Giuseppina 50

3. Portelli Giovanni Battista 62
   Portelli Bernarda w. 55

4. Stars Giovanni 63
   Stars Elisabetta w. 53

5. Mallia Giuseppe 63

6. Antignola Giuseppe 27
   Antignola Catarina w. 25

   Antignola Michel Angelo s. 4
   Antignola Rosolia d. 2

7. Bonello Michele 71

8. Mallia Michele 32

9. Piott Giuseppe 65
   Zammit Giovanni 50

10. Cauchi Salvatore 74
    Debon Domenico 72

11. Bonici Angelo
    Portelli Tommaso

---

[21] "Master of Works"
[22] ACCV, LSA, 1746-1764, no pag.

12. Grech Salvatore 70
    Agius Nicola

13. Schiavone Luca
    Micallef Pietro

14. Pace Antonio
    Grech Giuseppe

15. Agius Catarina 48
    Agius Rosolea d. 20
    Agius Beatrice d. 17
    Agius Francesco s. 12

16. di Gregorio Giovanni Battista 68
    di Gregorio Teodora w. 63

17. Dor Giovanni 78
    Dor Catarina w. 63

18. Manganaro Evangelista 73

19. Leone Giovanni 73
    Leone Anna w. 63

20. Damato Matteo

21. Farrugia Giovanni Maria 60
    Farrugia Rosa w. 50

22. Caruana Domenico
    Caruana Elisabetta w.
    Caruana Teresa Maria d. 1

23. Rizzo Salvatore 27
    Rizzo Anna Maria w. 22
    Rizzo Felice s. 4
    Rizzo Catarina d. 4
    Rizzo Giuseppe s. 1

24. Farrugia Giuseppe
    Farrugia Nicola s. 26
    Farrugia Teodora d. 24

25. Cachia Michele 54
    Cachia Natalizia m. 74

26. Buttigieg Pietro
    Buttigieg Evangelista w.

27. Vella Michele 72
    Vella Anna w. 67

28. Zammit Giovanni Battista 73
    Lia Lorenzo 28

29. Trevisan Giacomo
    Mifsud Andrea 77
    Zahra Gerolamo 70

30. Cannezzeri Giuseppe 60
    Cannezzeri Antonia w. 50
    Cannezzeri Maria Maddalena w. 8

31. Ravecchi Olivio 65
    Ravecchi Maria w. 64

32. Psaila Giovanni 54
    Psaila Maria w. 60

33. Zahra Paolo 62
    Zahra Maria w. 35

34. Lacenti Salvatore 18
    Cassar Giovanni 55
    Cassar Rosa w. 32
    Cassar Andrea s. 20
    Cassar Michele s. 18
    Cassar Giuseppe s. 16
    Cassar Ludovico s. 7

    Ventura Giuseppe 71
    Ventura Antonia w. 41

    Fenech Francesco 32
    Fenech Palma w. 32

    Debono Salvatore 64
    Debono Filippa w. 42
    Debono Pasquale s. 13
    Debono Francesco s. 5
    Debono Giorgio s. 2

    Portelli Giovanni 42
    Portelli Valenziana w. 40
    Portelli Teresa 32

    Schembri Michele 35
    Schembri Angela w. 32
    Schembri Catarina d. 8
    Schembri Giacomo s. 4
    Schembri Alessio s. 1

    Namura Giovanni 48
    Namura Eugenia w. 48
    Namura Nicola s. 11
    Namura Francesco s. 17
    Namura Nicola s. 11

Namura Gaetano s. 7
Namura Anna Maria d. 4
Namura Michel Angelo s. 1
Mallia Gregorio 63
Mallia Eugenia w. 58

Mallia Pasquale s. 23
Mallia Giovanni Battista s. 26
Mallia Teresa d. 17
Mallia Giovanni s. 15
Mallia Gaetano s. 13

APPENDIX XII

*List of all the 149 inhabitants of Fort Ricasoli in Eastertide 1797 (not including knights)
by family units, including names, state, and age[23]
N.B. w. = wife; s. = son; d. = daughter; ch = chaplain; v-ch = vice-chaplain*

Fra Adriano Leonardo ch.
Fra Gaetano Galea v-ch

Guberna Pasquale[24]
Guberna Margarita w. 54
Guberna Cristina d. 19
Guberna Giuseppe s. 14
Guberna Nicola s. 10
Guberna Vittorio s. 8
Guberna Francesco s. 6
Guberna Maria Vincenza d. 1

Editto Francesco
Editto Maria w.
Editto Maria Anna d. 21
Editto Giuseppe s. 20
Editto Salvatore s. 13
Editto Antonio s. 6

Galea Teresa (widow)
Galea Saverio s. 20
Attard Giovanni
Attard Gratia w.
Attard Catarina d. 11
Attard Maria Teresa d. 9
Attard Francesco s. 8
Attard Rosa d. 4
Attard Gaetano s. 2

Guzzivi Francesco
Guzzivi Rosa w.
Guzzivi Maddalena d. 13
Guzzivi Gaetana d. 11
Guzzini Catarina d. 7
Guzzini Gaetano s. 2

Spiteri Aloisio
Spiteri Concetta w. 22
Spiteri Giovanni s. 1

Rossi Regina
Rossi Antonia d. 20
Rossi Costanza d. 18
Rossi Giuseppe s. 10
Rossi Costanzo s. 7

di Luca Giovanni Battista
di Luca Maria w. 40
di Luca Gioacchino s. 14
di Luca Nicola s. 12
di Luca Massimo s. 10
di Luca Calcedonio s. 4
di Luca Gaetano s. 2

Azzupardo Giuseppe
Azzupardo Anna w. 30
Azzupardo Maria d. 10

---

[23] AAF, LSA Vittoriosa, 1797, ff. 39-40.
[24] Sergeant

Azzupardo Rosa d. 8
Azzupardo Emmanuele s. 4
Azzupardo Francesca d. 2

Mifsud Salvatore
Mifsud Maria w.
Mifsud Gratia d. 11
Mifsud Gioacchino s. 19
Mifsud Vincenzo s. 16

Darmenia Margarita 76
Darmenia Nicola (nephew) 13
Debono Felice[25]
Debono Vincenza w. 22
Debono Saverio s. 3
Debono Maria Vincenza d. 1

Spiteri Aloisio
Spiteri Clementia w.
Spiteri Giuseppe s. 8
Spiteri Michel Angelo s. 6
Spiteri Vincenzo s. 4
Spiteri Salvatore s. 1
Agius Maria (sister) 25

Grech Pietro
Grech Maria
Grech Antonia d.
Grech Paolo s. 3
Grech Rosaria d. 1

Scarpello Giovanni Andrea 38
Scarpello Marioa w. 37
Scarpello Giuseppina d. 13
Scarpello Giovanni s. 10
Scarpello Antonio p. 8

Sammut Calcedonio
Sammut Maddalena w.
Sammut Vincenzo s. 15
Sammut Salvatore s. 12
Sammut Giuseppe s. 10
Sammut Maria d. 5

Gulielmi Rosario
Gulielmi Vincenza w.
Gulielmi Teresa d. 18
Gulielmi Nicola s. 14
Gulielmi Feliciana d. 8
Gulielmi Egiodio s. 3

Minardi Vincenzo
Minardi Anna w.
Minardi Maria d. 18
Minrdi Salvatore s. 16
Minardi Antonina d. 11
Minardi Nicolina d. 9
Minardi Paolo s. 3

Balzan Clara
Balzan Francesco s. 37

Annati Giovanni
Annati Rosaria w.

Bugeja Tommaso
Bugeja Rosaria w. 27
Bugeja Natale s. 8
Bugeja Catarina d. 3
Bugeja Vincenzo s. 2

Ellul Gaetano
Ellul Giovanna w. 42
Ellul Vincenzo s. 22

Croce Luigi
Croce Maria w. 8
Croce Giuseppe s. 6
Croce Graziella d. 3

Manuele Francesco 33
Manuele Orsola w. 34
Manuele Nicola s. 11
Manuele Maria d. 9
Manuele Giuseppe s. 3

---

[25] Surgeon.
[26] ACCV, LSA 1765-1805, no pag.
[27] According to the 1797 count in Appendix XII, Antonio Mamo's age should read 47, while that of his wife.

Calleja Paolo
Calleja Santa w.
Calleja Luciano s. 12

Mangion Salvatore
Mangion Anna
Mangion Gaetano s. 8
Mangion Vittoria d. 6

Farrugia Grazia 30

Verrigio Regina
Verrigio Catarina d. 18
Verrigio Vincenzo s. 13
Verrigio Saveria d. 9
Verrigio Crispino s.

Polidano Lorenzo
Polidano Carmela d.
Polidano Nicola s. 3

Polidano Emanuele s. 1

Imbroll Antoio
Imbroll Angiolina w. 18
Imbroll Anna (mother) 80

Zahra Anna Maria 81

Mamo Antonio 43
Mamo Giuseppa w. 45
Mamo Vincenzo s. 20
Mamo Rosa d. 17
Mamo Salvatore s. 12
Mamo Vittoria d. 4
Mamo Giovanni Francesco s. 3
Mamo Gioacchino s. 0

Grech Giuseppe (Sergeant
Mallia Michele (Seargent

APPENDIX XIII

List of 14 Roman Catholic inhabitants of Fort Ricasoli in Eastertide of 1801, including family units; names; state and age.[26]
N.B. w = wife; s = son; d. = daughter

Mamo Antonio 50
Mamo Giuseppa w. 50[27]
Mamo Vincenzo s. 24
Mamo Rosa d. 21
Mamo Salvatore s. 16
Mamo Vittoria d. 9
Mamo Francesco s. 5

Pace Saverio 36
Pace Benedetta w. 27
Pace Emanuele s. 8
Pace Antonio s. 4
Pace Vittorio s. 1
Ellul Giuseppe 38
Falzon Antonio 30

Manuscript Sources
cited in the
Notes

AAF   Corrispondenza, 1701
AAF   Liber Status Animarum, Vittoriosa, 1702
AAF   Liber Status Animarum, Vittoriosa, 1715
AAF   Liber Status Animarum, Vittoriosa, 1797

AOM 109   Liber Conciliorum (1630-1633)
AOM 124   Liber Conciliorum (1681-1684)
AOM 131   Liber Conciliorum (1693-1694)
AOM 132   Liber Conciliorum (1696-1697)
AOM 133   Liber Conciliorum (1698-1699)
AOM 136   Liber Conciliorum (1706-1708)
AOM 137   Liber Conciliorum (1709-1711)
AOM 138   Liber Conciliorum (1712-1714)
AOM 139   Liber Conciliorum (1715-1718)
AOM 140   Liber Conciliorum (1719-1721)
AOM 141   Liber Conciliorum (1722-1724)
AOM 143   Liber Conciliorum (1728-1730)
AOM 144   Liber Conciliorum (1731-1733)
AOM 145   Liber Conciliorum (1734-1736)
AOM 146   Liber Conciliorum (1737-1739)
AOM 147   Liber Conciliorum (1740-1742)
AOM 149   Liber Conciliorum (1746-1748)
AOM 152   Liber Conciliorum (1755-1757)
AOM 154   Liber Conciliorum (1761-1763)
AOM 158   Liber Conciliorum (1773-1775)
AOM 159   Liber Conciliorum (1776-1777)
AOM 163   Liber Conciliorum (1784-1785)
AOM 257   Liber Conciliorum Status (1638-1645)

AOM 260   Liber Conciliorum Status (1657-1654)
AOM 261   Liber Conciliorum Status (1664-1671)
AOM 262   Liber Conciliorum Status (1672-1686)
AOM 264   Liber Conciliorum Status (1693-1699)
AOM 265   Liber Conciliorum Status (1700-1709)
AOM 266   Liber Conciliorum Status (1709-1716)
AOM 271   Liber Conciliorum Status (1755-1763)
AOM 272   Liber Conciliorum Status (1764-1772)
AOM 273   Liber Conciliorum Status (1773-1783)
AOM 274   Liber Conciliorum Status (1783-1795)
AOM 308   Atti dei Capitoli Generali (1631)
AOM 309   Atti dei Capitoli Generali (1776)
AOM 442   Liber Bullarum (1584-1585)
AOM 470   Liber Bullarum (1642-1644)
AOM 482   Liber Bullarum (1669-1670)
AOM 490   Liber Bullarum (1683-1684)
AOM 495   Liber Bullarum (1691)
AOM 497   Liber Bullarum (1693)
AOM 498   Liber Bullarum (1694)
AOM 502   Liber Bullarum (1698)
AOM 523   Liber Bullarum (1719)
AOM 533   Liber Bullarum (1729)
AOM 539   Liber Bullarum (1735)
AOM 616   Liber Bullarum (1794) tomo I
AOM 627   Repertorio delle materie contenute nel titolo "Salviconductus et diverse scripturae" de registri delle bolle di Cancelleria dal 1700 in avanti
AOM 635   Chirografi della camera del Tesoro e di Udienza A1 (1739-1756)
AOM 645   Registro dei decreti della Camera del Tesoro A (1667-1678)
AOM 647   Registro dei decreti della Camera del Tesoro D (1697-1706)
AOM 653   Registro dei decreti della Camera del Tesoro K (1760-1767)
AOM 1011   Volume contenente diverse relazioni, discorsi e sentimenti degl'Ingegneri riguardo le fortificazioni di Malta e Gozo
AOM 1013   Volume "Forte Ricasoli": mandati di lavoro
AOM 1014   Libretto "Trattenute delle paghe per la Cassa degl'Invalidi"
AOM 1015   Volume C contenente le deliberazioni della Congregazione di Guerra
AOM 1016   Volume A nel quale sono registrate le suppliche rimesse alla Congregazione di Guerra coi loro rispettivi decreti dal 1690 al 1705. Questo volume contiene inoltre varie opinioni d'Ingegneri intorno le fortificazioni che si proponevano in quell'epoca
AOM 1018   Altro Marcato D (1722-1732)
AOM 1019   Altro Marcato F (1732-1744)
AOM 1020   Altro Marcato G (1744-1763)
AOM 1021   Altro Marcato H (1763-1779)
AOM 1022   Altro Marcato I (1779-1788)
AOM 1023   Altro Marcato K (1788-1798)
AOM 1024   Volume nel quale sono registrate le suppliche rimesse al Commissario delle Fortificazioni dal 1734 - 1764

AOM 1051 Volume "Elezione dei Cavalieri Ufficiali" e formule di patenti G
AOM 1054 Memoria sulla sicurezza di Malta
AOM 1057 Volume nel quale sono registrate le paghe bimestrali fatte ai soldati delle torri marine F (1750)
AOM 1061 Volume contenente la consegna dell'Artiglieria fatta dal Cav. Fosiers nel 1785
AOM 1062 Volume contenente la consegna dell'Artiglieria fatta dal Cav. Fosiers nel 1790
AOM 1186 Suppliche Tomo v (1690-1721)
AOM 1187 Suppliche Tomo vi (1722-1735)
AOM 1189 Suppliche Tomo viii (1748-1758)
AOM 1444 Registro di lettere spedite dal Gran Maestro N. Cotoner (1669-1670)
AOM 1714 Regolamenti fatti nel 1797 pel governo spirituale, politico ed economice dello spedale dell'Ordine Gerosolimitano
AOM 1715 Officiale del Sagro Ospedale 1777 contenente una lista degli impiegati e pensionati dello Spedale col rispettivo ammonto dei salarj o delle pensioni
AOM 1763 Libro delle Ordinazioni e Regolamenti fatti per il Buon Governo dei Vascelli
AOM 1890 Libro Grande contenente il conto generale di tutta l'amministrazione e le spese per il mantenimento della squadra (1737-1739)
AOM 1897 Libro del Pane e Piazze Morte a Conto della Cassa degl'Invalidi, dal primo Giugno 1708 a tutto Aprile 1729
AOM 1928 Ruolo generale della gente accordata per le Navi ... dal 14 Ottobre 1703 fino al 23 Aprile 1705
AOM 1953 Diverse Scritture iv. Descrizione dell'edificio della Chiesa di San Giovanni
AOM 1987 Decreti e determinazioni fatte dalla Veneranda Assemblea dei Cappellani Conventuali, volume C (1684-1735)
AOM 6402 Volume Diverse Scritture A ...Una relazione del tenente Beretta sopra le fortificazioni di Malta; una memoria delle innovazioni proposte per le fortificazioni di malta nel 1670; una relazione dell'assedio di Candia che ebbe luogo nel 1667; ed un discorso sopra le fortificazioni proposte dal colonnello Floriani; ...
AOM 6430 Cariche in Convento
AOM 6534 Miscellanea
AOM 6535 Miscellanea
AOM 6543 Measures and dimensions of the works of defence of Malta and Gozo existing in reports of gunpowder magazines and in the testing of guns
AOM 6545 Account of the Treasury of the Fortifications, during the six months ending December 31, 1714
AOM 6549 Reports on the Garrison and Munition and Artillery posted on the bastions, forts, towers and castles. Some written in French; others in Spanish
AOM 6551 Reports and projects made by different Engineers (1633-1681)
AOM 6552 Volume on Same subject (1700-1715)
AOM 6554 Suggestions and reports on the Fortifications and defence of the islands (1633-1698)

AOM 6557 Memoirs on the fortifications of Malta and Gozo, with remarks dated about 1700

AOM 6558 Copies of several memoirs and annotations on the decisions of the Congregation of War, 1761

AOM 6560 Abridged history of the fortifications, in French about 1780

AOM 6565 Memoirs sur la Defence des iles de Malte et du Gozo

AOM 6571 Relazioni diverse A. Esame del racconto dei fatti della Congregazione di Guerra; del Promotor Fiscale; il Tesoro; ...

AOM 6574 Vertenze dell'Ordine di vario argomento (1698-1772)

AOM Treasury Series A 37 Registro dei contratti per la Fondazione Cotoner I (1676-1727); Registro dei Contratti dei Beni Rustici della Fondazione Cotoner

AOM Treasury Series A 45 (1) Registro dei Beni Urbani della Fondazione Cotoner dal 1 Novembre 1689 a tutto Ottobre 1690

AOM Treasury Series A 45 (3) Registro dei Beni Urbani della Fondazione Cotoner dal 1 Novembre 1693 a tutto Ottobre 1696

AOM Treasury Series A 46 (18) Registro dei Beni Urbani della Fondazione Cotoner dal 1 Maggio 1791 a tutto Ottobre 1792

AOM Treasury Series A 48 Conti dell'esigenze dei beni rustici della Fondazione Cotoner

AOM Treasury Series A 48 (19) Conti dell'esigenze dei beni rustici della Fondazione Cotoner dal 1 Maggio 1792 a tutto Aprile 1793

ACCV Liber Mortuorum III   (1690-1755)
ACCV Liber Mortuorum V   (1736-1837)
ACCV Liber Mortuorum VI   (1837-1875)
ACCV Liber Status Animarum   (1746-1764)
ACCV Liber Status Animarum   (1765-1805)
ACCV Liber Status Animarum   (1777-1786)

NAM Despatches 3, from S.o.S. Lord Liverpool to Governor Oakes   (1810)

NAM Despatches, out Duplicate 17, Governor Bouverie to S.o.S. Lord Glenelg (1838)

NAM Despatches, out from Governor Reid to S.o.S. Lord Newcastle (1850-1855)

NAM Despatches, out Duplicate 22, Governor Torrens to S.o.S. Lord Knutsford (1887-1889)

NAM Public Works Department 142
NAM Public Works Department 143
NAM Public Works Department 144
NAM Public Works Department 145
NAM Public Works Department 146
NAM Public Works Department 147
NAM Public Works Department 148
NAM Public Works Department bundle 578

NAM (Mdina) Police, Atti d'Istruzione KK, April-May 1889
NAM (Mdina) Police, Atti d'Istruzione LL, May-July 1889
NAM (Mdina) Procedimenti Criminali (1888-1889)

Bibliography
of Books, Articles and Newspapers
quoted or referred to
in the Text or Notes

Anderson, A., *A Journal of the Forces which sailed from the Downs in April 1800.* London 1802.

Attard, R., 'The Maltese Pirate Trial', in *The Malta Independent on Sunday,* (9,16,23 August 1998).

Azzopardi, V., *Raccolta di Varie Cose Antiche e Moderne Utili ed interessanti riguardanti Malta e Gozo.* Malta 1843.

Badger, Q.P., *Historical Guide to Malta and Gozo.* Malta 1869.

Balbi da Correggio, F., *The Siege of Malta.* Copenhagen 1961.

Baldacchino, C., *Goals, Cups and Tears: A History of Maltese Football.* Vol. I. (1886-1918). Malta 1989.

Blouet, B., *The Story of Malta.* Malta 1981.

Boffa, C.J., *It-Tlett Ibliet Matul l-Ahhar Gwerra, 1940-1944.* Malta 1976.

Bosio, I., *Dell'Istoria della Sacra Religione et Ill. Militia di S. Gio. Gierosolimitano.* Vol.III. Rome 1602.

Bowen-Jones, H., Dewdney, J.C., Fisher, W.B., *Malta: Background for Development.* Durham 1961.

Bradford, E., *The Great Siege.* London 1961.

Braun, H., *Works of Art in Malta: Losses and Survivals in the War.* London 1946.

Bruce, G.R., *Military Hospitals in Malta during the War.* Malta (no date).

Cardona, G., 'Mikiel Anton Vassalli', in *Pronostku Malti.* Malta 1976.

Cassar, G., 'The Proactive Role of the Planning Authority', in *The Times,* 11 February 1998.

Cassar, P., *Medical History of Malta.* London 1961.

Castagna, P.P., *Malta bil-Gzejjer Taghha.* Malta 1865.

Cavaliero, R., *The Last of the Crusaders.* London 1960.

Chamber of Commerce Sub-Committee, 'Ricasoli Bonded Stores', in *Commercial Courier,* 6 September 1982.

Chesney, A.G., *Historical Records of the Maltese Corps of the British Army.* London 1897.

Chetcuti, T., *Notizie Storiche e Patologiche Climatiche sul Cholera che divampò in Malta e Gozo nel estate del 1837.* Malta 1838.

Ciantar, G.A., *Malta Illustrata.* Malta 1780.

Cousin, R.J.D., *A Diary of the Siege of St Elmo.* Malta 1955.

Cremona, A., *Mikiel Anton Vassalli u Zminijietu.* Malta 1975.

Crocker, J., *History of the Fortifications of Malta.* Malta 1920.

Cutajar, F., *L'Occupazione Francese di Malta nel 1798.* Malta 1933.

Daily Malta Chronicle. Malta. 12, 14 April 1897; 26 March 1889; 2,19,26 April 1889; 3,7,14 May 1889; 26 February 1902; 10 March 1905; 7 December 1907; 26 November 1908; 23 January 1926.

Dal Pozzo, B., *Historia della S. Religione Militare di S. Giovanni Gerosolimitano detta di Malta.* 2 vols. Verona 1703, 1715.

Darmanin, A., 'The Mutiny at Fort Ricasoli', in *The Malta Independent.* 12,19,29 January 1997.

Darmanin, J.F., *The Phoenico-Graeco-Roman Temple and the Origin and Development of Fort St Angelo.* Malta 1948.

De Lucca, D., 'Baroque Town Planning in 18th Century Mdina' in *The Sunday Times of Malta.* 1 August 1976.

Denaro, V., 'Houses in Merchants Street, Valletta,' in *Melita Historica,* ii, no.3. Malta 1958.

Deschamps, P., *Le Chateaux des Croises en Terre Sainte.* 3 vols. Paris 1934, 1939, 1973.

Earle, P., *Corsairs of Malta and Barbary.* London 1970.

Ellul, G.V., 'The French Invasion of Malta: An unpublished Account', in *Hyphen.* No. 3. Malta 1978.

Faurè, G., *Storia ta' Malta u Ghawdex.* Malta 1913.

Fenech, D., 'Birgu during the British period', in Bugeja, L., Buhagiar, M., and Fiorini, S., eds, *Birgu: A Maritime City.* Malta 1993.

Ferrari, G., *Le Battaglie dei Dardanelli, 1656-1657.* Citta di Castello 1913.

Ferris, A., *Memorie dell'Inclito Ordine Gerosolimitano.* Malta 1881.

Ferro, H.A.R., 'The Battle of Valletta - 26 July 1941', in *The Malta Land Force Journal.* No. 7, July 1971. Malta.

Fiorini, S., 'Status Animarum I: A Unique Source for 17th and 18th Century Maltese Demography', in *Melita Historica,* viii, no. 4. Malta 1983.

Floriani, P., *Discorso Intorno all'Isola di Malta e di ciò che potrà succedere tentando il Turco tal Impresa.* Macerata 1576.

Fondazzjoni Wirt Artna, *Fort Rinella and the Armstrong 100 Ton Gun: A Brief History.* Malta 1994.

Galton, D., and Sutherland, J., *Report of the Barrack and Hospital Improvement Commissions on the Sanitary Condition and Improvement of the Mediterranean Stations.* London 1863.

Gravagna, L., *Ragguaglio sul Cholera Morbus.* Malta 1837.

Griffiths, W.A., *A Brief Outline of the Foundation and Development of H.M. Naval Establishments at Malta.* Malta 1917.

Guglielmotti, A., *Vocabolario Marino e Militare*. Rome 1889.

Guida Generale di Malta. 1881, 1882.

Guillaumier, A., *Bliet u Rhula ta' Malta*. Malta 1971.

Hardman, W., *History of Malta During the French and British Occupation*. London 1909.

Harlequin, Malta. 9 August 1838; 15, 20 September 1838.

Harrison, A.St.B., Hubbard, R.P.S., *A report to accompany the outline plan for the region of Valletta and the Three Cities*. Malta 1945.

History of the Royal Malta Artillery. Malta 1944.

Hoppen, A., *The Fortification of Malta, 1530-1798*. Edinburgh 1979.

Hughes, J.Q., *Britain in the Mediterranean and the Defence of her Naval Stations*. Liverpool 1981.

Hughes, J.Q., *Fortress: Architecture and Military History in Malta*. London 1969.

Hughes, J.Q., *Malta: A Guide to the fortifications*. Malta 1993.

Hughes, J.Q., *The Building of Malta, 1530-1797*. London 1956.

Keasing's Almanac, 1964.

Kohn, G.C., *Encyclopaedia of Plague and Pestilence*. New York 1995.

Kurat, A.N., 'The Ottoman Empire Under Mehmed IV', in the *New Cambridge Modern History*. Vol. v. Cambridge 1961.

Laferla, A.V., *British Malta*. 2 vols. Malta 1946, 1947.

Mallia-Milanes, V., *Descrittione di Malta Anno 1716: A Venetian Account*. Malta 1988.

Malta Army and Navy Directory, 1903, 1913, 1925.

Malta Census, 1901, 1911, 1921, 1931.

Malta, Corriere Mercantile Maltese, 9, 17-19, 22-24 April 1889.

Malta, Department of Information, *Malta Review*, 11, 28 April 1965.

Malta Drydocks Corporation, *Malta Drydocks: At your service in the Centre of the Mediterranean*. Malta (no date).

Malta Government Gazette, 14 February 1821; 14,21 June 1837; 12, 19, 26 July 1837.

Malta Independent (The), 16 March 1998.

Malta Mail and United Services Gazette, 1 August 1854.

Malta Times and United Services Gazette, 19, 26 December 1861.

Malta Times Broadsheet of the Mediterranean, 20 April 1840.

Malta Year Book, 1966, 1967.

Mediterraneo, 30 August 1838; 21 December 1861.

Micallef, J., *The Plague of 1676; 11,300 deaths*. Malta 1984.

Mifsud, A., *La Milizia e le Torri Antiche in Malta*. Malta 1920.

Mizzi, J.A., 'Fort Ricasoli to be turned into a Heritage Park', in *The Sunday Times of Malta*, 8 May 1994.

Murray, J. ed., *The Court and Camp of Buonaparte*. London 1831.

Ordine (l'), 13 December 1861.

Panzavecchia, F., *L'Ultimo Periodo della Storia di Malta sotto il Governo dell'Ordine Gerosolimitano*. Malta 1835.

Passerini, L., *Genealogia e Storia della Famiglia Ricasoli*. Florence 1861.

Portafoglio Maltese (il), 29 July 1854.

Porter, W., *A History of the Fortress of Malta*. Malta 1858.

Pullicino, P., 'Froberg's Regiment', in *Heritage*, ii., 481-483. Malta 1979.

Ramsey, W.G. ed., 'The Italian Naval Attack on Grand Harbour', in *After the Battle: Malta G.C.* London 1975.

Ransijat, B., *Assedio e Blocco di Malta*. Malta 1843.

Ratcliff, C., 'Carve Malta on my Heart', in *Malta News*, July 1974.

Reboul, G., *Giornale de Successi dell'Isole di Malta e Gozo. Compendiato da Ignazio Saverio Mifsud. (Compendiato a cura di V. Laurenza)*. Malta 1939.

Riley Smith, J., *The Knights of St John in Jerusalem and Cyprus, 1050-1310*. London 1967.

Roamer, in *The Sunday Times of Malta*, 11 April 1965.

Sammut, F., *Bonaparti F'Malta*. Malta 1997.

Samut-Tagliaferro, A., 'British Fortification and Defence', in *Archivum*, no. 1, Malta 1981.

Samut-Tagliaferro, A., 'A History of the Royal Malta Artillery, pt 1: 1794-1802', in *The Malta Land Force Journal*, no 10, 1-32, (April 1972). Malta.

Samut-Tagliaferro, A., *History of the royal Malta Artillery*, vol. 1 (1800-1939). Malta 1976.

Sanminiatelli Zabarella, C., *Lo Assedio di Malta, 1565*. Torino 1902.

Schembri, J., 'The Fortification of Malta - Fort Ricasoli', in *The Malta Land Force Journal*, no 7, 70-74, (July 1971). Malta.

Scicluna, H.P., *Documents relating to the French occupation of Malta in 1798-1800*. Malta 1923.

Scicluna, H.P., *The Church of St John in Valletta*. Rome 1955.

Shaw, C., *Malta Sixty Years Ago*. London 1875.

Soler, W., 'The Breakwater in Grand Harbour', in *The Sunday Times*, 26 June 1994, 38-41; 3 July 1994, 40-42; 10 July 1994, 44-47.

Spiteri, S.C., *British Military Architecture in Malta*. Malta 1996.

Spiteri, S.C., *Fortresses of the Cross: Hospitaller Military Architecture, 1136-1798*. Malta 1994.

Stilon, G.M., *Sul Cholera Morbus: Avvisi Medici*. Malta 1839.

Sunday Times of Malta (The), 4 May 1947.

Terrinoni, F.G., *Memorie Storiche della Resa di Malta ai Francesi nel 1798*. Rome 1867.

Testa, C., *Maz-Zewg Nahat tas-Swar*. 3 vols. Malta i 1979, ii 1980, iii 1982.

Testa, C., *The French in Malta: 1798-1800*. Malta 1997.

Testa, C., 'The French in Malta: 1798-1800', in Mid-Med Bank, *Report & Accounts 1989*, 29-51. Malta 1990.

Testa, C., *The Life and Times of Grand Master Pinto*. Malta 1989.

Thomson, D., *Europe Since Napoleon*. Harmondsworth 1972.

Times of Malta (The), 11 May 1942; 1 May 1947.

Torca (It-), 10 October 1982.

Tregellas, W.H., 'Historical Sketch of the Defences of Malta', in *Journal of the Royal Engineers Institute*, paper viii, vol. iii, no. 10. 1879.

Vassallo, G.A., *Storia di Malta*. Malta 1890.

Vella, A.P., *Storja ta' Malta*. Vol. ii. Malta 1979.

Vella, P., *Malta: Blitzed but not Beaten*. Malta 1985.

Vella Bonavita, J., 'Rinella Battery and 100 ton gun: Teenagers' Din l-Art Helwa Summer Camp 1969', in *Teenagers Din l-Art Helwa Quarterly*. Vol. 1, no. 1. (Autumn 1969), 25-28. Malta.

Vella Bonavita, R., 'The 100 ton 17.72-inch R.M.L. Armstrong Gun at Rinell Battery, Malta: A Brief Account and Description', in *The Malta Year Book*. 1978, 431-443. Malta 1978.

Wismayer, J.M., 'Fort Ricasoli', in *The Sunday Times*. 19 July 1998, 47-48.

Wismayer, J.M., *The History of the King's Own Malta Regiment and the Armed forces of the Order of St John*. Malta 1989.

Zahra, L., 'Fort Verdala and Fort Ricasoli', in *Malta News*. 4 February 1976, 3.

Zahra, L., 'The Story of Fort Ricasoli', in *The Sunday Times of Malta*. 6 December 1970, 30-31.

Zammit, T., *Malta: The Maltese Islands and their History*. Malta 1926.

Zarb, A., *Storia di Malta dalla Caduta dell' Ordine Gerosolimitano sino alla resa della Republica Francese*. Malta 1856.

Archival Maps and Plans
cited in the notes

National Archives of Malta - Ricasoli Plans:

6 Ricasoli No 4 Bastion No 5 D(efence) E(lectric) L(ight)
103 Fort Ricasoli Skeleton Record Plan. Proposed improvements to provide accomodation for RMA
106 Ricasoli proposed School, Malta. District East Sub district
121 Fort Ricasoli North. Layout of Bofors Gun Emplacement
127 Fort Ricasoli. Encroachment of sea between Nos 3 and 4 bastions (North of Recreation Establishment)
128 Fort Ricasoli. Proposed improvement to preparation room (Cook House, etc.)
129 Fort Ricasoli. (Married Soldiers Quarters 'A' Block) proposed addition of Bath Rooms
133 Ricasoli. [A(nti) M(otor) T(orpedo) B(oat) equipment 'C'] Elevations and Sections of new work
137 Fort Ricasoli. Proposal to re-appropriate wash-up as (Boiler House)
142 Fort Ricasoli. (A.M.T.B. Equipment 'A') details of Central Tower and Ammunition Hoist
146 Ricasoli. A.M.T.B. 'B' emplacement plan showing new work
220 Plan of cables, Fort Ricasoli
223 Record Plan of 20 Married Quarters Fort Ricasoli
228 Record Plan of Fort Ricasoli
235 Record Plan of 6 inch Breach Loading gun emplacement left ravelin
239 Record Plan of Fort Ricasoli
246 Fort Ricasoli. Proposed Recreation Room and C.
248 Plan and Elevation of House at Naval Rifle Range near Fort Ricasoli, showing the proposed two stages or platforms for rifle practice, also rain water tank of the capacity of 20 tons for service of Range and a drain around the House for the reception of stormwater

National Library of Malta - Maps and Plans:

Analytical Index 1

Place-Names quoted in the text

255

Analytical Index 2

Names of Persons quoted in the text